In and Out of Synch

L'Inhumaine (L'Herbier, 1924)

In and Out of Synch

The awakening of a cine-dreamer

NOEL BURCH

Scolar Press

First published in 1991 by

SCOLAR PRESS
Gower House, Croft Road
Aldershot, GU11 3HR, England

British Library Cataloguing in Publication Data
Burch, Noel
    In and out of synch: the awakening of a cine-dreamer.
    1. Cinema films
    I. Title
    791.43

    ISBN 0–85967–867–9

Publishers' Acknowledgements
The four essays in Part I, translated by Tom Milne, are reprinted from *Cinema: a Critical Dictionary*, edited by Richard Roud, 1980, by permission of Martin Secker and Warburg Limited and the Viking Press. 'Towards an Experimental Pedagogy' is translated from its first appearance in French in a journal published by the Comité d'entreprise of Electricité de France. 'Film's Institutional Mode of Representation and the Soviet Response' was originally published in *October*. 'Porter, or Ambivalence' was a contribution to *Le Cinéma Américain*, edited by Raymond Bellour, 1979; it subsequently appeared in *Screen*, in a translation by Tom Milne. 'Primitivism and the Avant-gardes' was first delivered as a lecture at the Whitney Museum in New York, and later appeared in *Narrative, Apparatus, Ideology* edited by Philip Rosen. 'A Dissentient Cinema?' was written for a collective history of the Japanese cinema. 'Notes on Fritz Lang's first *Mabuse*' first appeared in *Cine-Tracts* in a translation by Judith Mayne. 'Harold Lloyd vs. Doctor Mabuse' was a contribution to a compilation on Boris Barnet published by the Locarno Film Festival, 1985.

Printed in Great Britain by
Billing and Sons Limited, Worcester

Contents

Preface

The articles collected here were written between 1970 and 1985, a period during which my ideas – regarding film and much else besides – underwent extensive changes. It is therefore important to indicate the nature of those changes in order to enable readers better to relate these texts to one another.

The first section is composed of contributions to an Anglo-American film history, where these were somewhat out of place. I am pleased to be able to extract them at last from an inappropriately eclectic context. These articles belong to a first, 'formalist' phase, out of which had already come *Praxis du Cinéma* (1969), published in English as *Theory of Film Practice* (1973). This phase was characterized by a 'musicalistic' vision privileging the formal dimensions of the European art film. This approach was no doubt stimulating and fruitful to the extent that it placed a new emphasis on the *work of the signifier* at a time when this had been completely neglected by film theory since Eisenstein. However, such a complete neglect of content and of *how meaning is produced* was unacceptably reductive, both theoretically and practically. I have already taken the opportunity, notably in my new prefaces to the American and French reprint editions of *Praxis du Cinéma*, of expressing a more developed critique of that early stage of my work.

The second section consists of articles which belong to a ten-year exploration of what I regarded as alternatives to the Hollywood model. This latter was still viewed in this second phase as Bad Object, but by this time the 'art-for-art's sake' creed which had previously underpinned this dismissal had become amalgamated with a leftist Marxism, vaguely inspired by the French reviews *Tel Quel* and *Cinéthique*. The cinema of Japan, the experimental cinemas of the Soviet Union in the 1920s and North America in the 1960s and the pre-institutional cinemas of the primitive era (pre-1906) became privileged areas of investigation in that they seemed to offer possible models for radical film-practices in the capitalist

West that were artistically more acceptable (from the modernist standpoint) than classical documentary or socialist realism and less 'alienating', less 'manipulative', than the standard fictional format. During this period, the author moved close to British writers and film-makers whose concerns found expression in the reviews *Screen* and *After-image*, to both of which he was an occasional contributor.

Around 1979, I at last resumed film-making, the abandonment of which in the early 1970s had led to a *long detour through theory*. At the same period, a two-year stay in the United States revealed the intellectual ravages of the formalism which my early work – seriously overrated by the North American academic industry – had no doubt helped to encourage. Chastened by this experience, I found myself able to turn at last to issues of meaning and content, familiarizing myself with important English and American work of the 1970s which I had hitherto neglected. The two articles which make up the last section of this book are the most substantial efforts I have made thus far in this direction, one which will, I hope, be taken further.

NB

For Hannah

Part I
Forms . . . in the Firmament

M (Lang, 1931)

2 IN AND OUT OF SYNCH

1 Fritz Lang: German Period

Lang's career and the body of writing that has grown up around it, in France especially, present a double paradox. From 1920 to 1932, along with Eisenstein and Dreyer, Lang (1890-1976) was one of the principal architects of that *language sans langue* (language without speech) which, according to Christian Metz, is cinema. From 1933 onwards, exiled from Nazi Germany and settling shortly thereafter in the United States, he seemingly accepted all the (essentially regressive) inferences which the American sound film had drawn in particular from his best work in Germany; whether consciously or not, he identified himself with that anonymous being who was always much of a muchness, the all-purpose Hollywood director who turned out practically all of its product, whether made in California or elsewhere.

Since around 1950, however, a sizeable fraternity of (mostly French) critics and cinephiles, restricting themselves to an essentially thematic reading, have claimed to see no break between Lang's German and his American work, and argue either an exact parity between the two (*Moonfleet = Die Spinnen, The Big Heat = Mabuse*) or even the superiority of the American over the German films.

My purpose here is only incidentally polemical, and I shall not waste time demonstrating how and why *M* is not merely superior to *Fury* but belongs to an altogether different dimension. Instead, concentrating on the major works from Lang's German period, I shall attempt to define the nature of a series of achievements that matches the history of the cinema's crestline of discovery stage by stage.

First Stage: Mastering a System

Though dating from 1922, the two-part film *Doctor Mabuse, der Spieler (Dr Mabuse, the Gambler)* already marks, in my opinion a zenith in the gestation of a *literary genre within the cinema*. Its zenith, but also its terminal point: a whole line of similarly (but never quite so exemplarily) *transparent* cinema, including all the films Lang himself made after his departure from Germany, is rendered totally superfluous by this film. At the same time, however, *Doktor Mabuse, der Spieler* implicitly challenges this idea of 'transparency', for it is also an initial affirmation that articulations (here, changes from sequence to sequence, as opposed to 'matching' shot changes) can rate as entities in their own right, can be the components of an 'abstract' phenomenological discourse that may be read independently of the purely narrative discourse. This film, in other words, seems to me to be the precise point at which the cinema that reproduced the nineteenth-century novelistic discourse – and which postulated the essence of cinema, its vocation, as *being this reproduction* – defined its own limits and prepared to give way to that other complex, composite cinema which was both figurative and non-figurative, both artifice and reality, and whose first manifestation had probably been *Das Kabinett des Doktor Caligari* (*The Cabinet of Dr Caligari*, 1919), a film on which Lang had worked in its early stages.

My assertion that *Mabuse* tends essentially to reproduce the literary discourse may seem presumptuous, so I shall try to define this reproduction. The film is of course based on a serial by Norbert Jacques. But there are, after all, quite a number of cases where literary works have served as raw material for the elaboration of a cinematic form within which the 'literary' discourse as such does indeed still hold a real place, but no longer the one it held in the traditional novel, having become one code among several. For this reason I think an examination of the way this film *solicits the spectator's perception* would be more conclusive.

The reading of a novel written in the manner of Balzac or Zola involves 'forgetting' the reality of the printed letters as well as the functions of grammar and syntax: we are invited to share in the illusion, not that what we are reading is literally 'true', but that the characters in the novel are 'true to life'. We are, in other words, expected to maintain the same sort of relationship with them *as we do with the people around us*, being sorry for them, admiring them, being afraid of or for them, hating them, mourning their deaths and so on. The author's voice is of course often heard, explicitly or implicitly, but his comments almost invariably serve to enhance the 'credibility' of the characters through an expedient which consists in suggesting that the author maintains precisely the same relationship with his characters as that which he is trying to induce in the reader. The same is true of the cinema represented, in this respect, by *Mabuse*. Fifty years after being committed to celluloid, the portraits of Mabuse, the Countess Told, Attorney von Wenck and Cara Carozza are still as 'alive' and as captivating as they were in 1922.

It is in this sense that *Mabuse* was a consummation. For of course, long before *Mabuse*, this has been the ambition of practically every film made. But prior to Lang's first masterpieces, the cinema remained deficient in this area of novelistic credibility. Ince, Griffith, Perret and Feuillade all failed to endow their characters with the *density* that is the mark of their counterparts in novels and all Lang's earlier films, including the very Feuillade-ish *Die Spinnen* (*The Spiders*, 1919) are tainted with this same deficiency (which is of course a deficiency only from the standpoint of cinema as a literary genre).

How does this deficiency actually manifest itself, and how is it finally overcome in *Mabuse*? I have suggested that the reader's relationship with the traditional novelistic discourse is based on non-perception, on the 'invisibility', of the material articulations sustaining this discourse: in other words, syntax, grammar, and the perceptible form of words and symbols. In the cinema, this non-perception corresponds to a reading which 'sees' neither the edges of the frame nor the changes of shot – the two materialities which in fact tend to challenge the illusion of *continuity* that, as Robbe Grillet has very rightly pointed out, underlies the credibility both of the traditional novel and of the cinema which has adopted the same specifications.

For these two material realities to become 'invisible' in the same way as syntax and printed characters, however, a major obstacle had first to be surmounted *through artifice; what was not 'naturally' invisible had to be so rendered*. In particular, the spectator had to be persuaded that the pro-filmic space (which for a time was the same as the theatrical proscenium) could be fragmented, and that these fragments, passing successively before him in a space that remained constant (the 'window' of the screen), could constitute a *mentally continuous* space. For it was hardly more complicated than that: to achieve novelistic credibility, one had to be able to film objects or characters close up – to isolate a face, a hand, some prop, just as novelistic discourse does – without disorienting the spectator in his 'reasoned' or instinctive analysis of the spatial continuum involved at that moment, and also without drawing his attention to the artifices whereby his illusion of continuity was achieved.

During the cinema's very early days, of course, the idea of switching angles or bringing the camera in closer during the course of a scene – that is, introducing a discontinuity of viewpoint into the continuity of a scene – was inconceivable. At the same time, however, as *The Great Train Robbery* (1903) shows, the single fixed shot kept audiences too distant from the characters for them to acquire an individualized presence, and therefore any novelistic density. In Porter's film, the characters are so dwarfed within the frame that one cannot distinguish between them, and they remain anonymous. Such was the prestige of this novelistic density, however, that the obstacles preventing the cinema from attaining it had to be removed if wider audiences were to be attracted; and as a first priority, the camera had to be able to move in to show details of a scene once the overall view had been established.

This was the impulse that was to lead to the discovery of the basic principles of continuity articulations, following on the gradual realization that shots present themselves to the eye like the successive images in a comic strip, and that they can be linked to each other by specifically orientative elements (eyeline matching between people looking at each other, matching screen direction when someone leaves one frame to enter the next). Gradually, between 1907 and 1917, it became possible to maintain the illusion of continuity while resorting to fragmentation (to *découpage*), and to impose the illusion so strongly that the very *existence* of shot changes, like the edges of the frame, became totally obscured.

By 1922, every practising film-maker was more or less familiar with this system of orientation, though few of them so thoroughly as Fritz Lang. At the very beginning of *Der Spieler: Ein Bild der Zeit* (the first part of *Mabuse*), he films a dialogue between Dr Mabuse and his secretary – who is behind him – in a series of cross-cut close shots which isolates each of the men in turn *in a setting we do not see*. As an opening gambit this was a dangerous move at the time; yet thanks to perfect angular articulation between the direction of the secretary's eyes and of the glances Mabuse casts at him over his shoulder, the spectator can be in no doubt as to the relative position of the two men in the surrounding – and as yet hypothetical – space of Mabuse's salon. Dramaturgically, this opening sequence is exemplary, both in this perfect articulation which permits a close scrutiny of the characters from the outset, and in the striking concision with which the opening titles exactly pin down the two personalities and their relationship: Mabuse: 'You've been taking cocaine again'; Secretary: 'If you fire me, I'll kill myself.'

This demonstration of narrative mastery continues right through the celebrated second sequence of the film, with members of Mabuse's gang going about their business in alternating montage (one in a train, one up a telegraph pole, etc.), the continuity between all these shots in different settings assured by close-ups of synchronized watches. Technically, this complex narrative, unprecedented in its virtuosity, was at least as effective as one of Gaston Leroux's or Maurice Leblanc's best chapters. Let there be no misunderstanding, however: although the effect achieved would have been very much the same had this scene appeared in a novel by one of the best thriller writers of the day, the *means* employed by Lang are quite clearly *different* from those used in literature. Hence my conviction that in the cinema this process constitutes a *separate literary genre*, as autonomous in relation to the novel and the theatre as these two genres are in relation to each other. And it is this specificity in the dramaturgic cinema's means that reveals the germ of a cinema which would one day finally break free from the traditional novel.

One important aspect of this specificity is the immediate and total materialization of discontinuity whenever indication of this discontinuity answers a dramatic need. In other words, moving from one décor to another in a 'classic' novel usually involves a gradual process – describing the new setting, situating the new characters in it, and finally getting the new action under way – with the hiatus in reading introduced by a new paragraph or chapter contributing to the fact that these transitions are generally smoothed over. This is obviously not so in the cinema, especially if the use of what have come to be known as punctuating devices (the dissolve, iris in or out, fade in or out, designed precisely to soften such transitions in the manner of the novel and theatre) is as restricted as it is in *Mabuse*; for in the cinema, when these transitions take the form of simple shot changes, they are instantly perceived as radical breaks, as elements of extreme discontinuity.

This, of course, had always been so. But Lang was, I think, the first to exploit fully the dialectical possibilities in this introduction of an element of discontinuity within the narrative continuity. In Griffith's celebrated parallel montage for the final sequences of *Birth of a Nation* and *Intolerance*, the way the 'shot change' phenomenon functions in the succession of shots is usually purely arbitrary: the change of scene could easily have taken place a few seconds earlier or later, and one even feels that often these segments from scenes could be permutated without making much difference, for never at any moment in Griffith's use of this kind of montage does one sequence relate to the next through the shot ¬hange at the precise moment when it occurs. Directly on the level of perception there is consequently a total rupture, the only factor of continuity being one furnished purely by memory: the continuity linking together the characters and their acts in the context of the film as a whole. The result, to my mind, is a complete lack of tension and considerable uncertainty in the progress of the narrative, despite the supposedly 'rhythmic' (but can there by rhythm without directional movement and without tension-relaxation?) rapid succession of shots.

In *Mabuse*, on the other hand, where the basic organizing principle (first set forth in the sequence concerning the theft of the documents from the train) is in fact alternating montage, Lang always establishes clear relationships between the end of one scene and the initiation of another (or between the suspension of a scene and its resumption). This connection sometimes assumes the rather crude from of a question and answer ('Who can be behind all this?' asks a shot of Attorney von Wenck; 'Him!' answers a shot of Mabuse disguising himself); sometimes a rather more subtly cerebral counterpoint, when the thoughts or acts of one of the participants in this emotional quadrille worthy of Corneille (La Carozza loves Mabuse, who loves Countess Told, who loves no one, not even her discreet admirer von Wenck) lead quite naturally to the appearance of one of his partners. In a more general way, and no matter what its particular function, each sequence change takes over the relay, makes the necessary transmission of *narrative movement* (in the sense that one talks of the movement of a clock).

It should be stressed that all these transitions are purely dramaturgic: the 'plastic rhymes' of *Das Testament des Doktor Mabuse* (*The Testament of Dr Mabuse*; also known as *The Last Will of Dr Mabuse* and *The Crimes of Dr Mabuse*, 1932-3) were still to come. But they weave *specific* links across each sequence change, maintaining a constant presence (that of the narrative's movement *foward*, as opposed to Griffith's hesitations) in face of the violent rupture caused by the shot change in itself; hence the dialectical tension produced by each change of scene in the film, which on this level prefigures Eisenstein's dialectic. It is through the disposition of these privileged moments – as the scene articulations become here – that Lang organizes the 'respiration', the rhythmics of his narrative (and perhaps for the first time in the history of the cinema one can talk of a completely controlled rhythm).

Although what we are dealing with here is primarily a novelistic form (the main function of the structure and rhythm being to carry, to 'deliver' the narrative), a new and more strictly cinematic form – closer to opera than to literature – can be seen outlined in Lang's awareness of the dialectic potential of these ruptures in film, an awareness which was to become explicit in the trio of masterpieces to come: *Spione* (*Spies*, 1928), *M* (1931) and *The Testament of Dr Mabuse*.

Second Stage: Dissolution of the Code: Towards Montage

If the first *Mabuse* can thus be considered an end-stage not only in Fritz Lang's career but in the course of the cinema, *Metropolis* (1926) is undoubtedly a transitional work. It is also a fundamentally ambivalent film, in both style and ideology. Siegfried Kracauer and others have already demonstrated the ways in which this film is linked to the 'social criticism' peculiar to budding Fascism: the idealistic reconciliation of capital and labour, the deliberately derisory representation of the revolutionary act, the careful avoidance of any direct repression of man by man ('It's the Machine that has enslaved us; let's go back to real values . . .'). At the same time, however, the evident desire to denounce capitalist alienation has led some rather ingenuous critics, including Francis Courtade, to see *Metropolis* as 'first and foremost a social film, dealing with the class struggle' and showing 'what the life of the working classes would be under the Nazi régime'. At all events, as Theodor Adorno has demonstrated with reference to Wagner, an accomplished work of art can very well carry progressive and reactionary elements at one and the same time: it can be a faithful reflection of the ideology of the ruling class while offering forms, structures and aesthetic effects which are not only progressive or indeed revolutionary as far as the organic history of the particular art form is concerned, but also contain an implicit critique of the prevailing ideology, even prefiguring the advent of its antithesis.

I tried to stress earlier that the consequence, the *raison d'être*, of the orientation code mastered by Lang in *Mabuse* was to obscure the reality of the shot change in conditions of continuity (within a sequence). It was quite a different matter in *Metropolis*. Here, in the wake of the first French avant-garde (Gance, L'Herbier), Lang sets out to conquer Montage. The tripartite alternative – sequence shot, reverse angle, axial match – that defines the limits of the 'intra-sequential' style of *Mabuse* here loses its mandatory quality. Apparent instead is a desire *not* to conceal the shot change behind the 'natural' movement of the scene (bringing the camera in closer when the spectator is likely to want a closer look, turning it round so that he can see what is happening 'opposite') but to make it play a more positively *expressive* role. Here again, of course, we remain purely in the dramaturgical domain: montage, with Lang, is designed to stress the pathos of the action.

As an illustration one might cite the extremely effective sequence in which, trying to escape from Rotwang's clutches, Maria grabs the bars of a skylight and is filmed from various different angles in rapid succession. But another example, the meeting between Maria and Freder in front of the altar in the catacombs, will also indicate another important point. Their embrace is also filmed from a series of opposing angles, edited in a 'breathless' tempo. Here the shot changes are anything but invisible, all the more so in that Lang, apparently oblivious of the rules he had contributed so much towards consecrating, perpetuates some particularly glaring bad matches: almost systematically crossing the median line, he shows the actors from angles which mean that their respective positions on the screen are constantly reversed. Although these bad eyeline matches might at a pinch be said to enhance the desired effect, others – notably in the first scene between Fredersen and his son in the former's office – incontestably weaken it. Not even an involuntary echo of Eisenstein's dialectical use of good and bad matches in *Strike*, they seem simply to be inexplicable lapses; and they were to disappear almost completely when Lang more or less definitively abandoned the pursuit of Montage in his very next film (Montage in the cruder sense implied by the capital letter) to return to the problems of scene articulation (which is merely another aspect of montage in the wider sense). *Metropolis* is in fact at its most effective whenever montage, instead of attempting to assume an 'expressive' role within sequences (a simplistic interpretation of the expressionist doctrine?), confines itself to the task of providing narrative rhythm: for instance our first introduction to the Hall of Machines, seen in parallel montage with a scene in Fredersen's office, or the flash of Maria retreating before Rotwang along a wall, a shot inserted into a scene depicting the tribulations of Fredersen's son in the subterranean world. And after *Spione*, this was the track to which Lang was to return.

Third Stage: Considering the Ellipse – and Imposing It

Often neglected because of the stereotyped banality of its plot, *Spione* nevertheless marks a peak in the first great period of cinematic discoveries. Despite certain parallels with the first *Mabuse*, the area investigated here is essentially different. The film's metabolism is established through a systematic alternation of serenely discursive passages scrupulously respecting 'real time' with other moments so audaciously elliptical that they may have presented genuine difficulties to audiences of the period.

The ellipse and its evolution play a central role in the history of cinematic style. So that Lang's achievement in *Spione* may be seen in its proper perspective, it may be helpful to recall some basic concepts.

In language, properly speaking, an ellipse can be defined as the syntactic or stylistic omission of one or more words which the mind supplies more or less spontaneously. By extension: the art of abridgement or implication. In phrases like 'Each in turn' ('Each *must act* in turn'), usage has completely obscured our perception of the ellipse, and the elliptical form has substituted itself for the fuller version; at the other end of the scale, poetic ellipse (e.g. Mallarmé) sometimes leaves one unable to supply the missing words spontaneously.

The many gradations between perceived and non-perceived ellipse are also found in the cinema. In its cinematic sense, borrowed fairly freely from the literary definition, 'ellipse' has come to mean primarily 'a temporal abridgement'. One could of course call it the omission of one or more acts or events which the mind supplies more or less spontaneously. Cinematic practice suggests a more precise formulation, however: each time the circumstances of a shot change are such that, while establishing a chronological relationship between the two successive shots, it also – and by whatever means – suggests a time lapse between the end of one shot and the beginning of the next, then there has been an ellipse. This might be described as a strict definition. However, as we shall see later in examining the various manifestations of the 'elliptical effect' in *Spione*, the ellipse is often used in conjunction with another trope – synecdoche – whereby 'the detail signifies the whole'.

Now, in the development of the dramaturgic expedients already discussed, the ellipse played a major role, notably with a view to perpetuating the priorities presented by the traditional novelistic narrative.

Since the primitives presented each shot as an autonomous tableau, the shot change was always a break in temporal continuity, and consequently always an ellipse; but it was almost invariably the same kind of ellipse, essentially indeterminate in its time value, and syntactically equivalent to the inter-title 'Some time later' (in which it later came to be embodied). It was only with the introduction (notably by Griffith) of a sense of real continuity artificially created between shots by montage that the ellipse was to assume an entirely specific and diversified character in the face of this newly affirmed continuity.

Nevertheless even in Porter's films, despite the absence of this crucial element provided by the impression of perfect continuity, one can already see a rudimentary distinction in the respective time values of certain ellipses.

It is difficult in the present state of film research to trace precisely the steps whereby the progressive film-makers attained a genuine mastery, not of the ellipse as a stock figure of speech (this 'transparent' use was developed hand in hand with the code of orientation), but of a systematic manipulation of greater or lesser invisibility in the ellipse considered as an essential parameter in constructing a *découpage*. Even so it seems certain that, among the makers of silent films, Fritz Lang ventured furthest along this path with *Spione*.

The rapid series of shots with which *Spione* opens immediately places the film under the sign of the ellipse: gloved hands opening a safe/the hands placing documents in an envelope/a leather-clad figure riding on a motorcycle/radio antennae: waves radiating/a newspaper headline announcing the theft of secret documents/an official on the phone/a car on the road with chauffeur and passenger; another car overtaking it; a shot/the passenger crumpling up, a hand takes a briefcase from him/an official on the phone/another headline. For the space of a few shots the action then becomes less disjointed, though no less swift: reverse editing between harassed officials in the confusion of their office. Then the choppy movement starts again: another headline/two officials telephoning back and forth/a diplomat standing behind his desk/insert of a letter he is reading/a car stopping before an official building, a leather-clad man running up the steps and/going inside/erupting into the diplomat's office/title: 'I saw the man who . . .'/close-up of a window being pierced by a bullet/the leather-clad man falling/the furious diplomat exclaiming/title: 'Who can . . ./'. . . be behind all this?'/close shot of Haghi (Rudolph Klein-Rogge), then/a huge title: 'ME'.

From the outset here a sort of panorama of the field of elliptical modalities may be discerned. The two extremities already defined take precedence, of course, though not without frequent nuances which induce a movement in tight counterpoint to that of the narrative. To start from the beginning: the first two shots define an ellipse relatively determinate in duration; linked by the gloved hands, they are obviously separated from each other only by a few moments within the 'virtual' narrative time. The third shot introduces an ellipse of quite a different order: is this the same man, and the action therefore a continuation? His costume might suggest so, but this is mere assumption; the ellipse is therefore on the borderline between what I have described in my *Theory of Film Practice* as the 'small measurable ellipse' and the 'large indefinite ellipse', since the action in this shot could very well simply be occurring parallel to the first action, or even have no definite connection with it. But the following ellipse falls unmistakably into the second category: the radio waves are linked to what has gone before only by a relationship of causality (differing from the 'causal match' in that there is no illusion even of temporal continuity). Next come three similarly indefinite ellipses, then the murder on the highway introduces the first continuity cut; two more 'large ellipses', then the short reverse field sequence; two more indefinite ellipses, then an example of what one might describe with some justification as a 'spatial ellipse', because the alternate montage of a telephone conversation presents the temporal continuity and spatial discontinuity which in this stylistic context may be seen as symmetrically equivalent to the characteristics of the temporal ellipse. The sub-sequence that follows introduces what I consider to be the third main type of strictly temporal ellipse: although the match cut which takes us from the diplomat to the insert of the letter he is reading is decidedly in continuity, the next one *seems* at first to belong to the type of 'indefinite ellipse'. The entry into the building of the character (whose costume refers to the motorcyclist at the beginning) is accomplished through a match with a 90° angle change; then an invisible ellipse takes us into the preceding character's office, retroactively modifying our understanding of the previous articulation, which, instead of 'large indefinite' becomes 'small measurable'. As we shall see, this type of ellipse, which I have described as 'deferred', plays an important role in *Spione*. Finally, there is the close-up of the window being pierced by a bullet: although we tend now, conditioned by fifty years of sound cinema, to see it chiefly as a substitute for sound effects, in a silent context it also plays the elliptical role of synecdoche.

Although an overall analysis of the film is impossible here, attention should be drawn to what seems to me to be one of its keystones: the crucial stages in the first three-quarters of the main story (the love affair between Sonja and Tremaine, interrupted midway and relayed, as it were, by the short and tragic love of Matsumoto and Kitty) are marked by three 'cascades' of ellipses which are like so many echoes of the one used to open the film. As one might expect from the principle of variation adopted by Lang, these cascades are very different in kind. The first comes in Tremaine's apartment, after his encounter while disguised as a

Spione (Lang, 1928)

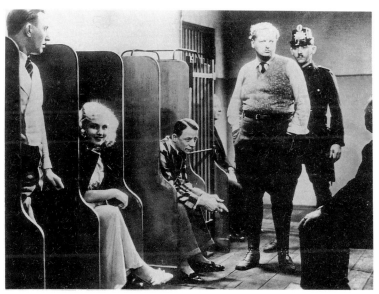

Das Testament des Doktor Mabuse (Lang, 1932–3)

tramp with Sonja, who tells him she has just killed a man. Once the police have gone, Tremaine takes a long look at himself in a mirror, and decides to spruce himself up before confronting the lovely lady hiding in his bedroom. There follows a series of almost crudely elliptical shots, in which reappears the idea not only of the synecdoche, but also of an 'expressive' ellipse-articulation (litotes): (1) a running tap; (2) a cake of soap being placed on a soap-dish (3) a towel being placed on a towel-rail; (4) a bath-thermometer being inserted into the water. The bath itself and the dressing afterwards take place off-screen, behind two shots in which Sonja searches the room into which Tremaine had shut her, and a third shot, of the manservant watching the door (another form of ellipse by insert, where the temporal abridgement occurs under cover of a 'third' shot; in this case the process is a dual one, Tremaine's ablutions being abridged in favour of the shot of the manservant).

But the most splendid cascade of ellipses of this type is probably the second in this 'series'. Under coercion from Haghi, Sonja writes and seals a letter for Tremaine which she addresses thus: (close-up) 'Hotel Olympic, Room 119/120' (dissolve)/close-up of the number on the door of Room 120/close-up of the letter held down by a statuette in Tremaine's room (we saw this statuette several times during Sonja's search) (dissolve)/close-up of the letter as presumably Tremaine reads it/(close-up) Tremaine's hand turns the letter over (at the foot of the statuette) and we read: '24 Park Street' (dissolve) in front of No. 24 a man arrives, back to camera – but it is not Tremaine, it is a 'Japanese' who furtively takes an impression of the lock under the eyes of a lookout linked telephonically (two inserted shots) to Matsumoto himself; and it is only after this interpolation that Tremaine himself arrives in front of the house in a taxi, with the 'Japanese' humbly opening the car door for him before moving away. Lang here displaces the 'logical' outcome of his abridgement, cheating our expectations by making the final ellipse at first definite (apparently it bridges the time lapse between Tremaine's reading of the letter and his arrival at the house), then indefinite (it is not Tremaine in front of the house, so this shot then seems to have no determinable temporal relation to the preceding one, and to be merely an associative link, a rhyme such as Lang often uses), and then, finally, reversing this again to show that we were right all along, definite (we were a few seconds ahead of Tremaine).

The third cascade preludes the other great sentimental encounter in the film, between Dr Matsumoto and Kitty, the treacherous *ingénue* sent by Haghi to seduce the Japanese. Matsumoto, who has just comforted Tremaine over Sonja's disappearance by revealing that she is a spy, remains alone on the pavement after Tremaine leaves. (1) a close-up of newspapers blowing in the wind; (2) repeat of the shot of Matsumoto; he holds out his hand; (3) close-up of a drop of rain falling on the hand; (4) repeat of the shot of Matsumoto; he starts walking; (5) close-up of posters torn by gusts of wind; (6) rain pelting down; Matsumoto enters the frame and passes Kitty, who is huddled in a doorway, her slender figure moulded by her soaked garment; (7) close-up as Matsumoto does a double-take and turns to the 'poor waif'. The configuration here is a novel one, for although only two of these shot-changes (4-5 and 5-6) are strictly speaking elliptical, the two earlier close-ups (the newspapers blowing, the drop of rain falling on the hand) have some of the characteristics of what one might call an elliptical movement, accelerating in pace and displaying in epitome the 'natural' stages of a storm-burst.

There is space enough here only to allude to the other aspect of the film: the many passages where, in striking opposition to the elliptical ones, time draws out, gets bogged down, where camera and montage linger lovingly over gestures, attitudes, faces, etc., almost as though only the narrowest possible area were to be allocated to the meagre prose of the story, the better to allow it to expand between a pyrotechnic poetry, often obscure, often built on elements superfluous to the narrative, and the languorous poetry of 'undue' gestures, of 'excessively long' shots, a poetry of time beguiled. Here we have an absolutely original dialectic that warrants more detailed examination.

Fourth Stage: Development of Rhyme

It is necessary for the coherence of this study to reverse chronology in the two last stages of Lang's German career. For despite the virtuosity it displays, *The Testament of Dr Mabuse* is far from achieving the same faultless mastery as *M*, made the year before.

On one very precise point, however, Lang's last German film makes a considerable contribution. I noted earlier of the first *Mabuse* that no matter how purely narrative their function, the articulations between sequences clearly heralded a cinema which would reject systematically transparent illusionism in that they revealed the continuous-discontinuous (dialectic) potential of spatio-temporal rupture in the cinema. And one can say that this sequel which Lang and Harbou decided to append to the narrative of their first masterpiece was also to be a continuation – and more particularly a development – of the formal approach inaugurated by it. Of course one finds the same type of articulations in *The Testament of Dr Mabuse* – by question and answer, by mental association, or simply by cause and effect – but one also finds a number of others not reducible in this way to the substance of the plot and which at the same time reveal, through the close links they maintain with the 'narrative' articulations, the existence of a much more general category of articulations between shots completely discontinuous spatially (in other words, between sequences).

This category I call 'rhyme'. And in *The Testament* Lang has subjected rhyme to a process of variation at least as rich as that undergone by ellipse in *Spione*. In order to gather some of the elements for a pragmatic definition of this protean and rather elusive figure, some of the aspects assumed by rhyme in *The Testament* should perhaps be listed. Some samples will, I think, also help to demonstrate that the distinction between narrative and 'plastic' rhymes, which may seem palpable when one passes from an examination of the first *Mabuse* to the second, is in fact probably a delusion, and that in the context of a dialectical analysis of a *composite* cinema (abstract-concrete, formal-narrative) only the general notion of rhyme has any real bearing.

Not surprisingly, the new dimension of sound greatly aided Lang in his task of extending this concept of rhyme. The passage from the first to the second sequence in *The Testament*, for instance, involves a musical rhyme: the deafening throbbing of some mysterious machinery, the only sound accompanying the scene in which the ex-policeman Hofmeister is spotted by two of the counterfeiters, 'changes into' the roar of a lorry starting up at the very moment when Hofmeister, thinking he has had a narrow escape, emerges from the warehouse-hideout. Here these two sounds 'rhyme' through their timbre and their sustained character, while the second differs from the first in pitch and volume (being sharper and weaker). And as we shall see, one of the essential characteristics of these rhymed articulations is in fact that the rhyme always (apart from exceptional cases, instanced later) reproduces the continuous-discontinuous phenomenon already described, but in the form of a 'resemblance-dissemblance' phenomenon. A few moments later, for instance, the crooks hurl a metal drum at Hofmeister which explodes in flames, and in the darkness that follows we hear a voice (talking about H Wagner's *The Walkyrie*) use the word 'pyre'; then we discover the speaker, Inspector Lohmann, in his office preparing to go on leave. Here the rhyme is in the nature of a pun – whose generic essence is precisely an opposition between resemblance and disemblance – but no matter how different in *substance* this rhyme is from the first example, the method of 'transmission' remains the same.

Further on in the film comes a remarkable succession of sequences, rich in rhymes of every kind, which will give some indication of the range Lang felt this device could cover. When the hero, Kent, and his girl are imprisoned in the 'curtained room' and hear the faint but unmistakable ticking of a hidden time-bomb, Lang turns to the last of a series of scenes depicting the quaintly bourgeois way of life of the members of the gang; here the irregular tapping of a spoon on a boiled egg echoes the regular ticking of the bomb. A few moments later, with the police already laying siege to the gang's apartment, a brief alternating montage is sketched between the gang's absurd attempt to escape by knocking a hole in the ceiling, and Kent's equally futile efforts to make some impression on the walls of his prison with a fragile penknife. Then, at the moment of surrender, the toughest gang member puts a bullet into his own brain; the police rush in; in close-up the hand holding the gun falls to the ground, and another hand enters the frame to seize the gun. Next comes another close-up with the gun in the same hand as though it were being examined. We then realize that we are in Inspector Lohmann's office, and that we have just witnessed a sort of rhymed ellipse, *retroactively perceived* (which in fact happens where both elements of the rhyme are identical, and where the rhyme can therefore only be perceived retroactively at the same time as the ellipse that divides it, because at the moment of articulation one of the conditions required to produce rhyme – spatio-temporal discontinuity – did not appear to be fulfilled). The scene continues with Lohmann, questioning one of the gang in his office, talking about 'the man who pulls the strings', and we are taken back again to the curtained room where Kent and the girl, having cut through a pipe, are anxiously watching the water level rise; but the first image that follows Lohmann's remark shows only the wooden cut-out figure used by the mysterious gang-member to sustain the illusion of his presence behind the curtain. With this single but fragmented scene alternating with a number of 'outside' scenes boldly and brilliantly dovetailed into it, we hear Lohmann mention for the first time the name of Dr Baum, the man whom Mabuse has posthumously turned into his slave; back in the room, we see, floating on the rising water and entering the empty frame, the loudspeaker which Baum, as the shadowy gang leader, used to address his henchmen. When Lohmann rubs his hands and exclaims 'Things are hotting up!' after telephoning Baum to lay a trap for him, our return to the room is followed almost immediately (the slight delay merely accentuating the rhyme) by the long-dreaded explosion, which, muffled by the mass of water, in fact frees the two lovers (in a way this rhyme is an inversion of the 'pyre' one at the beginning of the film). 'We're free!' cries Kent; 'Let me out of this cage!' echoes one of the gang members back at the police station, where Lohmann is arranging a confrontation with Dr Baum.

One can see quite clearly here how Lang runs the whole gamut of rhymes in order to bridge the disjunction between sequences with links that are as diversified as possible; hence the sense of a mechanism whose workings are as inexorable as they are constantly varied. Since *The Testament of Dr Mabuse*, these rhyming methods have been much used, and mostly abused, generally to titivate an articulation here and there. This is why they seem so gratuitous nowadays, and generally are inasmuch as they are not used with the same methodical variation as in Lang's film, which therefore offers a lesson still valid today, if not always through the excellence of its rhymes, at least in the attitude which governs their organization.

Fifth Stage: Large Scale Form

Unquestionably Lang's masterpiece, *M* provides us with one of the very first examples, along with *Battleship Potemkin* and *Vampyr*, of a composite form, simultaneously incorporating every aspect of a group of cinematic parameters and every moment of the film within a totally coherent combination.

The film can be seen as divided into nine clearly distinguished parts, each one having its own manner of functioning, obeying, one might say, its own laws. A certain number of general guiding principles circulate through the film as a whole, however, with those which govern the functioning of each part appearing in others, but according to a different prescription and with a different field of application. It is the very complex interaction between these principles which governs the form, or in the words of André Hodeir 'the mode of existence of a work which, while ensuring its unity, tends towards the greatest possible diversity'.

The nine parts of the film can be defined as follows: (1) the murder of Elsie Beckmann; (2) fear of the child-murderer spreads in the city; (3) police procedures and their inefficacy; (4) the underworld and the police pull together, each in its own way; (5) the two searches get under way; (6) the searches end; (7) M at bay – the building torn apart – M captured; (8) the police pick up M's trail; (9) the two trials.

As in all Lang's major films – with the exception already noted of *Metropolis* – the parameters productive of structures are essentially those relating to sequence changes (the same as changes of place in my analysis). It is through the arrangement of the frequency and 'degree of discontinuity' of those articulations, as well as the way in which their consistent element of *continuity* functions, that these nine parts are organized, both internally and in relation to each other.

Furthermore, the film is traversed by two broader movements which are, in a sense, independent of the division into parts. One of them, more or less constant, carries the film as a whole from the discontinuous towards the continuous. The other, which one might describe as recurrent, consists of a gradual 'unveiling' of the central character: it makes its appearance on seven occasions, always in a different tempo and aspect, but its overall progression through the film to the final 'nakedness' is constant.

These two broader movements, whose constituent elements naturally contribute to the particular style of the film, nevertheless derive directly from the terms of the theme that serves as a point of departure: an *unknown* murderer, *unseen*, making *intermittent appearances*, sows terror *on all sides* and *among all classes*; he is *progressively tracked down* and finally forced into a *sustained confrontation*. Nothing would be more misleading, however, than any attempt to reduce the form of the film or its style to a simple substantiation of this plot. As I hope to demonstrate, what we have here is a fully composite work, in which the structures retain their autonomous, 'abstract' function, but in symbiosis with the plot which they both support and challenge.

The murder of Elsie Beckmann

The film opens with a series of shots in three different settings which are nevertheless shown to be contiguous (the courtyard of a block of flats, where children are singing 'The Killer's Song'; the landing where the housewife who has just told off the children stops to speak to Frau Beckmann; and the latter's kitchen) and which provide from the outset a sort of surety for the continuity so often to be abandoned or subsequently challenged. Immediately after this, in fact, begins the first and one of the most subtle of the succession of alternate montage sequences ranged throughout the film and constituting one of its basic formal principles. Here, alternating with scenes showing Frau Beckmann going about her household chores and worrying about her little girl being late in coming home, we find two series of three 'insert' shots: the first series sketches a very condensed account of the little girl's journey to her death (leaving school; a police notice against which she bounces her ball and on which the killer's shadow falls; the purchase of the toy balloon), while the second comprises 'empty' shots emphasizing the girl's absence and accompanied by the mother's shrill cries (an angled shot down the empty staircase; the deserted attic with some clothes drying, Elsie's vacant chair). This second series, however, is heralded even before the end of the first, when this same shot of the empty staircase makes two anticipatory appearances, cut into shots of Frau Beckmann leaning over the banister. Furthermore, if this second series is 'clinched' by a shot (the empty chair) deriving from both the kitchen series and the 'cut in' series, this whole first part is similarly clinched by the pair of shots which, signifying through synecdoche the death of the little girl (the ball rolling on the ground, the balloon catching in the telegraph wires), also refer to the only two shots in the first series in which the killer was present (the poster, the balloon-vendor); the continuity between these new, isolated shots and the earlier series is ensured by Frau Beckmann's voice calling Elsie.

This part of the film also contains the first of the seven different and more or less progressive 'unveilings' through which we gradually move towards acquaintance with the killer, and which, taken together, compose a movement of approach essential to the general metabolism of the film. Here, from an off-screen presence (first appearance of the whistled tune) becoming a shadow on screen, the murderer gets as far as being seen in back view (the shot with the balloon-vendor); then the process is suspended, with the unveiling of the face not coming until much later, in successive stages.

Fear spreads in the city
Essentially, this part of the film comprises four comparatively elaborate sequences showing the effects of the engendered fear by the murder on the average citizen. Although radically disjunctive as regards both characters (who appear only in this context) and settings (completely isolated from each other and never seen again), this series is tightly fused by way of various rhymes, a device which reappears in amplified form later in the film. A man reads aloud a police notice before which a crowd is assembled, the same text continues first in the form of a radio broadcast, then, in the second sequence, is read aloud from a newspaper in a café, where the excited customers end by coming to blows, with the victim accusing his assailant of 'slandering reputations'. These words, on which the scene ends, rhyme with the 'What a slander!' uttered by a man whose apartment is being searched by the police on the strength of an anonymous letter. Finally, when this man, wrongfully suspected, says that the killer 'might be absolutely anybody in the street', these words instantly introduce the fourth episode of the series: a man is manhandled by a crowd as a result of a tragic-comic mis-understanding.

But just as important as this continuous-discontinuous movement are the three shots which *precede* this series: the first two, in which newsvendors raise the cry about the murder, recapitulate but also anticipate, since their cry is 'Who is the killer?' and the next shot (another example of the question-answer device) shows us the killer himself, sitting with his back to camera, writing a letter to the newspapers (one can barely see him; this is the first piece in a schematic unveiling (the second 'unveiling moment') completed only in Part 3). This shot also refers to Part 1, since we hear the whistled tune for the second time; and the next shot, introducing the series of four sequences, refers to the only other shot in the first part in which the killer 'appeared', since the poster in front of which the crowd is assembled begins with the same words as the one we saw earlier – '10,000 Marks reward: who is the murderer?' – with the typography ensuring that only these words are legible.

One can thus see how careful Lang is to weave a complex network of affiliations between the first two parts of the film, before embarking on this series of four comical sketches which involve not only a complete break in tone but a different narrative method.

Police procedures and their inefficacy

This part offers two subdivisions radically opposed in every respect. The first is one of the most discontinuous passages in the film: over the phone, the commissioner of police informs his minister of the extensive measures taken by his men, while we see his remarks illustrated by a series of very short and totally disjointed sequences. The other comprises the first (and for a considerable time, the only) long continuous sequence: a raid on one of the city's big whorehouses. It should be noted, however, that the continuous mode has already been introduced into the commissioner's illustrated report during the little comic sketch in which two eye-witnesses quarrel about what they saw; and that the portion of the long, two-part final sequence that takes place in the streets is introduced by overlapping of the commissioner's voice off screen ('But these measures have proved as ineffective as the nocturnal raids on underworld haunts') as though the illustrations were simply to continue. It is only when preparations for the raid are fairly advanced that we realize the narrative mode has changed yet again (and retroactive articulations of this type play a similarly privileged role throughout the film). It is also worth noting how this illustrated report is divided into several segments framed (asymmetrically) by shots of the commissioner and of the minister. Particularly striking here, however, is the insert of a close-up of the killer in his room, making hideous faces at himself in a mirror: a shot that it seems legitimate to take as the conclusion of the second 'unveiling' movement, which also started in the killer's room (these are in fact the only two shots in which we see him at home) in the shot showing him writing his letter at the beginning of Part 2; here again, though, given the facial distortions, his features are not completely unveiled.

The underworld and the police pull together

Simplistic in appearance, the structure here is perhaps the most complex in the film. After a purely narrative (transparent) and entirely continuous preamble (representatives from the various underworld organizations meet to discuss measures for dealing with the inconvenience indirectly caused them by the child-murderer), we embark on another (and very long) alternate montage series which takes up the rest of Part 4. At first sight the simple alternation – between a meeting of police officials trying to decide on more efficient measures, and the underworld conference which will result in a 'parallel action' – may seem platitudinous, not to say facile. But at a closer look one realizes that Lang has incorporated an extremely subtle variation principle which brings a whole range of oral rhymes into play.

The first rhyme is achieved through the completion of a sentence: addressing his colleagues, Schränker, the notorious crook presiding over the underworld meeting, says 'I am asking you . . .'/'. . . for your advice' finishes the police commissioner in the next shot. The first sequence involving the police ends on a very different rhyme, a sort of tit for tat retort: 'What we need,' a police officer says, 'is more and more frequent and tougher and tougher raids,' then he sits down/the racketeer immediately gets up to address the crooks: 'Informers! What we need is informers planted among the police so that we are warned about new measures in time.' A few moments later the Hustler maintains that 'the police ought to be looking elsewhere . . . because the man they want isn't a crook'/'Except during one of his fits, he's a man who probably looks like a respectable citizen,' an elderly police inspector continues, completing a rhyme that might be described as 'corroborative'. The passage which follows is the longest involving the police: uniquely, it ends in a cul-de-sac, with no liaison whatsoever with the next scene at the crooks' conference. As though to accentuate this break, the scene begins with a long silence in the smoky atmosphere.

Finally the pickpocket interjects a suggestion so completely harebrained that/a police officer cuts him off in mid-sentence with a 'contradictory' rhyme (and overlapping sound). But the officer's remarks are no more convincing, and an inspector says angrily, 'All this is getting us nowhere'/'That's no use', echoes the Hustler (rhyme through reiteration). As for the two articulations that follow, they are in perfect 'assonance', in the sense that the discourse passes from one setting to the other without any break in continuity, forming a perfectly unified whole. Then the Hustler acknowledges defeat: 'Well, what then?'/the police remain silent/so do the crooks/still the police are silent/and so are the crooks . . . until Schränker finally has an idea: 'We must catch him ourselves'/ And Inspector Lohmann, 'facing' him, echoes: 'There may perhaps still be a way . . .' Finally, in the last shot of the series, Schränker explains that the city's beggars must be mobilized (here the rhyme is no longer between two lines of dialogue, but has expanded to cover both sequences in their entirety).

It should be added that the spatial organization of the *découpage* here (the sequence of camera angles and distances) contributes to the creation of a sort of semi-illusion of continuity between the two settings, so that certain rhymes are further complicated by a slight delay in perception of the change in setting.

The two searches get under way
Essential though it may be, this part is very simple in style. Initially connected with what preceded it by Schränker's last words ('the beggars') – just as Part 4 was connected to Part 3 by the Pickpocket seeing the police wagons passing the window after the raid – it begins with sequences that are continuous and firmly linked to each other (all take place in the same building: the beggars' 'market'). In addition to the apparent purpose here of starting each of the main subdivisions with an affirmation of continuity, one finds from now on a progressive expansion of this sense of continuity up to the great final *séquence-fleuve*.

Next we move, bridged by the sound of a barrel-organ, to a shot which shows the beggar-musician watching over the children playing in a courtyard (an echo of the first shot in the film), and which is followed by three other similar tableaux. When we come after this to the corresponding police operations, they are set out not in this linear and directly elliptical manner, but by way of another alternate montage which reintroduces the killer, after his longest absence yet, in the most gradual of the seven unveilings. The first shot of the second series shows the killer leaving home furtively, huddled into his overcoat, hat pulled down over his eyes; we hardly have time to recognize him before he goes out of frame right. Almost immediately one of Lohmann's men enters left and goes inside the building. After this shot which introduces its two protagonists, the alternate montage begins: while the policeman gains admittance to Herr Beckert's room and submits it to a routine search, the killer (partially masked by the pile of fruit) buys an apple, stares hypnotized at a window-display of cutlery (close-up of the face, but it is blurred by glittering reflections in the glass), has his eyes drawn to a little girl whom he is about to follow; we hear his whistling off, but the little girl is rejoined by her mother and the killer hides in the doorway of a bookshop and then hurries (back to camera) to the terrace of a café, where, almost entirely hidden by a screen of ivy, he has a cognac to calm himself.

The final sequence in this series, which interrupts the alternate montage's to-and-fro, might perhaps be considered as a pendant to the two sequences at the beginning in which the policeman, after an exchange on the landing with the deaf landlady, finds himself alone in Beckert's room. What is incontestable, however, is the psychological movement here: the character retreating back into the shadows the moment the impulse is frustrated.

The searches end
The simplest of the nine parts, this one works basically through pairs of alternating sequences, if one excludes the first in which the policeman makes a routine report to Lohmann about Beckert (although this sequence can be taken as pairing with the last, in which the police move in to Beckert's room, to wait in vain for his return).

M at bay – the building torn apart – M captured
This part is the freest in the entire film. In a sort of fantasy on the original theme, each aspect of the film is reproduced, but on a reduced scale: the fourth unveiling is repeated (when the camera discovers M emerging from the shadows in the attic after the night-

watchman passes), as well as the principle of alternate montage, carried to climactic lengths but at the same time tailored to the 'recognizable' geography of the building, thus considerably attenuating its disjointed quality both spatially and temporally. On the other hand, it is here that one really finds oneself confronted by the killer for the first time – one sees him clearly, that is; the oral confrontation will not come till the end – while watching in close-up his desperate efforts to escape from his attic prison. And lastly, as already suggested, this part marks a great stride towards the absolute continuity of the final trial, in so far as alternate montage, restricted by the mental space-time, makes the ellipses much less obvious. Towards the end of this part, moreover, this sense of relative continuity is reinforced, contrariwise, by the only shot that violates it spatially: the teleprinter at the police station receiving the alarm signal when the nightwatchman manages to trigger it, which has the effect of accelerating the movement ending in the sixth unveiling, when M is discovered and again emerges from the shadows of the lumber-room (duplicating almost exactly the fifth unveiling, but 'in front of witnesses').

The police pick up M's trail
This extremely curious part is the only one whose exact beginning is in effect obfuscated. When the Burglar calls up for a ladder, filmed from above through the hole he has dug in the bank's ceiling, one might think – as he does – that some of his comrades are waiting for him up there; but when he emerges from the hole, he finds the police (off). Unknown to us, an ellipse had therefore separated this shot from the one preceding it; the other crooks left a good while earlier, and Part 8, presided over by the police, had already begun.

This eighth part is doubly (even triply) recapitulatory. Not only does the file which Lohmann is shown by his colleague Groeber resurrect the essence of the previous sequence (photographs showing the now deserted building where the action took place); this series of disjointed images commented on by a voice off is also a distinct reminder of the form of the first sub-division of Part 3. One might even hazard that the lengthy interrogations of the Burglar (used to frame his re-exposition) recall the gambling den sequence, both in their continuity and in the sort of relationships established between police and crooks. But at all events they undoubtedly form the penultimate stage in the film's takeover by the principle of continuity, which achieves absolute control during the climactic trial. Yet discontinuity is still present in three different ways: through the insert showing the famous hole in the ceiling when the Burglar protests that damage to property was all that happened; through the insert of the nightwatchman stuffing himself with sausages (a shot giving the lie to Lohmann's ploy of making the Burglar think one of his colleagues 'hit too hard'); and through the unexpected shot of Lohmann splashing water on his face in the lavatory where he has fled to recover from the excitement of what his prisoner has just revealed. Eventually this sequence ends on what seems to be a 'mental flash', apparently functioning like the inserts of the hole in the ceiling and the nightwatchman, and showing the exterior of the factory which the Burglar indicates as the place where the killer is being held. But as the next shot brings us closer to the factory, and a third takes us inside (inaugurating Part 9), the role of this 'flash' is retroactively modified, and rather than 'subjective' is seen to be 'objective' (the same device occurred in Part 6: in Lohmann's office, the officer who searched Beckert's room suddenly remembers the window-ledge/a close-up of the ledge, apparently 'mental' but in fact describing an ellipse, retroactively perceived when a policeman's hand holding a magnifying-glass enters the frame).

The two trials
The first is of course the famous virtuoso passage in which Peter Lorre as Franz Beckert/M confronts his accusers. This sequence is characterized essentially by an illusory continuity (a continuity imposed through the editing, in other words, rather than through actual continuity in the images) which is absolute and unblemished: no matter how closely one examines it, the duration of the action appears to correspond exactly to its screen time. Another important characteristic is that M *talks* for the first time. Hitherto he has uttered barely half-a-dozen completely non-committal phrases, and in the only scenes in which we had really been close to him (in the attic) he was silent apart from a few oaths.

We now come to the final, brilliant blending of the two movements that have run through the film: the movements towards continuity and towards the unveiling of M (the last stage visually in this unveiling being of course the moment when M himself tears off the coat covering his head to face his persecutors). In the context of this twin fulfilment, tokens of recall like the balloon floating in the air or the photographs of the murdered children are completely assimilated into the emotional movement, which naturally dominates here. This sequence stands alone, cut off from everything else. The concern for continuity, for unity, is such that when the police invade the factory, we do not see them – looking off-screen, the crooks slowly put their hands up – because any intrusion on screen by characters whose real (formal) role was completed in Part 8 would certainly have undermined the privileged autonomy of this sequence.

The film ends with the second, derisory trial: a shot of a court bench where the judge begins reading a verdict we do not even hear – a shot which, because of its total isolation in space-time, and especially because of its extreme brevity, even further accentuates the solemn finality of the preceding sequence while at the same time acting as a coda. But the final 'articulation' is the shot of Frau Beckmann which brings us right back to the beginning of the film: 'That won't bring back our children. They should be better looked after' (a line memorable for its formal role rather than its curiously moralizing tone).

Another masterpiece, already mentioned – *The Testament of Dr Mabuse* – and that was the end: a silence lasting some thirty films.
Translated by Tom Milne

1987
This article has been placed at the head of this section because it formulates the credo of my formalism as it stood at the time of writing *Praxis du Cinéma*. The notion that *Dr Mabuse* made the whole future of classical narrative film superfluous need hardly be dwelt upon, any more than the proposition that the 'essence' of *Mabuse* – or of any other silent Lang film – lay in its 'abstraction'. The assumption that *Mabuse* was the first convincing instance of film dramaturgy came from my ignorance of the cinemas of Italy (Gustavo Serena's *Assunta Spina* (1915)), Sweden (Sjöstrom's *The Girl from the Marsh Croft* (1917)), pre-revolutionary Russia (Protozanov's *Father Sergius* (1918)) and even France (Antoine's *The Earth* (1921)). For a very different approach to *Mabuse*, see Chapter 10.

More serious is the issue of Lang's place in the American cinema. Even if the general dismissal of Hollywood implicit in a number of comments here was ill-informed, the fact remains that a fuller familiarity with, on the one hand, the Hollywood films of the 1930s and 1940s and, on the other, the films made in Hollywood by Lang, does show that his work there was marginal and second-rate. The basic problem seems to have been that with the sole exception of the astonishing *You and Me* (1938), reminiscent of the Brechtian *Lehrstück*, he forgot that he was a European (unlike Edgar Ulmer, for example) yet remained incapable of more than the most superficial view of his adopted society. The critique of mob violence in *Fury* (1936) is far less penetrating, far more élitist and insensitive to American reality, than Mervyn Leroy and Robert Rossen's *They Won't Forget* (1937). *Hangmen Also Die* (1943) conforms far more to the traditional Hollywood stereotyping of Nazis and resistants than did the treatment of much the same theme by the American Communists Frank Tuttle and Lester Cole (*Hostages* (1944)) and it pales beside fellow immigré Jean Renoir's masterful study of collaboration and resistance *This Land is Mine* (1943). While he seems to have come closer to finding himself again in his strong remake of Renoir's *La Chienne* (*Scarlet Street*, 1945), *Human Desire* (1954), his reworking of the French Master's *La Bête Humaine*, seems to sum up his passive acceptance of the most reactionary Hollywood values of his day – unless its failings were simply due to his lesser aptitude at manipulating the system than Preminger's or Sirk's. Paradoxically, the formalist claims made here for Lang's German period are actually closer to the truth with regard to the academic formalism – in the sense of a highly crafted tissue of clichés – displayed by such films as *Secret Beyond the Door* or *Moonfleet*. And the implied assertion that the kind of artistic mastery which reached its zenith in *M* was left behind in Germany seems as accurate today as it did fifteen years ago.

2 Marcel L'Herbier

To write today in a manner neither contemptuous nor archaeological about Marcel L'Herbier (born 1890) is necessarily to assume the mantle of rehabilitator. At least this is so in Paris, the only place where his films are still likely to be seen.

Elsewhere, however, the masking, vignettes, and other technical devices of *Rose-France* (1918), the distorting lenses, selective *flous* and multiple superimpositions of *El Dorado* (1921) and the accelerated montage of *L'Inhumaine* (1924) might well be *recognized* by the underground generations; for they, at least, have deconsecrated the cinematographic image, so long held sacred under the reign of men like Bazin and Rossellini, and they care nothing for the peculiarly Parisian terrorism exercised by the disciples of André Breton, who are still busy paying off old scores, calling Germaine Dulac to account for *La Coquille et le Clergyman* and L'Herbier for his 'decadent' aestheticism.

A decadent aesthete the young L'Herbier undoubtedly was just after the First World War. As a man of letters, his gods were Claudel and Wilde (but also Villiers de l'Isle Adam and Proust); as a musician, his master was Debussy. As one might expect, he despised the cinema – until the day he suffered, like the rest of Parisian intelligentsia, the shock of DeMille's *The Cheat* (1915). Paradoxically, this first glimpse offered to Paris of a new cinematic dramaturgy – with a supple, quasi-invisible *découpage* or shot-structure which at last succeeded in fragmenting the screen space without shattering it – was to set L'Herbier, Gance and Epstein on a course which would lead them to the antipodes of the academic pole it actually signposted. In fact, only Delluc learned a direct lesson from this film. For the rest, including L'Herbier, it was the point of departure for an impassioned quest: the quest for that famous specific nature of cinema.

First stage: *Rose-France* (1918), 'a slim volume of verses published at the author's expense'. But although rooted in a literary-economic tradition derived from the nineteenth century, nothing could be further from the drawing-room aesthetics of *The Cheat* than this curious collage which mingles pretty postcards of pure 1914-18 camp with title cards copiously laden with verses culled from Charles d'Orléans and Péguy, the whole being packaged in an orgy of maskings, superimpositions and process shots which provoked Delluc to remark that 'L'Herbier is the finest photographer in France' ('perhaps to finish me for good', comments L'Herbier). This genuinely experimental film, which almost ruined L'Herbier, embodies an idea which casts even further than the major works to come: the idea of narrative as plastic by vocation. Here there is no dramaturgy, virtually no story, only a succession of symbolic actions articulating an 'impressionist' evocation through the indeterminately placed titles and inserts. But although this technique derives from *fin de siècle* conventions, it looks forward to our own times, to our concern with discontinuity, heterogeneous materials, irrational narratives. And beyond the frenzied patriotism it expands so faithfully, *Rose-France* emerges today as the 'visual music' dreamed of by L'Herbier, Gance and Dulac, and which three generations of critics and historians, preoccupied (quite justifiably, admittedly) by another approach to literature, were unable to hear.

A defeat for poetry, therefore, and an enforced return to *The Cheat*: to dramaturgy, in other words. First came the hack work designed to secure his position with Gaumont and to teach him more acceptable techniques (*Le Bercail* (1919) and *Le Carnaval des Vérités* (1919)) and then *L'Homme du Large* (1920), based on Balzac's *Un Drame au Bord de la Mer*. This time artifice made a reappearance (masks, superimposition, stylized lighting and framing), with the result that the natural landscapes inherited from the Swedish cinema are transformed into magnificent studio décors, nowadays unmistakably giving the lie to the naturalistic label that has stuck to this film for so long. Of crucial importance, too, is the idea adumbrated in the film that, through the mediation of the *découpage*, the shot-structure, dramaturgical methods can *also* be structure (music, according to the ideology of the time). For instance, a confrontation scene starting with comparatively brief shots and ending with a slow dissolve between the last shot and reverse angle, followed by an iris out, will inevitably bestow a double function on the *découpage*, appealing to the spectator in double guise: as narrative medium and as pure structure (rhythm), because this doubly 'cushioned' fall, in opposition to the previous progression along a series of peaks, carries the narrative, but at the same time asserts its abstraction. Thus the sequence where the father and son confront each other with the titles superimposed on the images (Henri Langlois compared these shots to ideograms) closely blends the visual and narrative functions.

It is easy to view the histrionics of Jaque Catelain, Roger Karl, Marcelle Pradot and the young Charles Boyer as grotesque; and it is true that with very few exceptions the French actors of the day did not adapt too well to the screen (which may be why Renoir looked to Germany for his Nana, just as L'Herbier did for his Baroness Sandorff – Brigitte Helm – in *L'Argent*).

Actually, Eve Francis and Philippe Hériat – playing what are in effect the leads in *El Dorado* (1921) – are among the handful of French actors from the period who are still watchable today. But irrespective of these questions of taste and fashion, the sequence-shot in which Eve Francis, racked by grief, falters slowly down a flight of steps, after having been thrown out of the villa belonging to her seducer's father – like the one in which she walks interminably along a huge white wall from long shot into close-up – prefigures the 'infernal *longueurs*' of Godard or Garrel. A first (provisional) landfall along L'Herbier's route, *El Dorado* contains, on the one hand, some spectacular *trouvailles* which have kept historians happy and can still excite the imagination today since they have never been followed up, and, on the other, more importantly, scenes structured with a spatio-temporal freedom far in advance of the period which foreshadow the birth of modern *découpage* in *L'Argent* (1928). Among the isolated *trouvailles* may be cited the shot where Eve Francis, day-dreaming on a bench before going on stage at the cabaret, is seen as a blur while the other dancers sitting on either side of her remain perfectly in focus; the arrival of Eve Francis in the Alhambra gardens against a background twice transformed by means of enigmatic dissolves which do not seem to affect her movement in any way; and the 'Cubist' split-screen in which the upper half of the image contains a shot of water filmed vertically from above, while in the lower half Jaque Catelain crosses the screen in long shot, presumably passing this same pool of water. Among the sustained *découpages* must be mentioned the two

L'Argent (L'Herbier, 1928)

El Dorado (L'Herbier, 1921)

sequences in the cabaret which open and close the film: the first handles the cut-in/cut-back mode of matching with unprecedented freedom, and the second is distinguished by a very skilful use of cross-cutting, with shadows from both stage and auditorium projected onto the backcloth behind which Eve Francis kills herself. Particularly remarkable, however, is the scene in the Alhambra in which Eve Francis secretly watches her seducer's movements among the pillars with his new mistress. Here the diversification of angles and distances, the contrasts between foregrounds and backgrounds, the use made of entries and exits from the frame, are an already remarkably assured affirmation of an attitude which would lead progressively to a rejection – from within the dramaturgical cinema itself – of *mise en scène* in favour of *mise en forme*.

These few references to the plot suffice to indicate that *El Dorado* is, in the figurative sense, a melodrama. But it is also a melodrama in the literal sense: the film, for the first time in the history of the cinema – and such incontestable 'firsts' are rare – was accompanied by a musical score composed with reference to the images and intended to be performed in constant synchronism with them.

Next come L'Herbier's two most celebrated films: *L'Inhumaine*, considered as the height of absurdity by his detractors, and *Feu Mathias Pascal* (UK: *The Late Mathias Pascal*; USA: *The Living Dead Man*, 1925), which the same detractors and the average historian are agreed in finding, all things considered, the best thing he has done. Today, while *L'Inhumaine* hardly seems to warrant such excessive severity, the slightly condescending accolade (second class) given to *Feu Mathias Pascal* totally falsifies historical perspective.

Curiously enough, both films have a feature which distinguishes them from the rest, although this trait has been very loosely attributed to L'Herbier's work as a whole: the mixture of styles. It is worth noting, first of all, that the generally high opinion enjoyed by *Feu Mathias Pascal* is bound up with a 'psychological' and dramaturgical justification of this anomalous element, while the opprobrium invariably encountered by *L'Inhumaine* – except among the more extreme devotees of camp – is primarily due to the fact that the admixture in this case is *pure artifice*.

L'Inhumaine was in fact a commissioned film, partly financed by its star, the singer Georgette Leblanc (who had almost been Debussy's original Mélisande in 1901) and intended as a showcase offering Americans examples of contemporary French art: painting, music, design, architecture, fashion, dance and, presumably, cinema. Each set was created by a different designer (Cavalcanti, Autant-Lara, Léger, Mallet-Stevens), and it is evident that L'Herbier deliberately attempted to mould the tone and development of each sequence in terms of the décor. Even the sequences shot in real interiors (the Ballets Suédois at the Théâtre des Champs-Elysées) or on location (the hallucinatory car rides) seem to be governed by this principle, which is, moreover, in no way aberrant in itself: now that the essentially composite character of cinema has begun to be recognized, one can say that a film subscribing wholly to it would not be running counter to the specific nature of cinema. In the final analysis, *L'Inhumaine* falls apart into a series of bravura pieces (some of them quite remarkable) which can only be considered in isolation. To my mind the lack of any underlying unity is due less to the framework provided by the script – admittedly weak by literary standards but nevertheless lending itself quite well to the discontinuity principle that conditions the film (L'Herbier says of this script that it was a 'figured base' on which to build 'plastic harmonies') – than to the inconsistency of the actors, who are after all the only elements of continuity in the film. Georgette Leblanc may have been too old for her role as a man-eating blue-stocking, and her acting is even more disastrous; and Jaque Catelain, who had a certain naïve charm in *Rose-France* and *L'Homme du Large*, is horribly miscast in the role of a passionate and worldly young scholar. Only the remarkable Philippe Hériat manages to bring conviction to his part (a musical comedy role as a Maharaja), and in some of the sequences in which he appears, no matter how divergent the styles, he contrives a semblence of unity which is entirely lacking elsewhere. It is possible that Darius Milhaud's score may have been a factor in lending overall unity; this, unfortunately, is something that cannot at present be verified.

Several sequences may be cited, however, to show how L'Herbier was continuing the experiments he had been conducting with exemplary persistence from the outset of his singular career. The artiste juggling a black and white painted cube on the balls of his feet is *encompassed* from every angle and distance, and the montage of this passage from the first sequence anticipates Eisenstein's analogous experiments by several years. Georgette Leblanc, venturing into the young scholar's bizarre house to pay her last respects to what she believes to be his corpse, is 'tracked' through a vast, bare set by a camera concerned to exploit to a maximum the possibilities of creating a new space by restructuring angles and by isolating the fields of vision from each other. Here again the *découpage* is both dramaturgy – the hallucinatory tension of this scene still works perfectly today – and a structural progression in itself. When the Maharaja, having substituted himself for Georgette Leblanc's chauffeur, races along the *corniche* with the *'inhumaine'* agonizing in the back seat of the car – victim of a poisonous snake hidden in a bouquet of flowers by the Maharaja himself – this extremely Feuillade-esque sequence is treated on the principle of a cyclical montage of variations, with the same shots recurring in a different order each time.

As for the famous accelerated montage of the long resuscitation sequence which climaxes the film, however – in a laboratory designed by Léger and staffed by dancers from the Ballets Suédois – it looks for once as though all L'Herbier has done is to take over one of the *idées fixes* of French film-makers at that time: to express movement, to create 'visual rhythms', by an essentially musical organization of extremely brief shots representing *inanimate* objects – a procedure based, it would seem, on the intuition that a static shot becomes pure duration and is therefore comparable to a *note value* in music. This (false) intuition had already inspired the sequences that today seem most debatable in that masterpiece *La Roue*. Not until the Russians would 'rapid montage' acquire a meaning, through the organic articulation of organic movements. The mechanical rigidity (even in movement) of the shots treated in this way in *La Roue* and *L'Inhumaine* results, despite frenzied accelerations, in a stilted static effect that is almost unwatchable today. There is confirmation here of a truth revealed to be fundamental: although there is an effective reality behind the cinema–music analogy, any mechanistic attempt to pattern a composite art on a homogeneous art is an error.

In this same sequence of *L'Inhumaine*, however, there is an experiment much more significant today (because it in fact draws attention to this composite nature): the insertion (in a tinted context: like most films of the period, it was tinted throughout) of very brief flashes of pure white and red which caused a contemporary critic to exclaim 'Tristan's cry comes true: I hear Light!' (The word 'psychedelic' hadn't been invented yet.)

Unlike *L'Inhumaine*, the subject of *Feu Mathias Pascal* had an unassailable pedigree: a novel by Pirandello no less. L'Herbier offered the part of Mathias to the excellent Russian émigré actor Ivan Mozhukhin (or Mosjoukine as he was known in France), and the project became a co-production with Alexandre Kamenka's famous Albatros company. It must be admitted that the dominant factor here is not the rigour of L'Herbier at his best, but the very free 'Albatros style' (e.g. Mozhukhin's *Le Brasier Ardent*, Epstein's *Le Lion des Mogols*, Volkoff's *Kean*): 'witty' camera angles and tricks, dream sequences shot against a black background, and so on. The film is made with great virtuosity, passing easily from rural *Kammerspiel* to comic fantasy by way of an excursion into expressionist comedy of manners. At the same time, everything here contributes towards the creation of that unity in diversity which was missing in *L'Inhumaine*: outstanding performances, beautiful photography, fine sets, a 'strong' plot. Yet the film is a retrograde step both in the history of the cinema and in L'Herbier's work. It takes us back to the notion of *mise en scène* being solely *at the service of a story*: it is *The Cheat* revised and corrected according to the Parisian-Russian aesthetic. The double function of the *découpage* which L'Herbier had already outlined in three of his films seems to be entirely missing here: each shot simply invents a new trick designed to display the Mathias-Mozhukhin character, and each sequence a new style which will 'reflect' the next stage in the story. But since cinematographic form was thought of precisely in these terms and no others for years, it is hardly surprising that where official history is concerned, *Feu Mathias Pascal* passes for L'Herbier's masterpiece.

His real masterpiece was to come very soon. In 1925, to offset the losses sustained by his own production company, L'Herbier made two commercial chores: *Le Vertige* and *Le Diable au Coeur*. When Jean Dréville, then a young admirer, taxed him with commercialism, L'Herbier replied that perhaps the period of experimentation was over; in his opinion 'the first avant-garde' (as it was subsequently named to distinguish it from the second: Man

Ray, Chomette, etc.) had lived out its life: it was time to pass on to serious matters. Dréville felt that this was a final abdication. And the project L'Herbier then had on hand might well have confirmed his fears: a Franco-German co-production with a bigger budget than the French cinema had ever known.

L'Argent undoubtedly marks the end of the period of experimentation, since it is itself the culmination of all these experiments – not just L'Herbier's, but those of the first avant-garde and even, to a certain extent, of the entire Western cinema (with the exception of the Russians). I shall therefore attempt a closer analysis of this masterpiece than those I have given here of other films of his.

My earlier statement that *L'Argent* gave birth to 'modern *découpage*' is based on the conviction that here, for the first time, the *style* (framing, camera placement and movement, positioning of actors, entries or exits from the frame, shot changes) systematically assumes a double role, dramaturgic and plastic, and that the interpenetration of these two functions creates an authentic cinematic dialectic, distinct equally from novelistic and musical dialectic, yet partaking of both.

The success of L'Herbier's undertaking was conditioned initially by seminal options in all departments: on the one hand, a novel by Zola in a tightly structured modern adaptation very different from the usual digest (the film runs for about three hours), and an international cast contrasting sharply with the actors in most French films not only by their physical presence but by their sober conviction (among the victims: Mary Glory, Henry Victor) or their controlled virtuosity (among the tormentors: Brigitte Helm, Alcover, Alfred Abel); and on the other, sets fantastic in size but extremely stark, with luminous photography accentuating this process of purification, and an absolutely unprecedented camera mobility.

L'Herbier claims that he made *L'Argent* because he hated money; and it is certainly true that the film, like the novel, is a sharp indictment of the cynicism of big business. At the same time, however, it was the enormous budget which not only determined the film's dramatic scope but made its formal ambitions possible (costly settings, camera movements necessitating the development of new techniques).

How does the dialectic that links these two axes of gestation function? One of L'Herbier's great achievements in this film is that not only was he the first to solve the tricky problem of the relationship between camera movements and shot changes, but he did so more effectively than anyone else until the Welles–Kurosawa generation.

In *L'Argent*, as in all cinema 'descended from *The Cheat*, the sequence of shots is at each moment a narrative vehicle. The camera movements, however, *inform* these shot changes on another level, establishing them as rhythmic or plasic elements. There are, for instance, a number of transition scenes set in the vast corridor of the bank where the characters keep a wary eye on each other as they pass under the white marble pillars; but although the look 'off' calls for a shot change according to traditional dramatic principles, the tracking shots which pursue or encircle the characters mean that these shot changes are seen to be obeying a double need: they indicate both a narrative movement (revealing what is seen, introducing new characters or new doorways) and a *formal* movement. For, although the camera movements themselves are never completely independent of the evolutions of the characters (and therefore participate in the dramaturgy precisely to the extent that they are subordinate), they do establish evidence of a frame in *constant and spectacular evolution* (owing to the expansiveness of both the movements and the sets which make them possible). Withdrawing to make disclosures, drawing closer to avoid them, gliding about in permutation and recomposition, these movements are completely devoid of the mentalistic function that has commonly been assigned to them since the introduction of the crane and dolly, for the *effect* they produce is unmistakably plastic. This is true not only of images in motion taken individually, but also of the totality of movements a sequence may comprise. At the same time the articulation of these movements, their 'broken continuity' spanning the cutaways which are dramatic in purpose *but which structure them* – like the flexible subordination of camera movements to character movements already mentioned – results in a crucial symbiosis: the dramaturgic and plastic functions are at once distinct and indissoluble.

Another manifestation of the same bivalence: the movement of characters within a fixed angle. In the long sequence in the Stock

Exchange restaurant where Saccard moves from table to table being introduced to all the characters who are to represent the power of money, the changes of shot and framing, whether static or in motion, are so tightly bound up with the unfolding of the plot that their functioning may at first glance seem to be univalent throughout. This is not so; it is merely that the instrument which animates them is no longer the same. Here this role is taken over by the entrances and exits from frame of the crowd of extras. Instead of being studiously 'realistic', and therefore invisible, as prescribed in studio-based films predicated upon the dialogue and the attitudes of the protagonists, these elements are stylized through acceleration or proliferation, and above all through a more or less precisely calculated spatio-temporal relationship to the elements of the *découpage* proper (changes of shot and camera movements), so that over and above their continuing dramatic function, the latter contribute to what one might call 'a superior rhythm'.

Sometimes the elements of the dichotomy appear horizontally rather than vertically. At the climax of the film, the confrontation between Mme Hamelin and Saccard introduces a series of cross-cut shots in close-up, interspersed with titles, which temporarily excludes any idea of a double discourse. But this series is then cut into by a brief track forward so that the frame is almost entirely blocked by the actor Alcover's elephantine bulk: a very striking visual effect, but one that is absolutely gratuitous by any direct dramatic principles, especially those established by what has gone before. The scene finally closes on a less tight shot of Mary Glory in which she is almost entirely hidden by a plaster bust in the foreground, while Alcover, very much in evidence, attempts to browbeat her: a dialectical situation created by the *découpage* which in a sense resumes the two preceding ones.

Fourthly and finally, let us examine a dialectical process which has been described – erroneously, to my mind – as metaphorical. When the aviator Jacques Hamelin takes off on the Atlantic crossing attempt that is to demonstrate the value of a new fuel on which the Stock Exchange is speculating, L'Herbier combines the two actions in a parallel montage, and *assimilates* them on the *découpage* level either by visual 'rhymes' (the propeller turning before take-off, followed by the rotation of the tiny central enclosure at the Stock Exchange under a camera diving vertically from a rope) or more particularly by a device arising from the 'subjective camera' principle (shots in which the camera skims over the Stock Exchange, cross-cut with shots of the aircraft flying over the aerodrome before departure). This sequence has been compared to the one in Gance's *Napoleon* where shots of the hero sailing stormy seas are intercut with, and then superimposed on, shots of the equally stormy Convention; the double structuring of this sequence – both metaphorical and plastic – is certainly superb, but it does not involve the dramaturgic dimension (in the material sense implied here): at this point in the film, only destiny links Napoleon to the Convention. What we have here is akin to the 'montage of attractions' as demonstrated in *Potemkin* (the stone lions) and *October* (Kerensky's bronze peacock), where the organic unity of the discourse is ultimately sacrificed to the metaphorical message (whatever the considerable interest in other respects of these devices in both Gance and the Soviet film-makers). Moreover, when Gance's camera swings like a pendulum over the delegates' heads in the Convention, no spatial orientation is established between the two actions. In *L'Argent*, on the other hand, the cross-cutting situates the aircraft 'above' the Stock Exchange in a continuum which may be imaginary but is none the less material. Furthermore, consistent with the principle that underlies the whole film, the texture here too is dramatic materiality, with no verbal metaphor intervening (it is this very aircraft that is the object of concern to the Stock Exchange). This sequence also throws new light on the film as a whole, particularly when considered in relation to the other three sequences described: for we are confronted here, in a radicalized form, with the opposition between an idea of continuity which bridges shot changes, and an idea of discontinuity introduced on another level by these shot changes. This dialectic, which is the very essence of all cinema, manifests itself throughout *L'Argent*, notably through the parameters cited above; but it is in this sequence that its presence makes itself felt most sharply, for although the aircraft and the Stock Exchange become increasingly *present* in relation to each other as the sequence builds ('imaginary' continuity), there can be no doubt as to the discontinuity between these shots in terms of narrative space. The structure of this sequence was further stressed by one of the first attempts to provide sound effects for a film. When

L'Argent was first shown, it was accompanied by gramophone records alternating the sound of an aircraft in flight with the noise of the Stock Exchange.

For over forty years established film historians, parroting the contemporary view, have described *L'Argent* as a ponderously boring white elephant. It is only recently that the evolution of cinematographic language has enabled us to *see* a film which must have remained totally *invisible* at the time. Such purgatories are not uncommon in art. To be understood, Bach had to wait for Mendelssohn and Liszt.

Of all the many preconceptions about L'Herbier's work, the least erroneous is probably the idea that his career really ended with the coming of sound, even though he made twice as many sound films as he did silents. At least one remarkable effort from the early sound period deserves to be noted, however: *Le Parfum de la Dame en Noir* (1931), a film totally forgotten today. Distinguished by its disorienting effects (mirror images, spatially elusive sets, fragmented *découpage*) and by some wonderfully inventive sound (the mysterious noises which silence the hallucinatory hubbub at the sinister dinner), this very personal adaptation of Gaston Leroux's novel seemed to herald a career in sound films as brilliant as his silent days had been. After two years of voluntary inactivity, however, during which he turned down numerous offers, L'Herbier finally agreed to film a successful 'boulevard' play, *L'Epervier* (UK: *Bird of Prey*, 1933), followed by two more of the same, *Le Scandale* (1934) and *L'Aventurier* (1934).

What had happened? L'Herbier himself has explained with remarkable lucidity:

> It is sometimes hard to know yourself what you did or what you didn't do. What is certain, however, is that when sound came, conditions of work became very difficult for a film-maker like me. For economic reasons, you couldn't consider making sound films like the ones we had done in the silent days, sometimes even at our own expense. You had to exercise a good deal of self-censorship, and, as far as I was concerned, even accept forms of cinema which were the very ones I'd always avoided. Because of the dialogue, we were suddenly obliged simply to can plays . . .

Raoul Walsh claims that his master, Griffith, simply didn't know how to adapt to the 'new language'. Maybe. But it is curious to note the number of great film-makers who, like L'Herbier, made one or two very fine and very important films *after* the coming of sound, only to lapse subsequently into distressing conformity. It was between 1928 and 1931 that Epstein, Lang and Sternberg made their masterpieces, reaching heights they were never again to attain. After completing nine films between 1920 and 1929, and then his masterpiece, *Vampyr*, in the early years of sound, Dreyer had to content himself with one film every ten years for the rest of his life. Let there be no misunderstanding, however: L'Herbier's career needs no excuses. *L'Argent* earns him his place among the masters.
Translated by Tom Milne

1987

Leaving aside some errors of judgement (for example, the underrating of *Feu Mathias Pascal* and the dismissal of *Le Vertige*), it seems reasonable to correct a few historical errors. The impact of *The Cheat* on Parisian high society was due at least as much to its scabrous subject-matter – the film had been banned in most states of the Union – and to its sympathetic portrayal of the rich, as to the American technical advances which it revealed. Delluc, as both critic and director, was much less impressed by this film than by the Westerns of Ince, and it was Gance, with *The Tenth Symphony* (1917) and *Mater Dolorosa* (1918), who drew the most direct lesson from DeMille's famous shocker.

More generally, this article and other writings which I devoted to the first French avant-garde suffer from my ignorance at the time of the overall context of French production in the late 1910s and 1920s, when the work of Antoine, Baroncelli, Cavalcanti, Poirier and Volkoff loomed at least as large as that of Epstein and L'Herbier.

And finally, a recent viewing of *L'Affaire du Collier de la Reine* (1946) indicated that L'Herbier's sound film production is perhaps not nearly as negligible as was assumed here.

3 Sergei M. Eisenstein

Eisenstein frequently compares his work to the work of Marr. Just as Marr seeks the roots of the spoken language, Eisenstein seeks the roots and forms of the development of a cinematographic language . . . Well, is it not a reasonable problem to be preoccupied with film language and to experiment in this field in order to create a new theory and to test it in his own film production? . . . I feel that it would be well to furnish Eisenstein with an empty studio and let him experiment to control his theories.

This was how Nikolai Lebedev, then head of the Institute of Scientific Cinematographic Research, defended his colleague Sergei Eisenstein (1898-1948) before the All-Union Culture Creative Conference of Workers in Soviet Cinematography held in Moscow in 1935. Lebedev was, it seems, Eisenstein's only champion. His critics, on the other hand, were many and distinguished: Dovzhenko, Pudovkin, Trauberg, Yutkevitch, Vassiliev. Of what was Eisenstein accused? Of intellectualism, of preoccupation with problems too far removed from Socialist development, and above all of having made no film for seven years. Yet it was Lebedev rather than this distinguished opposition who was right. Eisenstein, the ex-engineer, was first and foremost a man of science: the first great theorist of film practice, the first great teacher, he remains the man who defined – thirty years before anyone else, in both his early writings and his silent films – the essential cinematographic phenomena. And if he remained silent as a film-maker during the first seven years of the Stalinist era, it was doubtless because he knew in his heart that the price for the reappearance of his name on the screen was recantation: his self-criticism published, the film-maker plunged into academicism while the researcher retreated entirely into the 'abstraction' to which he had been prematurely consigned. This tribute to Eisenstein the researcher is therefore dedicated to the memory of Nikolai Lebedev, who foresaw the recantation but could do nothing to prevent it. Researcher, I repeat – for the mistake made by the members of that conference in 1935 is surely repeated today in the prevailing view of Eisenstein's films as no more than slightly *passé* classics. Like Lebedev, I shall try to restore the perspective.

In the early 1920s, when the young Soviets of Eisenstein's generation were turning toward the cinema, cinematic 'language' was in a period of gestation and still far from the rigid codification it was to undergo. In the wake of Griffith, Ince, *et al.*, the Americans were perfecting the grammar of space-time continuity (matching eyeline, screen direction, movement) which enabled them to fragment the proscenium space without disorienting the spectator or destroying the illusion of this ambient space. At the same time, however, *montage* was born, and with it another, essentially *dialectic* cinema.

After *The Birth of a Nation* (1915), parallel montage was used not only for dramatic purposes (two different, distant actions shown alternately: a technique dating from Griffith's *After Many Years* in 1908 and used by him chiefly to create suspense – a practice criticized by Eisenstein in 'Dickens, Griffith and the Film Today' in *Film Form* for its ideological implications and formal simplifications) but for 'everyday' purposes as well. At the beginning of *The Birth of a Nation*, when the two young Northerners arrive on a visit to their Southern friends, the characters inside the house are shown alternately – shot for shot – with those outside. In so far as 'direct montage' is concerned, however – implying not only temporal continuity but also spatial contiguity – the foundations for this double continuum were still too insecure in 1920: eyelines and fragmented movements still often matched badly or not at all, and, generally speaking, the rules for 'theatrical' *découpage*, which were to become sacrosanct in a few years' time, did not exist objectively – even though the need for them was felt by many film-makers – except as *possible guides*. (It is significant in this connection that in France at least, the script-girl, a traffic policeman whose job is to see that the rules are respected, did not form part of the technical crew until around 1927.) This was one of the factors which encouraged the clean sweep policy favoured from the outset by several young Soviet film-makers, especially Eisenstein and Vertov: only a clean sweep of all pre-existing cinema made sense in this total revaluation of everything which was to be the heritage of the October Revolution for almost fifteen years.

As a concrete example, when Eisenstein used contradictory angles in his first feature, *Stačka* (*Strike*, 1924-5), in showing how the spying foreman is sent sprawling by a huge metal wheel dangling from a crane cunningly manipulated by a group of playful workers, his prime consideration was not the violation of some rule of spatial continuity. (On the surface of the screen, the wheel changes direction several times in a manner inconsistent with the continuity of its 'real' motion, while the relative positions of wheel and foreman are on several occasions 'illogically' reversed.) On the contrary, Eisenstein felt the value of this sort of 'dialectic' montage – in which an inherent continuity (present in the spectator's mind by virtue of the 'real' logic of the scene) is opposed to an actual discontinuity (defined here as being on the surface of the screen) – to be self-evident; he saw it as being inherent in the versatility of the camera (as opposed to the theatre's fixed frontal viewpoint) and in the possibilities of montage. Today, to the average spectator as well as to the average specialist, a moment of cinema such as this seems the height of artiness, a serious violation of the 'basic rules', acceptable for once as a touch of genius on Eisenstein's part but too showy, confusing and anti-realistic for the modern eye. The fact is, however, that Eisenstein recognized this orientation-disorientation dialectic as one of the film-maker's basic tools.

At the time of *Strike*, however, this recognition was merely implicit. Eisenstein's explicit preoccupations evidently lay elsewhere:

> The attraction (in our diagnosis of the theatre) is every aggressive moment in it, i.e. every element of it that brings to light in the spectator those senses or that psychology that influence his experience – every element that can be verified and mathematically calculated to produce certain emotional shocks in a proper order within the totality – the only means by which it is possible to make the final ideological conclusion perceptible. The way to knowledge – 'Through the living play of the passions'

– applies specifically to the theatre (perceptually) . . . Approached genuinely, this basically determines the possible principles of construction as 'an action construction' (of the whole production). Instead of a static 'reflection' of an event with all possibilities for activity within the limits of the event's logical action, we advance to a new plane – free montage of arbitrarily selected, independent (within the given composition and the subject links that hold the influencing actions together) attractions – all from the stand of establishing certain final thematic effects – this is montage of attractions. 'Montage of Attractions', reproduced in part in *The Film Sense*.

These two extracts from Eisentein's first published article (printed in 1923 while he was working with the Proletkult Theatre) restate the basic principles of a concept that was to remain a constant with him for fifteen years; after *Oktjabr* (*October*, 1927-28) and 'Methods of Montage' (1929, in *Film Form*) it was to become 'intellectual montage', but would not be explicitly denied until 1938 ('Word and Image', in *The Film Sense*). This concept derives from the dialectical intuition – also felt to differing degrees by Pudovkin, Kuleshov and Vertov – that the juxtaposition of two *heteroclite* images (drawn, in other words, from two distinct spatio-temporal continuums) produces 'a third image': inherent, mental, but pre-eminent. An intuition of cardinal importance. But in his first film (*Strike*) especially, the conclusions Eisenstein drew from it concerning montage in its strictest sense that is, the putting together of *shots* – were less dialectical than mechanistic and *metaphorical*. A shot 'foreign' to the action is joined to a shot or group of shots '*in situ*': this adds an 'imaged' dimension by 'illustrating' the words which might be used to *qualify* the initial action – a verbal detour which, when it functions in isolation, tends to obliterate the material aspect of the images, leaving only the meaning or, to borrow a term from Eisenstein's later vocabulary, the *pathos*.

For example, the shots of police moving into action against the strikers are followed by a shot of a lemon-squeezer being used by one of the factory bosses. Or again: the final sequence of the workers being massacred is intercut with documentary shots of a bull being butchered in a slaughterhouse. A nuance is already evident from these two examples. In the context of the film, the bosses taking tea around a table form an integral part of the basic material; we have had this scene before, and it embodies one of the two poles in the political conflict which is central to the film. So, although it is grafted onto the police repression by way of parallel montage, this scene also possesses its own 'references'; consequently the metaphor here also functions *simultaneously* as a privileged junction-point between two separate 'currents', thus contributing to the overall form of this segment of the film. The slaughterhouse scenes, on the other hand (like the shots of animals used to characterize the police spies), are extraneous to the film – extraneous to the form – and their purely 'adjectival' introduction violates what one might call the 'continuum of verisimilitude', even contesting the idea that the film is a locus endowed with its own unity. Eisenstein himself (in the article already cited) was in due course to point it out, regarding it as a mistake.

To my mind, the real 'trouble' here is the mixing of two temporal systems: one dynamic, steadily advancing, and the other static, irregular, non-evolving. An admixture like this disturbs the spectator conditioned to expect unity in temporal systems, or rather, the illusion of unity. From a non-normative viewpoint, however, and provided the unequivocal and simplistic transposition of verbal metaphors is avoided, this admixture can be extremely fertile in itself; as witness Lupu Pick's masterpiece *Sylvester* (1923), which is entirely predicated on a non-metaphorical alternation between a carefully modulated progressive time (the back-shop drama) and a completely static time ('documentary' shots of the town celebrating New Year's Eve). As we shall see, moreover, these two stages in the montage of attractions were to combine with Eisenstein – notably in *October* – in a dialectic whose complexity long went unnoticed.

What makes *Strike* an astonishingly prophetic film, however, is the disparity between the sequences (a corollary of the disparity between shots inherent in the 'attractive' concept, and consciously extended by Eisenstein 'to the level of the scenario'). For this notion of provoking ruptures of style, tone and indeed the 'attitude of the camera' within the filmic material itself has made a vigorous reappearance with Godard's work. Although Eisenstein later described as 'Leftist deviations' the juxtaposition of the acrobatic eccentricities of the police spies with the measured sobriety of the workers, or of spontaneous, pragmatically edited scenes (the water-hose sequence) with more fastidiously structured episodes (the cavalcade of soldiers on the 'balconies'), to the contemporary eye these juxtapositions reveal a new organizing principle capable of leading to an effectively 'materialist' cinema. (For example, the documentary shots and theatrical monologues, both set in opposition to a sort of pseudo-psychological intimism in Godard's *Deux ou Trois Choses que je sais d'elle*, or the constant changes in 'camera attitude' in his *Le Gai Savoir*.)

Eisenstein himself in fact heralded this deeply revolutionary vision when, as though anticipating his own questions, he wrote in 1925 about *Strike* (translated into French as 'Sur la question d'une approche matérialiste de la forme', in *Cahiers du Cinéma*, no. 220-221):

> The form and elaboration of the contest in terms of the subject-story – in our case the process, applied for the first time, of scenario montage (that is, constructing the scenario not on the basis of dramatic laws universally recognized as valid, but by expounding the content in ways which determine the structure of the montage as such; for instance, through the organization of 'newsreel' material), and the correct choice of visual angle in relation to the material – proved in our case to be the consequence of a *fundamental formal understanding of the material* proposed; of the fundamental 'artifice', in other words, formally innovative, which the *mise en scène* brought to the construction of the film, an artifice which had been determined (historically) first.

Possibly in reaction against the general 'eccentricity' of *Strike*, the montage of attractions disappeared almost entirely from *Bronenosec Potemkin* (*The Battleship Potemkin*, 1925), or rather, is given a uniquely privileged position: the only example is the stone lion which seems to rear up in protest against the massacre on the steps (unless it is protesting against the answering salvo from the *Potemkin*'s guns: such ambiguities, as we shall see, are the strength, but also the price, of 'intellectual' montage). Even then, the three shots constituting the metaphor really form part of the film's central concern, which is with montage in its more accepted material forms,

SERGEI M. EISENSTEIN 51

and particularly with 'direct' montage: in other words, the fragmentation into clearly differentiated shots of an action conceived as continuous.

For Eisenstein at this time, the shot change was the cinematic event *par excellence*, providing the specific character of filmic development. He could not conceive of a scene without numerous shot changes, even where the need for them could, from a narrative or even dramatic point of view, be eliminated by clever staging (in an article at this time he made fun of film-makers who resorted to shots 'running as long as 12 metres' – 20 seconds!). Of all Eisenstein's films, it is in *Potemkin* that the dialectic character of these shot changes is now most obvious. Each sequence appears to respect the sense of 'real' time as it unfolds – continuous time, that is – as well as unity of place (this is so in the 'action' sequences at least; by way of contrast, certain transitional or parenthetical sequences are treated elliptically). Certain academic minds – even Eisenstein himself at one time – interpreted this predilection as a return to the classical theatre's dusty old law of the three unities. A sorry way of attesting to the cinema's impeccable pedigree while missing the most important point. For this spatio-temporal continuity cannot be dissociated from the element of discontinuity kept continually present through the innumerable changes of shot. How does the dialectic that can be found in this 'symbiotic opposition' work?

In *Potemkin*, each change of shot (or succession of changes) cutting across the continuity of the action has its own characteristics, depending on the nature and the intensity of the conflict it inevitably introduces. For it is in conflict that Eisenstein finds the essence of the shot change: graphic conflict, conflict of planes, conflict of volume, conflict of space, conflict of light, conflict of tempo.

In the opening sequence – 'the crew's quarters' – there are graphic oppositions between the hammocks, from one shot to the next (but also within the same shot: for Eisenstein, one is an extension of the other), which create the dominant tension, essentially determining the rhythmic contribution of each shot change. But on this another dialectic superimposes itself: the conflict between, on the one hand, the continuity of the action (the spying quartermaster making his rounds, the reaction of the rebellious sailor), and, on the other, its extreme fragmentation into particles of time which constitute both integral parts of this continuity, and autonomous plastic entities, dependent on the graphic conflicts between the hammocks, from one shot to another and from changes in shot scales, but also on certain 'bad' matches. The effect of repetition, of prolongation in the brief 'overlapping' shots showing the sailor's movement of revolt, is one which will be considered more fully when we come to *October*.

Although the dialectic method is perhaps seen at its most naked in this sequence, many others function in an identical manner. For instance, the sequence on the quarterdeck with its frequent use of non-dramaturgical matches (not serving to advance the action in any way, yet distinctly perceptible in themselves), with its close-ups interconnected by the way heads turn, by the glances directed off-screen, by isolated gestures which seem to 'match' one another – these movements as a whole forming a sort of continuous system which overlays the cuts. Or there is the messdeck sequence, with its conflict of movement between shots (edited against the beat) from the suspended planks serving as tables.

As for the celebrated Odessa Steps sequence, Eisenstein has analysed it himself ('The Structure of the Film' (1939), in *Film Form*), notably in terms of the opposition between ascending and descending movements (within the frame), but in the light of what he calls the 'pathos', a somewhat idealistic notion which seems to me to come down to a justification of the 'form' in terms of the effect produced. From a dialectical point of view, however, this sequence seems to me quite distinct in character from those already cited. The crew's quarters and the quarterdeck, in particular, offer an enclosed space whose overall topography is constantly 'present' on the screen, despite fragmentation in the editing, because orientation in screen space is respected, and because Eisenstein frequently resorts to long shots which between them 're-situate' the close-ups, no matter how isolated these may be. Even in the sequence where the yawls sail towards the battleship, although the respective positions of the people on the wharves, the battleship and the yawls are merely implied (by cross-cutting), we still get the impression that we recognize spatial relationships pre-existing the successive impressions conveyed on the screen.

In the Odessa Steps sequence, on the other hand, this sense of a pre-existent space – from which the close-ups could have been 'extracted' – is severely shaken, perhaps for the first time in the cinema over such a lengthy sequence, which doubtless explains the extraordinary shock effect it had at the time. In point of fact, not only do we never at any moment see the steps as a whole, not only do the soldiers seem to be descending an endless flight of steps, but the entire sequence is splintered into detail shots, some of which 'match' with others – are extracted from the same space, in other words – thus forming 'clusters', but most of which are linked together only by the movement that traverses the screen, subjectively continuous (in its driving impetus) but objectively discontinuous (in its direction, its speed and its 'support'). What we have here is therefore an essentially dialectic space whose only existence comes from the succession of shots, so completely is the sense of a coherent ambient space broken down. The perambulator running away from the dead nurse falls not so much down a flight of stone steps as from one image to the next. Even the soldiers' feet seem to advance in a space quite distinct from that in which the guns are raised to fire. Even the scenes at the foot of the steps, seen in longer shot, seem to occur in a separate space, for this swarming confusion has nothing in common with the incisive arabesques of the closer shots.

There is, however, nothing very mysterious about this unusual spatial impression: the profusion of 'non-situated' close-ups – or clusters of close-ups – and the absence of topographical references (both related to the fact that the only spatial concern of a dramaturgical nature is the distinction between ascending and descending and not the precise situation of an incident on the steps) combine to create a space which not only challenges the fixed frontal viewpoint, but also abolishes the sense of a material (spatio-temporal) continuum, and does so within a place and time that are nevertheless established as circumscribed. This was an absolutely decisive step which was to lead, a few years later, to one of the great turning-points in cinema: the affirmation in Dreyer's *La Passion de Jeanne d'Arc* of a cinematic space totally irreducible to any synthetic representation whatsoever – the final emancipation from the theatrical space of the nineteenth century.

Without undue insistence on the reality of these works, one can find a dialectical dimension in the very progress of Eisenstein's thought and practice through his first three films. For in *October*, the

Strike (Eisenstein, 1924–5)

October (Eisenstein, 1927–28)

metaphorical discontinuity of *Strike* (montage of attractions) is wedded to the continuous-discontinuous montage principle of *Potemkin*, creating an extremely complex 'apparatus' which is probably the high point of Eisenstein's art but which still presents, it seems, considerable difficulties.

The two basic figures which determine the functioning of almost the entire film are present from the first sequence, the dismantling of the statue of Alexander III. When the ropes which topple the statue are pulled taut, this action is splintered into half-a-dozen shots, taken from various angles and distances, with the action repeated integrally each time. This overlapping effect, already noted in *Potemkin*, was in fact also present in *Strike*, where it was used more daringly but also more crudely in *October*. The ignominious exit of the spying foreman (from the latrine where he has been trying to eavesdrop on the agitators) is shown twice in successive shots; certainly a flagrant violation of the rules of continuity, which as I have noted had been formulated for only a few years, but also an incongruity echoing 'bad' matches in Feuillade's films of the same period (and perhaps due simply to clumsiness). In the domestic scene which leads to the decision of a worker's wife to sell some personal possessions in order to feed her family, on the other hand, this principle of reiterated gestures assumes a dominant role: when the woman goes out of the door, for example, and the husband goes angrily back to bed, the montage has them repeat their action. But in *Strike* one feels that the process is still subject to the demands of dramaturgical expression: it is what Eisenstein would call a 'trick' to stretch out in time an action he wishes to stress. (Notable in this respect are the axial matches showing a workman falling onto some metal shavings: his contact with the deadly spirals is seen first in medium shot, then again in close-up, with the processs repeated in reverse as the man gets up.) The same thing is true of *Potemkin*, although the technique shows considerably greater mastery and flexibility, and no longer suggests even remotely the possibility of an error. (Note, particularly the scene in which a sailor – the first sign of open revolt – throws down the plate with the provocative inscription: the action is shown in three or four shots taken from angles so close to each other that they clash, which accentuates even further the artificial aspect of this gearing-down device).

It was only with *October* that this technique began to give rise to more complex developments, starting with the dismantling of the Tsar's statue: the repeated collapse in fragments of the huge effigy echoes the successive resurgences of the ropes, while at the same time these shots are governed by a progressive impulse comparable to that underlying the more disparate shots of the Odessa Steps sequence. Here, then, is the first synthesis. But this principle of 'stretching' was to find its full justification in the justly celebrated sequence where the bridges of Petrograd are raised to cut off the workers' quarters from the rest of the city. Whereas the *découpage* of the tightening ropes and falling statue respected the singleness of viewpoint (all these shots 'match' each other in direction and in the relative positions of the objects) while destroying the continuity of temporal flow, the opening of the bridge is filmed and edited from contradictory points of view, so that even the continuity of direction, never rationally in doubt from the action, is constantly challenged on the surface of the screen itself. This of course is a reprise of the technique from the crane scene in *Strike*, but used here, thanks to the repeated overlapping, in conjunction with an extreme stretching of 'real' time. To this structure is added a further complexity, for the sequence as a whole in fact operates on two distinct temporal levels, thanks to parallel montage (and here again we find the temporal functioning of the metaphor spun out at the end of *Strike*): on the one hand there is the level of 'logical' progression, which includes the bourgeois citizens mockingly watching the scene, and on the other the level of slowed-down, splintered progression, arbitrary and basically unreal, as the bridge is opened. The way in which this second temporal stream flows from the first, eddying away in an oneiric maelstrom, then blending again with the 'normal' time as the dead horse and the carriage fall, makes this sequence a truly exceptional moment in cinematographic art, as well as an admirable demonstration of the cogency of Eisenstein's dialectical concepts.

But to return to the opening sequence of *October*: as the ropes are pulled taut, we also see reaction shots of the crowd watching the operation. Soon, however, these 'literal' shots give way to 'figurative' shots of other crowds – mutinous guns, brandished scythes. Here we are undoubtedly back with the montage of attractions, in its most radical guise: the only connection the visual content of these shots has with the action is metaphorical. There is, however, a vitally important difference from the slaughterhouse of *Strike*; these shots, which cannot by any logic be situated in front of the condemned statue (for that space is known to us, we have 'inspected' it), are nevertheless situated there by way of one of those imaginary spatial relationships which are peculiar to the cinema: cross-cutting. The metaphor changes character, becomes more direct: what is being said is no longer 'here men are massacred as (elsewhere) cattle are', but 'you who are tearing down this statue, millions of peasants and Soviet soldiers are your witnesses, watching you.' The ideological difference is undeniable; the material difference is manifest. The montage of attractions has become dialectic, in so far as it is motored by a conflict in the spectator's mind ('I know that these three crowds cannot be assembled at the same time in front of this statue, yet that is the main impression I receive'), a conflict simultaneously resolved and sustained on the surface of the screen.

This is not the only way in which the montage of attractions contributes to the overall dialectic of *October*, despite a curious tendency among the most lucid commentators on Eisenstein's work to join the film-maker in his belated (and deliberate?) blindness concerning the way these processes really function. Jean Mitry, for instance, in his book on Eisenstein:

> At the Second Congress of Soviets, during the storming of the Winter Palace, the conciliatory speeches by the Mensheviks are intercut with shots showing hands playing harps. The idea, purely literary in fact, is to turn what the Mensheviks are saying into a lyrical whine, a song designed to lull listeners to sleep. But if the idea is valid, though rather mannered, one may yet wonder: what are these harps and harpists doing amid the objective reality of the congress? Again the film-maker's artifice transgresses reality for a figure of speech drained of its living content.

Equating the method here with the use of the slaughterhouse in *Strike*, Mitry fails to recognize the dialectical relationship which binds these images together. For although the relationship that first appears is indeed simply a figure of speech – when, following the shots of the Mensheviks, the harpists' hands are seen in non-situated shots – a different kind of relationship is established between these shots and those of the delegate who is sleeping with a blissful smile on his lips and who hears – this is an impression physically imposed by the sequence of shots – the 'celestial' music produced by the harps. Here the relationship between the images is no longer simply metaphorical but material (because implying a concrete act of perception), with the harps *situated* in the 'auditory space-off' belonging to the shots of the sleeping delegate. But this is not all: although the introduction of a stone cherub – as foreign to the 'real' locus as the harpists – into the montage at this precise moment is another example of *intellectual* association (harps = angels), on the syntactical level this statue undoubtedly belongs to the sleeping delegate's dream, and also acts in a *material* transition to the Winter Palace effected through an ostensible axial match which appears to situate the cherub among the columns towering over the Palace gates. A course like this, comprising successive and constantly differentiated tensions and resolutions, leads much further, it seems to me, than the univocally metaphorical montage of attractions, making it function dialectically alongside other equally 'valid' (as Mitry would say) dramaturgical elements within a specifically cinematic structure: both materiality and pathos, in other words, abstract and concrete, intellectual and perceptible.

A third development of the montage of attractions may be noted: the sequence in which, strutting to the doors of the Tsar's apartment, Kerensky is compared through montage to a mechanical peacock spreading its metal feathers. At first glance, what we have here seems to be a perfectly straightforward metaphor. The shots juxtaposed here, however, are not isolated and therefore univocal ones, but clusters of shots put together along the lines projected in *Potemkin* (short, overlapping shots which splinter the movement), so that the same 'rippling' motion, already evoked, runs through the clusters of shots at one frequency, and through the whole sequence at another, establishing a material (visual) link which completes the mental link, throwing a dialectical bridge across the open breach in the 'continuum of verisimilitude'.

Finally, as I have said, it was in *October* that the montage of attractions achieved its final transformation, characterized by Eisenstein as 'intellectual montage'. The clearest example in *October* is probably the one cited by Eisenstein himself: the sequence of the 'gods' ('Methods of Montage' in *Film Form*). For

Eisenstein, however, the intellectual cinema had yet to be born. We know that he dreamed of filming *Das Kapital*; in other words, of moving towards the essay film, where didactic message and formal discourse converge totally – a notion taken much further by Vertov. When General Kornilov attempts his monarchist *putsch* against the provisional government, we see three titles: 'In the Name of God and Country'/'In the Name . . .'/'OF GOD!' Then: the tower of the baroque church/a carved fresco of the martyrdom of St Sebastian/ the tower framed diagonally to the right/the tower framed diagonally to the left/various close shots of the fresco/statue of Buddha/statue of a Tibetan sage wreathed in smoke/dragon mask with open mouth/statue of Buddha/mask/Buddha. Then a title: 'In the Name of Country'. Eisenstein explains:

> These pieces were assembled in accordance with a descending intellectual scale – pulling back the concept of God to its origins, forcing the spectator to perceive this 'progress' intellectually.

Studies of the 'semiological' perception of images are not sufficiently advanced, even today, to justify the expression of definitive opinions (put forward by numerous commentators, including Eisenstein himself) as to the validity of this idea. Of the particular example quoted, it can simply be noted that, as far as I am aware, the explicit 'message' as defined by Eisenstein is very rarely perceived. In so far as dialectic is concerned, this sequence seems to me to operate only on an intellectual level, and only if the shots are reduced to list form as above, whereas Eisenstein suggests – not in connection with cinema – that true dialectic is a complex phenomenon comprising at least two levels, intellectual and visual. Finally, missing here is the dimension of humour which is almost invariably associated with the montage of attractions in *October*, and which is the mainspring of an important dialectic defined by Alain Robbe-Grillet as 'the internal sabotage of structures by themselves' (a humour whose role is evident in the introduction of the harpists and the cherub, and which is so singularly lacking in the final sequence of *Strike*).

Furthermore, the problem of intellectual montage (and of the montage of attractions in general) is allied to the much greater problem of the silent cinema postulated as an 'autonomous language' capable of faithfully fulfilling all the functions of written language. All the great film-makers were deeply preoccupied with this problem during the late 1920s, but each time an attempt was made to create this 'language' that would function as prose, the result was, paradoxically, a complete 'poetic' abstraction, irrespective of the degree of purely plastic cohesion in the filmic discourse. Kirsanoff's *Ménilmontant* is a remarkable example: in attempting to present not merely a 'story without words' (eliminating all explanatory titles), but also the thoughts, impressions, fantasies and even intentions of the characters, while capturing place and atmosphere, all in the spirit of 'poetic realism', Kirsanoff achieves an 'obscurity' worthy of *L'Année Dernière à Marienbad* in certain passages, because the message doesn't come across (probably, in fact, for fundamental perceptual reasons). In these same passages, on the other hand, the purely cinematic style is so rigorous, the images so beautiful and their 'evocative' intensity within the montage so great (though in a sense absolute: evocation without object), that one suddenly finds oneself confronted by great cinema in the contemporary sense – doubtless despite the film-maker's conscious intentions, for (Epstein's astonishing intuitions notwithstanding) it seems hardly likely that anyone at that period would have been aware of the problem in precisely these terms. As in fact is proved by the example of Eisenstein himself, who in pursuing the elusive ideal of intellectual montage often achieved results analogous to Kirsanoff's. (For instance, the introduction in the bridge sequence in *October* of a battered stone face; an attraction effect which undoubtedly had a very precise meaning in Eisenstein's mind, but which now seems no more than a very striking, privileged moment of rupture in the dual progression of this sequence.)

This 'myopic' examination of Eisenstein's two masterpieces, *Potemkin* and *October*, must not be allowed to obscure the extraordinary power of the overall conception sustaining them: in other words, their form. In this respect the two films are in fact diametrically opposed. Whereas *Potemkin* is constructed as a block that is simultaneously compact and veined by a network of cracks (the shot changes) whose relationship to the inexorable progress of the action is analogous (if more complex) to that between the shapes of the pieces in a completed jigsaw puzzle and the picture it represents, one might say of *October* that the pieces have been scattered and then reassembled in a vast collage which no longer bears the immediate connection with the story of the film (or history itself) that characterizes the roughly hewn discourse of *Potemkin*; a collage in which large clusters of shots still persist, reminiscent of the 'plaited' articulation of *Potemkin*, but where the form (as in *Strike*) owes more to the logic of mosaic. One may even claim this (after Christensen's *Häxan*, and more particularly the first films of Vertov) as one of the first examples in cinema of an open form, which seems to determine its own shape even as it unfolds with the untrammelled ease of an exercise in free association; in a sense this process of spontaneous growth, sometimes monstrous, constitutes the antithesis within a vast dialectic which incorporates (into cinema) all the rest, and whose thesis is history itself. It is doubtless because of this unusually disjointed and desultory development that the average spectator, accustomed to a single level of discourse and to assuming a more passive role in relation to the succession of images he is offered, finds *October* 'tiring on the eyes'. When Eisenstein says ('Word and Image' in *The Film Sense*), referring to montage in general, that 'The strength of the method resides also in the circumstance that the spectator is drawn into a creative act in which his individuality is not subordinated to the author's individuality, but is opened up throughout the process of fusion with the author's intention', it is very probable that he was in fact referring to the constant critical collaboration necessary for any adequate viewing of *October*.

This mosaic form and open discourse reappear in *General 'naja Linija* (*The General Line*, 1926-29), begun before *October* but completed after it, and retitled *Staroe i Novoe* (*The Old and the New*) to diminish the resonance of what were considered to be its ideological deficiencies. Perhaps because of the fragmented circumstances in which it was made, perhaps because the criticisms levelled against it doubtless had to be taken into account, the film never achieves the extraordinary unity which makes *October* a masterpiece; it tends on the contrary to fall into a series of set-pieces and stylistic exercises, some of which are of great interest for what they reveal about Eisenstein's methods. It is of course difficult to discuss these passages without taking Eisenstein's analyses into account, and more particularly the categories he established. At the same time it is clear that in many cases both analyses and categories, though seemingly scientific, are purely subjective in origin. This applies in particular to tonal and overtonal montage – *a posteriori* attempts to explain the formal method of sequences that are essentially impressionistic in character (in which an accumulation of shots, in other words, aims to create an *impression* through the sum of their pictorial content, independently and often in the absence of any dialectical conflict): see, for the first, the fog scene in *Potemkin*, and for the second, the religious procession in *The General Line* (cf. 'Methods of Montage', in *Film Form*).

In point of fact, the repertory of *dialectical conflicts* referred to earlier seems to me to account most satisfactorily for the experiments conducted in *The General Line*: graphic conflicts ('cubist' opposition between the spouts filmed from various angles in the cream separator sequence); conflict of perspectives (the old woman sitting in front of a hut, where the use of different lenses means that the perspective changes from shot to shot: although the essential components of the composition remain the same – the woman and a wooden bird's nest – they are differently placed, and more particularly differently *spaced* each time); and finally the conflict which Eisenstein describes as being 'between matter and viewpoint', to wit, the distortions occasioned by certain lenses: the sequence where the tractor is repaired and the machine, while remaining perfectly recognizable, radically changes its morphology from shot to shot through changes in viewpoint associated with the use of a wide-angle lens which enormously foreshortens the perspective.

After 1929, it becomes extremely difficult to follow Eisenstein's development of the grandiose concepts that emerged from his first four films and were formulated in essays written at the time. Quantitatively, certainly, the greater part of his theoretical work dates from the 1930s and 1940s, but more than anything else these writings reflect the ultimately insoluble conflict between Eisenstein's own aesthetic and the constraints imposed not so much by Stalinism proper (Stalin himself was one of Eisenstein's greatest admirers in Russia, and it was probably thanks to him that Eisenstein was able to make his last two films) as by a historical-political situation which made a certain conception of art useless, wasteful and, in the final analysis, harmful. To my mind, it was this conflict that was to lead Eisenstein further and further away from contemporary realities and concrete cinematic problems, and cause him to seek refuge in eschatological considerations; often extremely illuminating, admittedly, but shedding light mainly on painting, literature, or at best an almost entirely imaginary cinema conceived as 'a universal synthesis of arts and cultures' and ensconced a thousand leagues away from the dialectical and materialist cinema he had experimented with and theorized about from 1924 to 1929.

As for the films made by Eisenstein during these difficult years, his work between 1929 and 1938 is of course irretrievably lost. *Que Viva Mexico!* (1930-32), victim of Upton Sinclair's incomprehension as a progressive writer turned producer for the occasion, exists only as a series of rushes; whether preserved at the Museum of Modern Art or 'edited' by hands as clumsy as they were well-intentioned, these rushes add practically nothing to our knowledge of Eisenstein's ideas and methods. In the case of *Bezhin Lug* (*Bezhin Meadow*, 1936), apparently completed but suppressed by the political machine, and later destroyed (supposedly by water during the bombardment of Moscow), the sequence of frame stills put together by Alexandrov is perhaps more suggestive – notably of the way in which Eisenstein was then attempting to *encompass* a given 'tableau' as completely as possible (for instance the opening sequence: the dead mother on the cart, the boy, the grandfather, framed in shots of a dozen different sizes – a technique that derives from certain sequences in *Potemkin* but also looks forward to the academicism of *Alexander Nevsky*).

The most interesting record we have of these years of silence is Vladimir Nizhny's book *Lessons with Eisenstein* (1962). Compiled from shorthand notes of the classes taught by Eisenstein at the State Institute of Cinematography, this book reveals what may be considered as the outcome of Eisenstein's direct preoccupations with cinema. It includes, in particular, an important extension of the dialectical notion through the Eisensteinian concept of *the montage unit*. This consists simply of a group of shots filmed so that they match one another, either through eyeline or because they show the same things from the same angle. Nothing particularly original here, since the idea is basically the same as the American 'master shot', a technique designed to reinforce the screen orientation code discussed at the beginning of this article. Eisenstein, however, makes an essential distinction, providing for the deliberate use of bad matches to challenge the orientation thus established, either to pass from one montage unit to another during a sequence, or as a privileged moment of rupture within a given unit. Admittedly, from the humanist point of view he always adopted, Eisenstein justifies these techniques purely in terms of their dramaturgical function. This concept is strikingly illustrated in the Odessa Steps sequence (the baby-carriage 'falls' from one montage unit into another) and later became an integral part of the stylistics of Antonioni.

Another chapter of *Lessons with Eisenstein* is equally prophetic, in that it contains the first formulation of 'non-montage' (or the 'shot-sequence'): an episode of *Crime and Punishment* filmed – on paper – in a single shot, absolutely in the manner of Welles or Skolimowski. Very long takes involving complicated movements were already in use at the beginning of the sound period, of course – *Scarface, Die Dreigroschenoper* – usually for reasons of expediency since no one yet knew much about editing the soundtrack. But none of them reveals the kind of virtuosity envisaged here in staging movements for a sequence where the camera in fact remains entirely stationary.

Unfortunately, almost no trace of these ideas can be found in Eisenstein's last two films, *Aleksandr Nevskij* (*Alexander Nevsky*, 1938) and *Ivan Gronznj* (*Ivan the Terrible*, 1941-46), where the montage unit is indeed used, but shorn of the dialectic of good and bad matches, reducing it to an exact equivalent of the Hollywood master shot.

Alexander Nevsky marked Eisenstein's return to film-making after the *Bezhin Meadow* disaster; I would have preferred to pass over it in silence as one of the most profoundly retrograde films ever made by a film-maker of stature. But since a statement like this demands some sort of substantiation, it is worth noting on the one hand Eisenstein's complete abandonment – under pressure, admittedly, of developments in the Soviet cinema as a whole, effective as soon as sound films gained a foothold – of the 'typage' principle (the use of non-professional actors), as well as of 'the mass as hero' in favour of 'positive heroes' played by professional actors; and on the other hand, his adoption of a style articulated exclusively on axial matches and cross-cutting. The parallels with the

Hollywood star system and master shot are so obvious that they require no comment. The result is a stilted and academic film (for example, the sequence with the Teutonic Knights at Mass: a vast, conventional tableau, filmed in a series of detail shots, always from the same angle). Even the Battle on the Ice, celebrated for its 'montage', in fact breaks down into a series of stiff tableaux in which bombastic actors execute a series of mechanical gestures, and which seem to have been precariously stuck together end to end according to a rudimentary technique which almost deliberately excludes any reference to the dialectics of the silent days. As for Prokofiev's famous score, quite apart from its intrinsic musical weakness, the dialectic between images and music into which Eisenstein tried to integrate it is based on notions of audio-visual perception totally outdated even then, and nowadays apt to raise sniggers.

There is an interesting study to be made of the way in which the sound revolution affected the Soviet cinema. For although it marked a serious regression, exactly as it had in the capitalist world, it may not have been for the same reasons. Even if one disregards the pressures peculiar to the Stalinist machine, it is obvious that the political content of a film is necessarily less verbalized and therefore less explicit in a silent film; consequently the first Soviet films, by virtue of their silence, were less open to attack from ideological experts accustomed to dealing in words. In *October*, the arguments offered by the agitators when faced by the Tartar troops of Kornilov's 'Wild Division' could legitimately be summed up in four lapidary titles: 'BREAD! PEACE! LAND! BROTHERHOOD!'; but after the coming of sound such arguments had to be scripted and spoken in full, to avoid accusations of evading a problem that was now technically 'soluble'. The political order laboured henceforth under the illusion that the cinema was directly within its grasp. In any case it was probably in part this explicit quality in talking pictures that led to serious retrenchments by all the Soviet film-makers as soon as synchronous sound appeared on the scene, as well as to Eisenstein's conviction that talking pictures meant the inevitable eclipse of montage.

So we come to *Ivan the Terrible*. Undeniably allied to *Alexander Nevsky* – through its epic character, the role played by the music, and even its style (more tightly knit, admittedly, but based on the same academic application of the same forms) – the uncompleted trilogy which closed both Eisenstein's career and his life is, though hardly the masterpiece claimed by orthodox histories, infinitely more convincing than the earlier film. This conviction, however, stems simply from a 'consolidation' of the straightforward, univocal texture of *Nevsky*. Cross-cutting and axial matches again predominate, with an almost total respect for screen orientation (the bad matches in screen position which do occur, notably in the sequences of Ivan's 'death agony', are due to quite fortuitous incompatibilities between Eisenstein's totalitarian conception of composition and the narrow margin allowed for 'cheating' by the principle of continuity). It is true that the shots are often longer here than in *Nevsky*, and the shot changes consequently a little more privileged, mitigating the sense of absolute uselessness aroused by the *découpage* in the earlier film, but the straightforwardness of the montage – the way in which shot changes are sandwiched between phrases exactly like the caesura in the old declamatory forms – underlines the kinship between this film and the most archaic forms of opera, whereas Eisenstein's silent films had, whether consciously or not, already adopted the modern dialectic between formal and dramatic discourse of *Tristan, Pelléas* and *Wozzeck*.

It is characteristic of the distance separating Eisenstein's later essays from his practice as a film-maker that in 'Word and Image' he in fact outlines the theory of sound-image dialectic on the basis of the *dislocation* (in Pushkin's poetry) between the syntactic pauses within a sentence and those within a line of verse. He seems to have wanted to apply this idea to the relationship between music and image, but the astonishing thing is that he failed – or did not want – to realize that its most obvious application in a sound film is to the relationship between image and dialogue.

Historians have in fact drawn attention to the extent to which Soviet society in the 1930s and 1940s was characterized by a return to archaic forms; and it is perhaps in the light of this observation that the most pertinent overall reading of *Ivan the Terrible* can be made. But such artistic exercises, like the 'return' to old musical forms effected by Carl Orff during the early days of Nazism, are a far cry from the liberating experiments that distinguished the incomparable first period of Eisenstein.

What is left today of this enterprise that remains unique in the history of the cinema? In the afterword he wrote in 1929 for a pamphlet on the Japanese cinema by Nikolai Kaufman (published in *Film Form* under the title 'The Cinematographic Principle and the Ideogram'), in which he defined the pre-cinematographic principles embodied in various aspects of traditional Japanese culture, Eisenstein ended with this heartfelt appeal:

> In its cinema Japan . . . pursues imitations of the most revolting examples of American and European entries in the international commercial film race. To understand and apply her cultural peculiarities to cinema, this is the task of Japan! Colleagues of Japan, are you really going to leave this for us to do?

It is almost as though this appeal was heard. For in the same year, Ozu's first silent comedies are a striking reflection of Eisenstein's preoccupations, and his influence is apparent on a number of Japanese film-makers of the 1930s. Through the importance he attaches to shot changes and in his very personal conception of the dialectic of bad matches, Kurosawa must undoubtedly be considered Eisenstein's heir. And following in Kurosawa's footsteps, a new generation of brilliant experimentalists, led by Oshima and Yoshida, are attempting to extract from the whole body of cinema dialectics a means of entry into the dialectic of history which ultimately escaped the Soviet giant.

In the West, however, this heritage continues to be regarded with suspicion. Here is Jean Mitry again, on the raising of the bridge in *October*:

> This kind of montage is no longer possible today. Objective reality must be respected *above all*. Meaning should not be extracted at the cost of distorting things represented, but only through an event apprehended in concrete reality.

What we have here is a loud and clear affirmation of the myth, for so long universally accepted in the West, of the cinema's 'naturalistic' vocation. But the young Eisenstein who wanted the cinema to reveal its artifices, and who consequently pushed them to their ethical and aesthetic extremes, helped to lay the foundations for all the constructions which are now permitting the cinema to rediscover *its* reality. Although the compositional style may be outdated today and the 'dramatics' on occasion a little simplistic, Eisenstein's *attitudes* towards his art, and his rigorous scientific dialectic, offer an inexhaustible source of inspiration for the young film-makers of today and tomorrow.

Translated by Tom Milne

1987
The lip-service paid here to Marxist vocabulary – 'dialectic', 'materialist' – will, I hope, not mislead readers as to the resolutely formalist (and idealist) thrust of this article. More seriously in need of correction today is the underlying assumption that the Soviet cinema ceases to be of interest with the coming of sound. In recent years it has become possible in the West to see many films from the early and even the later 1930s which show that the debates which went on in Soviet film circles, the criticism of the formalism of the 1920s, did not sterilize Soviet film production as has so often been claimed, that films signed 'Barnet', 'Raizman', 'Medvedkin', etc. in no way dishonour the great heritage of the 1920s, either aesthetically or ideologically.

4 Carl Theodor Dreyer: the Major Phase

Whatever the merits of the eight films which Dreyer shot in Scandinavia and Germany before going to France to make *La Passion de Jeanne d'Arc* (1928), this film, like three of the four sound features that were to constitute the rest of his life's work (he died forty-one years later!), is as much at odds, both formally and aesthetically, with what we might call the dominant ideology of cinema, as those eight silent features were, on the whole, consistent with it. A film like *Master of the House* (1925), sensitive and charming though it is, descends directly from the narrowly dramaturgical branch of the *Kammerspiel* family; its charm and sensitivity are the qualities of a pantomimic literature, and we are dealing here with purely dramaturgical film-making. Indeed it is the radical cast of Dreyer's successive departures from the ideal of invisible direction that presumably explains the tragically unbalanced profile of his career: nine features in nine years; five in forty.

Hailed as an 'artistic masterpiece' by even the most mediocre critics of the era, it is perhaps time that *La Passion de Jeanne d'Arc* were defined not as some strange freak of genius but in terms of its material contribution to film art. For it is the first film to have embodied, explicitly and uncompromisingly, an awareness that spatio-temporal continuity in film is a convention, that orientation to pro-filmic space is obtained through artifice and *that it is as such that these factors are the keys to film as an autonomous art-form.* True, it can be argued that two years earlier Eisenstein had achieved just such a demonstration. To my mind, however, *The Battleship Potemkin*, though a far more complex work than *Jeanne d'Arc*, involving as it does a great variety of (often contradictory) approaches to formal problems which, in many instances, Eisenstein was the first to raise, does not, precisely for these reasons, possess the exemplary, laboratory-like rigour of Dreyer's film.

Less ambitious here than Eisenstein or Vertov, Dreyer none the less went straight to the core of what was then and, in a sense, still is, *the* problem. 'Granted,' he says in effect with *Jeanne d'Arc* that thirty years of film-making have gradually taught us to analyse, to break down 'proscenium space' (i.e. the long shot, the 'situation shot' which potentially contained the close-up, the 'detail') in such a way as not to disorientate the spectator in his remembered perception of that space (through eyeline, screen-position and screen-direction matching). Granted, too, that the spectator has long since become accustomed to reading this analysis as an organic, undifferentiated whole. What if we now proceed to do away entirely with proscenium space (and radically curtail our use of its chief auxiliary, the direct match); what if our shots relate to each other *only through the device of the eyeline match*; what if the spectator has no remembered cognizance of an overall spatial continuum to which to refer; what, in short, if the representation of pro-filmic space as a global concept is left entirely to the imagination?

Jeanne d'Arc is, of course, famous for its close-ups. Careless critics, in fact, have often described it as a film made up entirely of close-ups. Apart from the fact that this is quite untrue (the range of shot sizes is relatively large, from medium long shot to extreme close-up), this description has generally implied, in the minds of its authors, a definite ethical and ideological reading of Dreyer's basic formal strategy, i.e. the 'close-up' regarded as the shot size best suited to capturing those 'significant details' of human behaviour which give the film its 'psychological depth'. Now this reading, significantly enough, harks back two decades to the candour of the early pioneers, striving to make the close-up 'work' (and ultimately succeeding through the code of orientation) solely in order to surmount what seemed to be film art's dramaturgical 'deficiency' by the standards of the nineteenth-century novel form. In short, Dreyer's film was read, and is still often read, as primarily 'transparent' film-making: its essential statement is purported to concern only such matters as the saint's behaviour before her judges, as mediated by Dreyer, his actors and his camera. The basic formal strategies present are regarded merely as more or less active but essentially subservient ingredients.

Nonetheless, the hasty conclusion (or rather: the idealized memory) that the film is composed only of close-ups is not without meaning, for it actually reflects a perceptual reality. Indeed, one of the principal impressions produced by a close-up is that of an exclusion: one is conscious of *not* seeing what is around the frame, in particular of not seeing what the subject of a close-up might be looking at, an impression which most people would agree 'normally' diminishes as shots become larger and more *self-contained*, as they tend, in other words, towards the 'situation shot'. However, it is precisely in this respect that *Jeanne d'Arc* is no 'normal' film, for all its shots, regardless of their size, function in this way: one is aware of an ambient space which one cannot see, which is never shown.

The film's key formal strategy may be summed up thus: it contains absolutely no situation shots to 'map out' the topology of the main setting (the court-room). The first shot, a fairly wide-angle tracking shot, could be regarded as 'figuring' the conventional situation-shot; but in fact, its downward tilt is such that it in no way *describes* the set as a whole. We only really see the floor and a few people around the edges; but we have the impression that we have seen the court-room in its entirety. This sleight of hand may well have been designed to alleviate the abruptness of the film's novelty, but in so far as it also offers us an illusory description of an illusory space, it is completely compatible with the film's overall formal conception.

Nor are there situation shots of the four subsidiary settings – Jeanne's cell, the cemetery, the torture chamber, the place of execution – in which the action of the film is understood to be unfolding. The successive shots depicting this action are linked almost excusively through eyeline matching, and the spatial continuum from which they are extracted is in fact purely illusory; it exists only in the spectator's mind, never as a comprehensive image on the screen. The shots are laid out like so many picture postcards suspended in a void; they are linked materially by the 'threads' of eyeline but are irreducible to any all-encompassing tableau. More than any other 'continuous-action' film before it, *Jeanne d'Arc* is irreversibly the sum of its parts: it is a linear projection, as it were, of a three-dimensional model.

In varying degrees, this is true of all films, if we except such extreme cases as Hitchcock's *Rope*; but in 'transparent' (commercial) cinema, the filmic discourse is so conceived as to hide that fact. Herein lies the key to the exemplary quality of *Jeanne d'Arc*, gravitating as it does towards the opposite pole, laying bare the essential two-dimensionality of spatial rendering in film as well as the actual flatness of pictorial representation on the screen (perspective here is designated as an artifice – as in *Gertrud,* 1964) – through compositional techniques which recall primitive painting.

Of course, the film would be a limited achievement indeed had Dreyer confined himself to this large-scale corroboration of Kuleshov's famous experiment in screen-direction matching. However, whereas Kuleshov never applied his theoretical formulation of the continuity match in any but the most rudimentary illusionist way, Dreyer tacitly inferred from it a dialectical form. For indeed, once a film has been established as a series of *separate shots laid end to end* rather than a 'somehow' undifferentiated, holistic rendering of an action, its organizational principles – the various ways in which these shots are related and articulated – come almost automatically to the fore and occupy a position of equality alongside the narrative organization *per se*, especially when, as here, the narrative has largely been reduced to its own abstraction (i.e. to the numerous intertitles which reproduce schematically the minutes of the actual trial). It is the overall interplay between these two organized systems that I call, taking my cue from Eisenstein, a dialectical form; and Dreyer's film is one of the most clear-cut examples of such a form. To convey adequately the formal texture of *Jeanne d'Arc* would require shot-by-shot descriptions of long sequences. Instead I shall confine myself to an enumeration of the parameters which Dreyer makes use of.

As befits a dialectical apparatus, these parameters take the form of conflicting pairs: camera fixity as against camera movement; camera movement in a given direction as against movement in another; subject movement as against fixity (or as against movement in another direction); one shot size as against another, more or less contrasting size. Now these are, of course, banal components; few films are without them. However, embodied as they are by those stripped, abstracted, radically autonomous images, the parameters listed above become extremely apparent, and this conspicuousness in turn lays bare the fact that they are subjected to a constant process of variation: series of deliberately similar matches alternate with series of systematically diversified groupings, etc., and though apparently more empirical than the

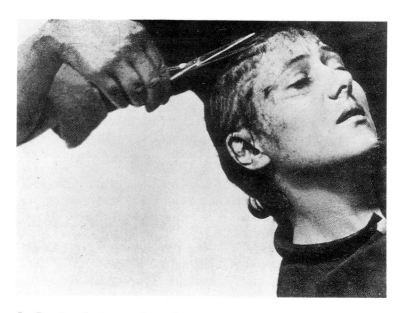

La Passion de Jeanne d'Arc (Dreyer, 1928)

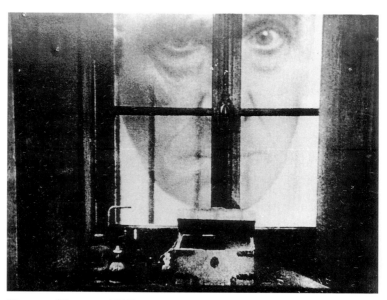

Vampyr (Dreyer, 1932)

comparable variation plan found in *Gertrud* the phenomenon is clearly perceptible.

One further parameter which enters into this variation-form deserves special attention as it is not really a part of 'common grammar': it involves the varying degrees of 'correctness' in eyeline matching, which is almost the only type of continuity cut used in the film. It is generally felt that the 'most correct' eyeline match involves the 'paired subjects' looking off camera at exactly the same angle of incidence. Though never over-stepping the bounds of 'correct' *directionality* (a left-directed look always responds to a right-directed one), Dreyer considerably varies this angle of incidence (the furthest limits being a look almost into the lens in response to a look directed ninety degrees to the right or left).

To complete my surveys of the dialectical functions at work in *Jeanne d'Arc*, I must describe one more important conflict which, though less definably structured, pervades the entire film: a conflict between the carnal and the abstract which I regard as summing up – albeit on a very impressionistic level – the essence of film art. It has become a commonplace to point out that Dreyer's refusal to use make-up on his actors results in the close-ups showing skin-grain, blemishes and perspiration. This refusal is inevitably ascribed to Dreyer's concern for 'reality' (as opposed to the 'studio-ridden' artificiality of most silent films) and regarded as the physiological complement of that psychological realism judged to be primordial among the film's statements. And indeed, at one stage of 'the creative process', this assumption may have been relevant. However, from the analytical standpoint, what seems far more significant to me is that these representations of flesh, as truly carnal as any that have been committed to film, are set forth within a completely non-realistic, almost unphysical pictorial context (most often the figures are seen against pure white backgrounds, with only an occasional lighting effect or isolated décor element as surrogate for the 'environment'), not to speak of the abstraction inherent in that 'linear projection' of an illusory spatial continuum already mentioned. To my mind, the basic tension which underlies the film stems from this conflict of the carnal with the disembodied which Dreyer manages to sustain even through the final coda, in which the eminently physical uprising of the populace and its bloody repression by the soldiers still inhabit that same abstracted, 'shot-to-shot' space (and this in spite of the fact that it contains the largest shots in the film), still obey the same editing principles, which are here simply augmented to this larger scale of representation.

La Passion de Jeanne d'Arc, by virtue of the extremes to which its seminal options are carried, by virtue too of their essentially *reductive* character, is experimental art in the strictest and noblest sense of the term, restrictions or even prohibitions being placed on certain parameters so as to explore others more fully. *Jeanne d'Arc* does not *contain* its experiment, it is substantial with it.

In contrast, Dreyer's next film, *Vampyr* or *An Adventure of David Gray* (1932), though a direct outgrowth – and development – of the conception which gave life to the previous film, is a *work* of unparalleled complexity; it remains today one of the most modern of all narrative films, if modernity is to be measured in terms of a profound compatibility with contemporary aesthetics as a whole. Just as *Jeanne d'Arc* was built upon shot-to-shot spatial relationships that may be described as 'open', so too the generative principle of *Vampyr* is an open *temporal* relationship between shots and a modal variation thereon.

Like *Jeanne d'Arc* in this respect, *Vampyr* contains I believe, only two really direct cuts, i.e. cuts in which the same space or fragment thereof is common to the two successive shots. And while the reverse-field figure at times provides an ostensible guarantee of temporal continuity, it is cross-cutting which is the predominant figure by far (to the point of actually 'absorbing' the reverse field), either as a protracted, reiterated back-and-forth movement or in its more abbreviated form: the cutaway shot. Now, cross-cutting, as we know, was a device originally developed for purposes of dramatic exposition and expression: its aim was to convey a feeling of simultaneity about two actions separated in space whose developments were known or sensed to be in some way interdependent (the simultaneity being either literally chronological – e.g. the final sequences of *The Birth of a Nation* – or merely metaphorically so – e.g. the basic conceit of *Intolerance*).

During the 1920s, Fritz Lang laid the groundwork for an abstracted approach to the spatially discontinuous cut, but Dreyer's use of it in *Vampyr* is far more radical, perpetually challenging as it does the very notion of temporal continuity implicit in the narrative. Furthermore, the specifically definable formal function filled by such shot changes is considerably greater even than in Lang's masterpiece, *M*, for by using them throughout the film, not only as inter-sequential articulations but after almost every individual shot, Dreyer was able to develop a whole system of modal variations, playing on the principle of spatio-temporal discontinuity in nearly all its conceivable varieties, and establishing itineraries by which one mode gives way to another in the course of a given series of repeated shots.

Perhaps the most remarkable example of the way in which Dreyer 'explodes' the continuity of the reverse-field figure is the sequence in which the two sisters, Léone and Gisèle, are face to face in Léone's room after she has been rescued from the vampire in the park. The elder sister is seated in a high-backed wooden chair; Gisèle stands facing her. The shots of Gisèle include the back of the chair in the foreground, signifying Léone's presence, to be sure, but Léone herself is completely hidden by the dark wood. Dreyer comes as close as possible to the over-the-shoulder shot without actually drawing on its primary function, which is to *situate* two face-to-face characters in a single shot; visually, each girl is emphatically alone, all the more so since their eyelines do not quite meet (indeed it soon turns out that Léone is not looking at her sister at all, but at some manifestation of the shadow people in the ceiling). And here, as elsewhere in the film, the number of shot changes far exceeds what might be regarded as a dramaturgically economical figure: thirteen reversals for three short lines of dialogue: 'Oh, if only I could die!' – 'No, no . . .' 'Oh yes, it's all over for me!'

If I have laid emphasis on Dreyer's handling of the reverse-field, it is not because of any preponderance of this figure in the film. I simply wish to make it clear that the emphatic fragmentation of shots which characterizes the film as a whole is present even in those passages where the guarantee of spatio-temporal continuity is normally strongest. Thus, these reverse-field series may be regarded as constituting one pole of the modal variation mentioned earlier; the other being the 'pure' cut-in shots of the sky and of such metaphoric images taken from outside the film's 'narrative space' as the skulls and skeletal hands in the 'blood-letting' sequence. Far more representative of the film's overall texture is the passage that immediately precedes the Lord's final seconds. Having witnessed the murder of the Lord by the shadow-people, David Gray, accompanied by the elderly man-servant, bursts into the drawing-room where the old nobleman lies dying; the coachman is seen hurrying down a flight of stairs; close-up of the Lord; the nurse comes down a hallway; close-up of the Lord; in a close-up, David Gray finds a cup of tea on a table, picks it up; a door opens and two hitherto unseen women servants enter the drawing-room; medium shot of the Lord on the floor, with the man-servant kneeling beside him; the nurse and Gisèle, the younger sister, are seen looking over a banister; then Gisèle comes down the stairs; close-up of the women servants crying; medium close-up of Gisèle entering the room; David Gray tries to make the dying Lord swallow a spoonful of tea.

This should give some sense of the extreme fragmentation to which Dreyer has subjected this narrative tissue, a process which is far more sophisticated than cross-cutting *à la* Griffith or even the ingenious rhyming techniques of Lang. Indeed, it will be noticed that the systematic thwarting of shot-to-shot, sequential logic in the manipulation of the elements that go to make up this passage implies definite structural aims. Particularly significant in this respect are the two shots of the coachman and the nurse, apparently running towards the scene of the tragedy but never arriving. Dreyer has created a kind of dialectic of temporal uncertainty through his unique temporal fragmentation. For indeed, while the spatial organization of successive shots may be defined in terms of a variation on the cutaway, the temporal relationships between shots can be described only in terms of a principle of uncertainty.

The shot change which involves Gisèle coming to the drawing-room is 'elliptical', and indeed, taken out of context, nearly any given pair of contiguous shots in the film could be analysed in terms of the ellipsis. However, the fact that nearly every shot change has this elliptical quality tends to eliminate what is specific to ellipsis, i.e. its *dialectical character*, which normally asserts itself through the contrast with the full range of standard continuity cuts (cuts on movement, concertinas, etc.). To take a comparison from music, it is absurd to describe as dissonant a totally non-tonal work, since dissonance as such is meaningful only in the context of a tonal work, where it coexists with *consonance*. Moreover, nearly all the ellipses in the film belong to *the same mode* (they are achieved through the cutaway as opposed to what can be a more obtrusive and more specifically variable form of time-abridgement: cutting directly from one stage of a given action to a later stage), and the nature of this mode is such that they are, perceptually, of equivalent 'value'. As exponents of transparent cinema have long observed, it is only too easy to 'cheat' on the duration of off-screen action: the elapsed time between two shots from a given action-line separated by one or more cutaways seems to have a neutral, immaterial existence, it is time elapsed and nothing more, it has no specific perceptual duration attached to it. Now, in Dreyer's film the elliptical cutaway is practised so often that we quickly come to accept the successive fragments of a given narrative action as constituting the whole of that action and the very notion of time-abridgement seems to disappear. Dreyer has created an 'illusory', abstract time continuum in this film comparable to the illusory spatial continuum developed in his *Jeanne d'Arc*. Just as the separate shots in the previous film are related only at the surface of the screen, so too the shots in *Vampyr* are temporally related only in terms of projection time.

The other major formal option in *Vampyr* concerns what I have called the 'roles' assigned to the camera. Here again, we are dealing with a variation principle, for the camera's role is continually changing, either from one shot to the next or within a given shot, so that this structure may be said at times to be in unison with the spatio-temporal organization of the shot changes themselves, at others to be set in counterpoint 'against' it. First, however, I must define what is meant by the 'roles' of the camera.

The notion of a 'subjective' camera is a familiar one. It is usually defined in terms of its dramatic efficacy and with reference to an ethos of 'identification': the spectator is put into the character's shoes. *Vampyr* contains extensive use of the 'subjective' camera, as does nearly every narrative film in the history of cinema. But in this film Dreyer was the first, I believe, to designate it as one of several clearly defined and alternating camera roles, thus effectively refuting the ethos of identification contained in idealist criticism's definition of the subjective 'camera-eye'. Here it becomes one perfectly objective function among others that can be defined on an equal footing, whereas for idealist criticism it has always been a privileged, 'humanist' function.

The camera can, of course, assume many roles than those

which Dreyer assigns to it in *Vampyr*, and the three distinct camera attitudes which I detect in this film may or may not be basic: the camera can, as I have said, 'look through the eyes' of one or the other of the characters; it can make itself 'voyeur', in other words behave in such a discreet 'distant' way towards what is being filmed as to make us 'forget' its presence; the camera can be 'author', in other words its 'gaze' can be so oriented as to stress the fact that there is someone behind the camera who knows what is going to happen and who, at times, chooses to anticipate the actors' behaviour, even to the point of guiding our attention away from the characters – from the object of the camera as voyeur – when it is felt that a break with 'objectivist' illusionism is dramaturgically and/or formally necessary.

Now, in so far as I am justified in saying that this parameter is subjected to a variation treatment, it is in the myriad ways in which these roles are made to succeed each other and to *modify one another retrospectively*. And Dreyer's concern for systematic diversification is in this way apparent. The opening episode provides some excellent examples. It is important to see how the structuring of the shot change modes and the role-changing interact, often overlap, but are nonetheless separate phenomena which must be analysed successively before their interrelationships can be understood.

The introductory shot of David Gray has the neutral quality of what I call the 'voyeur' attitude. Its sole function is to present the main character, already established as such by the preceding title, and it is the relationship between David Gray and the camera in this shot which establishes the norm of illusionist 'voyeurism' (the keystone of transparent cinema), all departures from which will henceforth need to be analysed in terms of one of the other roles which I postulate for the camera in this film. The first shot of the sign on the inn, in so far precisely as it breaks off the 'action' with no apparent justification, is undeniably an 'author's' intervention, implying, as we shall soon see, 'I know where he is going.' The shot of the tap-room is more complex: it begins as another suspenseful 'author's' intervention ('This place too has something to do with our story'), but then, when David Gray peers in at the window, the camera assumes, momentarily, two roles at once: it is watching David Gray's actions with 'voyeuristic' reserve but at the same time its gaze is identified with his (David Gray's own role is, moreover, that of a voyeur, see below). We might also note that this is only one instance in which the camera's 'subjectivity' is not dependent upon the impression that it has actually replaced one of the characters in space. In the next shot, a pan along the roof of the inn and then down to where David Gray stands looking up, we have another type of role-change within the span of a single shot: the initial cut back to the roof has a subjective quality (David Gray had looked up), but the movement across the roof, seen from an angle which does not correspond to his point of view, brings us back to the 'author's' attitude. So does the pan downward (again: 'I am going to show you something'). But when the camera settles on David Gray, it resumes its 'objectivist' role. Subjective again is the shot of the maid-servant at the skylight, even though, again, the angle is not compatible with David Gray's actual point of view; here again it is enough for the camera to be 'looking' at what the character is looking at to establish its 'subjective' role. The cut to the first shot of the man with the scythe doubly restores the camera in its role as author, because it abruptly diverts our scrutiny from what certainly seems to be the mainstream of the action, because of the heavily symbolic possibilities of this image injected into a basically 'straightforward' context. The second shot in this cutaway series still retains this exceptional quality, but after the man with the scythe has begun to ring the bell for the ferry and we have cut back again to David Gray at the inn, the remaining shots in this subsidiary series, integrated into the primary action through the continuing sound of the bell, come to be witnessed by the same 'voyeuristic' camera that is watching David Gray. The camera retains this role until the close-up of the chamber-maid in the hotel room, manifestly seen through the eyes of David Gray (she is looking more or less towards the camera); and the last two shots of the man with the scythe at the ferry are seen subjectively 'through David Gray's eyes', while in the intervening shots David Gray, the voyeur, is seen by 'the camera as voyeur'.

The rest of this first section of the film is perhaps even more interesting from the point of view which concerns us here. After David Gray has pulled down the blind, the camera pans with him as he moves to examine a weird Germanic painting. A 'subjective' close-up isolates this 'icon', but the pan from the figure has something of the 'author', while the candle which enters the frame from below re-emphasizes the 'subjective' role. The cut to a side-angle shot of David Gray looking at the picture brings us back into the objective 'voyeuristic' mode. This prevails throughout the shot as our hero hears strange mutterings, and well into the next as the camera follows him through the door and on to the landing where he goes to investigate. Another cut shows us a completely unsituated bit of ceiling, with the top of an opening door low in the frame; the low angle of the shot gives it a subjective cast at first (David Gray when last seen was looking up), but the pan down from the ceiling which follows and which ends on a horribly disfigured man coming through a door on crutches, effectively does away with all trace of subjective verisimilitude: no person's gaze would ever follow such a path; the whole shot is strictly an 'author–camera' contrivance, and at this point our impression of this frightening tableau is that of a radical cutaway, an 'author's image' *which David Gray has not (yet) seen*. However, when we cut back to him, he is hastily retreating down the steps (which we had not seen him climb), presumably frightened by the mysterious figure above, so that, once again, we have a retrospective change in the camera's role (but how much of the previous shot was subjective?). The camera retreats ahead of David Gray into the room; he shuts the door and goes out of shot. And again the camera shifts from voyeur to 'author' as it trucks rapidly in for a close-up of the key in the lock, in *knowing* anticipation of David Gray's panic-stricken afterthought: his hand suddenly darts into the frame to give the key a comforting twist.

This last type of role-change through camera movement is one of the film's most characteristic and original traits: in many instances the camera, which has doggedly followed a character about the set in the best 'invisible' tradition, will suddenly leave him or her without apparent 'reason' and wander off, either to pick up another character at some considerable distance or take up a stand in some corner of the set, focus on an empty wall or doorway and *wait*, 'knowing' that someone will soon appear. One remarkable example of this occurs when Léone, heeding the vampire's call, has risen from her sick-bed to wander out into the park, and David Gray and Gisèle hurry after her. The dolly movements are complex but the role-change that concerns us occurs when David Gray exits from the shot through one of the French doors; the empty frame keeps moving until it reaches the far door, then stops to wait until the old man-servant and his wife have entered the frame, preparatory to his joining in the chase.

Idealist criticism has been hard put to cope with these movements and more generally with the role-changing phenomenon of which they and the cutaways are so often the vehicle. A typically idealist reading refuses to envisage the presence of sheer artifice at the heart of the film, is reluctant to read these organizational processes for anything but their fictional effect, or to understand that these role-changes move in and out of the fiction and that the film is *not* reducible to its fiction.

On the level of interpretative analysis, I should say that the film may be regarded as David Gray's own fantasy, a waking dream whose erotic character is only thinly disguised. This strange hero is totally passive throughout: with two exceptions he *does* absolutely nothing, he is pure voyeur, and the events that he is watching take place in the manner of the classical erotic fantasy: their logic is that of desire, and their 'elliptical quality' corresponds, on this level, to the day-dreamer's impatience to be done with the connectives and 'get on to the next exciting bit' (which would tend also to confirm our observation on the structural level that the ellipses are neutral, lacking in tension). In this connection, it is not uninteresting to point out that the subject of *Vampyr* was proposed to Dreyer and the film commissioned by the young man who plays the role of David Gray in such a convincing torpor: Baron Nicolas de Gunzburg. However, while this psychoanalytical interpretation is undeniably a part of any complete reading of such a complete work, it would be a great mistake to reduce the film's form to the project of rendering this subjacent 'story', at least as great as to reduce it to purely dramaturgical functions. This film is a truly composite work, as only very few films are; it has a purely abstract, 'musical' dimension, closely associated with the dramaturgical but by no means reducible to it.

Vampyr is one of the three or four richest, most complex films in the history of narrative cinema. The organizing principles I have described are applied throughout the work and not just in the passages I have analysed. Moreover, there are others, I am sure, that I have not yet discovered. Only a shot-by-shot analysis on all the successive levels can do the film justice.

Vampyr was shot in 1932. It seems significant to me that this film, which was perhaps the highest summit of film-making to that date, should also coincide with the end of the first great creative period in European films (1919-32). The commercial victory of sound contributed to the subsequent swift triumph of filmed theatre and 'transparent' cinema in all its forms. How closely related to this development was Dreyer's silence during the first ten years of what we can only call 'the dark age' of cinema in the West? His flirtation with Grierson and the General Post Office film unit (1933-35) was an obvious mistake, and it is not surprising that no film came out of it: the aesthetics of the British documentary were completely at odds with his sensibility, despite the attraction he felt for its ethos.

But, ultimately, it was back in his native Denmark, during the very bleakest period not only of European cinema but of European history, that Dreyer was at last able to make his second sound feature, *Vredens Dag* (*Day of Wrath*, 1943). To my mind, the real mystery of those ten years of silence lies not so much in the silence itself but in the *distance* separating the two films that bracket it. For *Day of Wrath*, probably the best known of Dreyer's sound films, is a totally academic work, made according to all the precepts of transparent cinema, with only a shot here or there to recall superficially that he had once made *Jeanne d'Arc* and *Vampyr*: the long sequence-shot at the beginning, which contrasts favourably with the flat, perfunctory reverse-field that characterizes most of the film, is like a pale memory of some of the beautiful moving shots in *Vampyr* – but without the dynamics of role-changing, and when this principle does reappear fleetingly, it is in the form of back-and-forth pans that occasionally relieve the monotony of the reverse-fields but fulfil exactly the same function.

One of the most damning pieces of evidence against traditional idealist criticism has been its failure to see *Day of Wrath* for what it is: not simply an 'inferior' film – in fact, if one accepts the purely literary norms that so often pass for cinematic criteria, it is a 'beautiful story, beautifully acted' – but a work of a completely different *species* from *Jeanne d'Arc, Vampyr* and *Gertrud*.

Only two years later, in 1945, Dreyer had an opportunity to make another film, this time in Sweden: *Två Människor* (*Two People*), based on a play by one Martin Glanner. It is difficult to tell what this film would have been like had Dreyer not completely lost interest in it before he even began shooting – he was deprived at the last minute of his chosen actors. The film is an unbelievably awkward compilation of every imaginable cliché of filmed theatre (truck-ins to emphasize emotional build-ups, two-minute takes which end for no other reason than that the actors have started to move, etc.). Only in the rather long post-credit 'montage' exposition of the story background, done with newspaper clippings laid over rather lovely tabletop compositions of lab equipment, is there the faintest echo of *Vampyr*.

It is wonderful to see how closely Dreyer's career follows the profile of Western cinema as a whole: at the height of the experimental 1920s, he makes the most rigorously experimental film of all; at the end of the brief period which saw the efforts of the great pioneers crowned with a formidable series of brilliantly accomplished and complex films ushering in the sound era – films signed Vigo, Sternberg, Lang, Renoir, Pudovkin – he made the most brilliant and complex of them all. Then, at perhaps the lowest ebb of that dismal period when transparent cinema in all its poverty reigned supreme, his first film in ten years was exemplary in its demonstration of the blind alley down which film had gone. And yet of course the 'Dreyer miracle' was still to come: twelve years later, at the age of sixty-five, he was able to mirror, in his own way, the timid rebirth of the art of film – in America with the first works of Brakhage *et al.*, in France with Tati and Melville, in Italy with Antonioni, in Scandinavia with Bergman – by suddenly producing *Ordet* (*The Word*, 1955), a film which, transitional and uneven though it may be, nonetheless reveals Dreyer *remembering who he was*, rediscovering the meaning of form and paving the way for *Gertrud* (1964), which was to celebrate not only the most productive seventy-fifth year that any artist since Verdi has had the privilege to enjoy, but also an old man's staggering contribution to the second generation of major post-war film-making (Godard, Hanoun, Resnais, Straub).

Already in *Vampyr* and *Day of Wrath*, Dreyer had evinced a certain fascination with long takes (indeed, the slight interest offered by the latter film resides in a few extended shots, such as the discovery of Herlofs Marte hiding in the attic). In *Ordet* – which lasts 124 minutes and contains only 114 shots – this tendency becomes a full-blown style. Although the 'one shot per sequence' principle is predominant, it is not always respected (in particular, the meeting at the tailor's house is divided into several shots). The notion of the changing camera roles reappears here with some frequency (whereas it was almost totally absent from *Day of Wrath*), yet somehow it does not play a decisive part, precisely, I think, because of the small number of shot changes – most of them coinciding with sequence-changes and involving fades or dissolves (the bulk of the role-changes in *Vampyr* came through shot changes). Consequently, the type of movement which, in *Vampyr*, was analysable from the role-change standpoint seems here to tend towards a different kind of experiment, involving surprise effects of a more meticulously articulated kind than those of *Vampyr*. I do not think it is possible to define Dreyer's attempt at formal elaboration in *Ordet* as an overall attitude or set of attitudes, and the two very interesting examples which I shall give are not really representative: there are only a few figures of this sort in the film. Still, they do show Dreyer back at work after twenty-two years, and deserve our attention if only for this reason.

The first example occurs very near the beginning of the film. Johannes, the visionary, has risen in the middle of the night to go out onto the moor. His two brothers and his father, dressing hastily, follow him at some (undefined) distance. Dreyer cuts from a shot of the three men in medium long shot coming towards the camera and *looking towards the camera*, to a medium long shot of Johannes, also facing the camera, preaching to the elements from the top of a wind-swept rise. At this point, the spectator inevitably feels that Johannes' pursuers are still behind him. In the middle of his speech, the camera begins to track off to the right. For seconds, we see only the tall grass sliding by, until we come upon the other three men, as close to the camera as Johannes had been, 'stalking' him through the grass. Now there was of course already a good deal of disorientation in *Vampyr*, but it was a part of the general ambiguity. Here, on the contrary, it is at the very centre of an elaborate *mise en scène*.

A similar effect, also obtained through movement – camera movement and framing are the only active formal parameters in this film – occurs in the next sequence. The father comes into the parlour and the camera pans to the right with him until we discover his daughter-in-law Inger grinding coffee. They exchange a few words about Johannes. Then the camera leaves them and pans again (still to the right but 'all by itself') to another door as Johannes comes into the room and, moving with the continuing pan, goes to a chest of drawers, lights two candles that he finds there and takes them in his hands while his father (off-screen) questions him about what he is doing ('I am the light of the world,' Johannes answers, 'but the darkness does not understand that'). As he carries the lighted candles to the window, opens it and places them on the sill, the camera pans with him to the right (Father: 'What do those candles mean?' – Johannes: 'It's so my light can shine into the darkness'). And followed by a pan to the left, he leaves the room by another door. The camera pans back to the window with the two candles. Inger comes into the shot, takes the candles, snuffs them out, goes back to the chest of drawers (pan to the left), puts them in their place, then comes up to the table where we now discover Mikkel, as well as his father, sitting and waiting for their coffee. She serves them and again they discuss Johannes. At this point, Anders comes into the shot, and since we have heard no door-sounds, we must assume that he, like his brother, has been in the room all along.

The successive discoveries of the presence of the two other sons during the scene with Johannes is quite characteristic of the film's more elaborate sequences, and their association with the role-changes seems to confer upon the latter a function very different from that which they had in *Vampyr*. In this same spirit, the back-and-forth pans (in lieu of reverse-field series) which already appeared in *Day of Wrath* (and even in one or two sequences of *Vampyr*, constituting in his earlier film a peculiar association of the 'subjective' and the 'author's' camera), are here developed to a high degree of structuralization. I refer, in particular, to the long shot sequence in which Anders discusses with Mikkel and his wife the obstacles between himself and the girl he loves, and in which the camera moves back and forth several times between the characters but no longer in the mechanistic way of *Day of Wrath*; for here each movement involves some variation of composition or number of characters.

Lastly, I must also mention the constantly varied leitmotiv of carts crossing the frame which serves as a kind of punctuation (at times integrated into the action-line, at others not) throughout the film, and which was one more sign that Dreyer was striving in *Ordet* to elaborate abstract sub-structures to sustain and complement his remarkable dramaturgy, even though we are far from the through-conceived form of *Vampyr* and *Gertrud*.

Gertrud is one of the most difficult films of post-war cinema. Booed by a fairly sophisticated audience at its world première in Paris, it has been shown publicly in very few countries and still meets with hostile puzzlement from even the most favourably disposed spectators. In no other film perhaps is there such a wide breach between the 'libretto' and the 'music'; indeed, it is like an opera in which all the words might be spoken so that one would have a tendency to regard the music as secondary or not even hear it at all. The text of the film is taken from a play by Hjalmar Söderberg, a Danish disciple of Ibsen, and Dreyer made no effort to modify the rather archaic quality of the dialogue or what seems today to be a somewhat naïve approach to the theme of women's condition in society. Not surprisingly, most audiences seem to read *Gertrud* solely as filmed theatre, and the occasional spectator who professes to like it will almost invariably be found to have been drawn to the play as such, to the actors, the theme, etc. However, despite superficial appearances, the play is *not* the film. Though respecting quite rigorously the text and architecture of the original, Dreyer has built another structure 'into' it, and it is at the locus of the quasi-operatic coexistence of these two organized wholes, which are almost completely autonomous, that we find the actual result of Dreyer's work, which, in spite of his textual fidelity, is ultimately as far removed from the Söderberg play as Debussy's *Pelléas* is from Maeterlinck's.

I distinguish three basic options underlying the tectonics of the film. *Gertrud* is well known for its very long takes, and while one cannot speak of a 'one-shot-per-sequence' approach, most of the film's eight sections are composed of only a few shots. Now it has generally been stated or implied that these shot changes are incidental, that the essence of the film's texture is in the camera movements and framing, which are, indeed, of vital importance. All Dreyer's sound films have generally been felt to be the work of a director for whom 'editing' (i.e. the shot change as formal function) is secondary. Like Mizoguchi (of whom the assertion is largely true), he is purported to be an exponent of what Japanese critics, borrowing more or less accurately from the French, call *photogénie* as opposed to *montage*. As we have already seen from our examination of *Vampyr*, nothing could be further from the truth. And in *Gertrud*, Dreyer has adopted a drastically strict organizational attitude towards the shot change. Here again we are dealing with a variation structure: Dreyer has contrived to vary continually and, with certain restrictions, absolutely, the modes of matching in this film. By this I mean that, generally speaking, each mode is used only once in the course of the film or, when occasionally a mode does recur, it is in such a different context that the principle of diversification is respected on the combinatory level. Of course, the mode of a match is in itself a binary parameter. A few examples: cutting from an exit frame right to an entrance frame left as against (for example) cutting from an exit frame right to a shot in which the same character is already in frame; cutting on a standing-up movement as against cutting on a sitting-down movement, a 'concertina in' as against a 'concertina out'; cutting from a one-shot to a two-shot as against cutting from a one-shot to a long shot (this type of figure predominates in the speech-making section of the soirée held in honour of the poet Lidmann).

With regard to this through-variation on matching modes, one of the film's pivotal moments occurs near the beginning, during the 'confrontation' between Gertrud and her husband, Gustav, when she tells him that she is in love with another man. This episode contains the only series of reverse-field shots in the entire film (with one important exception; see below); it constitutes a kind of 'liquidation' of the reverse-field figure and, above all, of the 'three-dimensional' space which it implies. All the rest of the film is shot according to a principle of strict frontality. This confrontation is one of the nodal moments of the film, in that here the two continua, 'libretto' and 'music', as it were, become consubstantial. The privileged dramaturgical function of this set-up and of the resulting eyeline matches is obvious, since this is the only really 'face to face' dialogue until the very end of the film: otherwise, the characters tend throughout not to look at one another. Its structural singularity is equally clear, since elsewhere the diversification of modes is an autonomous phenomenon, an arbitrary structural premise (not unlike Resnais' *a priori* decision to place the main character of *Je t'aime, Je t'aime* in the middle of the frame at all times), and the choice as to *which* mode should come *when* seems to have been primarily determined by 'blocking' contingencies and by the topography of the set.

The second and third seminal options, closely interconnected, concern camera movement and framing. It has presumably been noticed by others, so obvious is the fact, that each shot in *Gertrud* is made up of a definite number of prolonged *stations* – absolutely static frames in which neither camera nor characters move at all – separated by passages of extensive recomposition in which both characters and cameras move with considerable amplitude; there is no camera-nudging, no incidental actors' 'business'; the dichotomy óf movement and fixity is absolutely clear-cut. This observation leads, quite naturally I think, to the next step in a reading of the film, one which reveals a second 'editing scheme' superimposed over the structure offered by the shot changes. I am convinced that if lantern-slides were made of each of those 'fixed stations' and shown one by one in the order of their appearance on the film, they would constitute a perfectly coherent editing scheme without the inverted commas; in other words all the matches would be harmonious and 'correct'. This is an obvious *parti pris*, respected with utter rigour; in this respect, it is a completely original attitude and is one of the main factors at the origin of the impression of radical stylization which the film cannot fail to produce, even on its detractors.

The third option concerns the composition of those static stations. Again it has often been remarked that the characters almost invariably sit or stand facing the camera at a considerable distance and along an axis which runs essentially parallel to the plane of the camera, or rather of the frame. Moreover, in many instances, there is present in the picture, in the background, some 'projection' of the frame (a painting on the wall, a doorway) also running parallel to the plane of the frame. Hence the characters, at most of their 'stations', are presented in an extremely flat space (a flatness enhanced by the low-contrast lighting and the depth of focus) while at the same time they seem to be *inscribed* in a veritable demonstration of (foreshortened) linear perspective. In this sense, Dreyer's film may be said to belong to a long-established though rare tendency in film-making which has sought to arouse in the viewer an awareness of the duality of cinematographic representation – the projection on a *flat surface* of an *image of depth* which is all the more convincing as it is constantly 'verified' by movement – a tendency the importance of which was theorized as early as 1916 by Hugo Munsterborg in his pioneering book of phenomenological analysis, *Film*; and which was rendered explicit by the makers of *The Cabinet of Dr Caligari*. And while many non-narrative or non-figurative film-makers (especially in the United States) have made such problems the centre of their work, I believe that no narrative film-maker has succeeded so completely in integrating this duality and its apprehension into the formal tissue of his film as a whole. The dramaturgical implications of this symmetrical frontality are undeniable: Phillipe Parrain defined them thus:

> The rigour with which the frame in *Gertrud* is divided in half (*most of these frontal 'stations' are two-shots*) does not correspond to a style of presentation only; it also serves to emphasize the characters' isolation, the element in their relationships of 'incommunicability', to use a word that has become fashionable.

It remains for me to point out the importance of the one other 'violation' of the principle of frontality: a brief return, at the end of the film, to the reverse-field figure of the beginning, but expanded here to the inordinate scale of Gertrud's unlikely parlour (a scale exaggerated by a wide-angle lens) in the scene of the final parting between the heroine and the scientist. Here again, Dreyer displays his awareness of the structural and dramaturgical advantages of both the singularization of a given figure – visually and spatially this moment is unique – and the recurrence of a structural motif at privileged moments in the course of a work; an awareness which I regard as one of the sure signs that he is one of the few really major contributors to the development of a specific film art.

1987
The condemnation of *Day of Wrath* formulated here can only be wrong. Many of Dreyer's silent films – *The President* and *Michael* most notably – are of more than passing interest.

It is undeniable that the relationship of tension which Dreyer, in his best work, established *vis-à-vis* the standard language of European and American films is at the root of his poetics. But such analyses as these are of little use in themselves, isolated as they are from such issues as gender definition (cf. Mark Nash, *Carl Dreyer, BFI*, 1977).

Part II
Forays . . . on the Fringes

The Man with a Movie Camera (Vertov, 1929)

5 Towards an Experimental Pedagogy

To begin with, two historical observations: first, from 1895 to around 1912 there stood beside the motion picture screen in Europe, the United States and elsewhere, a person known as the *lecturer*, a common adjunct of animated projections at the fairground, where this function was performed by the barker who attracted spectators to the stand or tent before the show. The lecturer presented and commented upon the film/performance, with an eye both to captioning the images for the audience and to *helping it to decipher them*. After 1908, however, and in step with the development of the system of editing, framing and lighting that we identify with the Institutional Mode of Representation, in step with the concomitant linearization of narrative and with the constitution of the star-system, in step with the strengthening of the *diegetic effect*, in short, the lecturer's presence became increasingly *importunate*, so that he was gradually relegated to the junk heap of history. Western history, that is. For in Japan, the lecturer, whose cultural antecedents are quite different (the *bunraku* doll theatre, in particular), was to hold his place until 1937, the year of the belated, final disappearance in that country of the silent film. And in Thailand, the lecturer still exists today.

Secondly, around 1930, the advent of synch sound in France seems to have profoundly modified the social composition of the cinema-going public, bringing at last into the picture palaces the bulk of a middle-class audience that had always scorned an art which, unlike *their* theatre, was *speechless* (and this influx was one of the chief factors in bringing about a decade of canned theatre). At about the same time, the first socialist country, where films were produced and viewed in quite different economic and social conditions, also began converting to sound. The changes that took place in the Soviet cinema between 1929 and 1936[1] – and which, there too, reoriented the nature of production for several decades – were of course determined in part by the political transformations familiar to all. And yet, it is just as certain that in a society where politics was in command, the relationship of those in charge of ideological questions to cinema was profoundly modified by the advent of synch sound, a technology which at last gave *specialists of the Word* a cinematic competence which until then could be legitimately claimed only by specialists of the image.

Between the death of the lecturer and the birth of synch sound has been located the gradual emergence of 'the Language of Cinema'. Today, the idea of a *natural language of cinema*, welling up spontaneously, inexorably, from a kind of original chaos – an idea which was for many years an intangible postulate of critics and theoreticians, including that school of semiology which today can be qualified as classical – is no longer acceptable. I, for one, wish to replace it with the notion of an Institutional Mode of Representation (IMR), implying that this 'language' is *only* that of a culturally and socially circumscribed institution. And I claim that this institution has existed only since about 1910, *in the West*, but not necessarily elsewhere[2], for, we now know that *something else came first*. This 'something else' was the Primitive Cinema, whose audience was largely popular in Europe and in the USA[3] a cinema whose system of representation owed more to the arts 'of the people' (*Images d'Épinal*, melodrama, street story-tellers, circus, magic lantern, etc.) than to the bourgeois theatre or novel; a cinema which, for this and other reasons, was scorned in most countries until at least 1910 by the middle-classes, who, at best, delegated into those dark places of iniquity their children, escorted by their maids or grandmothers.

For over ten years, cinema took the form of series of autonomous tableaux, many of which were organized neither in accordance with the norms of classical perspective, nor around a *centring subject*, which proposed a narrative that did not necessarily obey the principles of linear causality and which seldom delineated *characters* in the usual (psychological) sense. The contradictions that quickly developed were ultimately to lead to the linearization of the signifier via editing, to a centripetal organization of the image, to the constitution of the persona via the close-up and the star-system, to a codification of shot-sizes, etc. (They also engendered incongruities which today seem astonishingly 'modern': see in particular the films of Porter.) But the Primitive Mode was to produce its own masterpieces, films which owe their beauty solely to the full development of the 'way things were seen then'; witness the admirable *Kentucky Feud* (1905) by Billy Bitzer, soon to be Griffith's cameraman, but whose camera's 'raw stare' preserved here, in ten hyper-realist tableaux, *distanced* both literally and figuratively, a real-life folk saga of the period, producing a film which seems to anticipate both Brecht's *In the Jungle of the City* and Godard's *Vivre sa Vie*.

And we know now that elsewhere there was something else taking place. There was the cinema of Japan, where thanks to the absence of any colonization, cinema remained, for the first thirty-five years, a direct extension of traditional modes of representation, at the opposite pole to those of our Western bourgeois age (but still close, twenty years after the *Conquest of the Pole* and *Fantomas*, to the Primitive Cinema of the West with, in particular, its own lecturer, the *benshi*). In Japan too there subsequently developed, from around 1930, a filmic mode of representation which was specifically Japanese. For example, Ozu exploded *diegetic space as environment* (which was how occidental IMR practices conceived it), in particular by systematically violating the rules of eyeline matching (the keystone of shot-reverse-shot) and raising pictorial flatness to a principle of *mise en scène*. Shimizu radicalized the archetypal Japanese narrative – de-dramatized, non-linear, 'topological' – and along with Mizoguchi, and many other, lesser-known directors, spurned the close-up and even editing itself as the West had conceived them since Griffith, preferring long takes and wide-angle shots which called for an *exhaustive reading* (again somewhat in the manner of the Primitive Cinema of the West).

And we know now that 'on the fringe' also there was something else taking place. There was *The Cabinet of Dr Caligari*, in which the flatness of the screen was stressed *at the same time* as the impression of depth was being demonstrated (characters moving towards or away from the camera, 'through' what appears in every other respect to be the 'pure surface' of Expressionist woodcuts); in which the spatio-temporal autonomy of the successive tableaux was also emphasized – that is, in contradiction to the system that was already dominant by 1919, but consonant with Primitive Cinema, via the expressionist *Stationentheater*; and in which the homogeneity of narrative was challenged through a remarkably ambiguous ending (how can the characters whom we encounter once more in that same phantasmic setting, possibly belong to what we are nonetheless told is the film's primary level of reality?) And still within the silent era, there was the trumpet blast of Dziga Vertov's *Man with a Movie Camera*, the zenith of an all too brief career wholly devoted to the critique and 'deconstruction' of the IMR and to an attempt (no doubt Utopian, see below) to elaborate a pedagogy not only *by* but *of* the image (inscription of the process of production, dismemberment of the linear discourse, designation of the image as surface, etc.)

And finally (though I can mention here only a few of the many benchmarks which have made it possible for us to read alternative practices in general), there was the New American Cinema: Brakhage challenging the representational nature of the 'live' image; Warhol subverting Institutional formats, organizing the disturbing encounter of pro-filmic time and projection time, reviving the Primitive acknowledgement of frame-edge as material boundary of the spectator's view; and above all, Snow, the greatest figure of the movement, testing in all his films the limits of the very concept of diegesis.

All of these alternative practices underpin, today, our awareness of the historical and cultural determinations of a mode of representation which we spontaneously experience as *natural*. They underpin our ability to relativize and analyse it for what it is: i.e. a *construction* founded on the linearization of the signifier, on the closure of the diegesis, on the production of the flat filmic image as haptic space and of the diegesis as environment centred around the *isolated* spectator-subject, on the presence, the centrality and the psychological 'tri-dimensionality' of the pro-filmic persona, and finally, on the synch voice as 'soul' – as *guarantor* of the whole.

Now, and only now, we can pose clearly the problem addressed by the title of this article: *Can and should mass-targeted audio-visual propaganda depart from the IMR and the secondary codes which have come to be associated with it?* Given that the social divide with regard to the cultural heritage is such that the vast majority of working people today only relate spontaneously to the IMR, can any pedagogy/propaganda *indulge* in such a departure and still remain effective? And how can this other effectiveness be measured?

Of course, the first three questions must go hand in hand with another: Why depart from the currently dominant system when it constitutes a vehicle of pedagogy/propaganda whose effectiveness can be empirically verified? And the two other questions prompt a contrary reflection: Can one really consider that the (relative) ineffectiveness of the established system in this area has been demonstrated, thereby justifying a departure from it?

Actually, of course, these questions are most often raised in a different form, which is far less interesting to us here: Even granted that the IMR is an effective propaganda vehicle, is it not necessary to depart from it for reasons which, in the last analysis, are of a *moral* order, for reasons of 'revolutionary purity'? Since the Institutional Mode is based, after all, on 'manipulation', 'fascination', 'illusion', etc., does one have the right to seek to convince people, however successfully, however much in the name of ideas that are 'correct' (i.e. from the point of view of the working class and its allies, for example), by means of a 'false' language? This issue will be recognized by many readers. It informed, in particular, several remarkable art-works signed 'Jean-Luc Godard'.

So first of all, apropos of this very issue, let us dispel a possible misunderstanding. There is an approach which for an individual artist (or group of artists) consists in pursuing, on the basis of personal ideological goals, *vanguard* modes of pedagogy/ propaganda. Now, the insertion in our society of such products inevitably takes the form of cultural consumption, reserved for a certain type of public under very specific conditions. Even if such undertakings can be of major importance to the cinema as an art, *as well as for the development of mass pedagogy/propaganda* – acting as a kind of laboratory for them – they will not be regarded in this article as pertinent. For my working hypothesis is that with the development of the class struggle as we know it, and with the development too of the possibilities of the audio-visual media, an essential problem in France today is that of a *mass* pedagogy/ propaganda. By 'mass pedagogy/propaganda' I mean pieces of work commissioned by representative collectivities (party, trade union, municipality, association, mass organization) which are readable by their memberships, and which are solely designed to serve these collectivities' ideological objectives.

Now, while the Kino-delia and Kino Pravda series of revolutionary newsreels produced by Vertov and his team during the early 1920s correspond fairly well to this definition, projects like Kino-eye (1924) begin to seriously depart from it, whilst *The Man with a Movie Camera* falls outside it, utterly unreadable as it was for the vast majority of Vertov's contemporaries, whether they were illiterate peasants in Kazhakastan or sophisticated literati in London. And yet, it is these late silent films of Vertov, and particularly *The Man with a Movie Camera* – now that we have learned to decode them – which contribute, more perhaps than any others, to our understanding of the IMR and of the possibility of alternative modes of representation in general. It is they that provided what remains today the most fertile laboratory for the pedagogy/propaganda film, even if, in their own day, their double-pronged effort at consciousness-raising – ideological as well as purely visual ('We want to educate the senses of the masses', said Vertov) – was desperately Utopian. No film, in and by itself, especially if it involves the principle of *tabula rasa*, can possibly achieve this.

One last introductory remark: I have outlined above the general principles of the IMR, its basic strategies and some of the primary codes attached to it, in terms of the model offered by the classical narrative film *which provided the historical space in which this system was constituted*. However, it could be easily demonstrated that the IMR dominates the classical documentary film as well. The documentary voice-over differs essentially from the Primitive lecture in that it is an articulated component of the 'aural universe' of the film (music, atmos tracks, etc.), that is to say it is *in* the diegesis the way God is said to be 'in the world' (is it not sometimes referred to as 'the voice of God?'). The voice-over centres the documentary diegesis the way the main character centres that of a fiction film. The Primitive lecturer, on the contrary, was *in the cinema* and *outside the film*, his voice necessarily interfered with the images he read, and which he designated as images, *from without*, thereby 'neutralizing' much of their diegetic potential. A classical documentary is eminently *readable* (in the Barthesian sense) by virtue of its centripetal imagery and of its production of screen-surface as haptic space (all the rules of framing and camera placement apply just as well as to the narrative film). Finally, of course, here too synch voices play the role of 'underwriters of the real' (notably in the modern *cinéma verité* type of reportage). It is for these and other reasons that, in the last analysis, the usual distinction between fiction and documentary (cf. the perennial opposition between Lumière and Méliès, whose works are, in fact, merely two different aspects of the 'Primitive Mode of Representation') is irrelevant for anyone wishing to break with the illusions fostered by classical criticism and historiography – a fact which is admirably demonstrated by Vertov's 'mixing of genres' in *The Man with a Movie Camera*.

In view of all this, is it possible at present to give direct and unequivocal answers to the questions adumbrated above? I, for one, think not, especially because of the absence (to my knowledge) of any scientific means of measuring the effectiveness of audio-visual pedagogy/propaganda. Above all, we cannot answer them when formulated in this abstract way, independently of any specific, concrete practice. If, however, I have set them forth in these terms, it is for the sake of clarity, and also because recently they have so often been posed in this way, especially by film-students and audio-visual political activists. However, standing a fashionable slogan on its head, I would say that in this area a *detour via practice* is unavoidable. This is because, for the moment, we have little more to go on than practical experiments (theoretical reflection in this area having been mainly informed by prescriptive leftist moralism). The bulk of these experiments do not allow us to conclude that the IMR and its auxiliary codes are ineffectual, for example, when it comes to putting across ideas to which a part of the population is resistant, stimulating discussion, etc. The remaining experiments have indicated only a few of the ways in which a vanguard pedagogy/propaganda might vie with the pragmatic effectiveness of one employing the IMR and its secondary codes. Here, however, one must, as always, bear in mind that the measurement of this effectiveness remains wholly subjective. For example, in the case of the member of a political cadre who considers that this or that audio-visual object reproduces or fails to reproduce the 'correctness' of an 'equivalent' leaflet or speech, or that of the spectator who does or does not recognize (identify with) the form given to what he has seen and heard, his judgement is bound to be overdetermined by his relationship to the audio-visual media, a relationship which of course is bound to be a function of the societal dominance of the IMR. Yet equally subject to caution is the judgement of the specialist, practician or theoretician, whatever his relationship to the IMR, whatever his practice, precisely because of his non-representativeness in an area where only the behaviour of social groups can possibly be of significance.

For the moment then, I will confine myself to a description and a summary analysis of three experiments which have come to my attention, setting down a number of reflections concerning the lessons for tomorrow which might be drawn from them.

One of the few truly decentralized organizations tolerated by the monopolist state is Télé-Promotion Rurale, consisting of a dozen units, each assigned to one of France's agricultural regions. Their task is, on the one hand, to provide the three public television companies with a certain quota of broadcast hours per year dealing with 'the problems of rural society' and, on the other, to place at the disposal of representative organizations in each region the audio-visual tools necessary for educational campaigns aimed at alerting peasants to the need to assume their own problems more fully. Since these activities are financed by the State, it is obvious that in the current political framework it is naturally out of the question to challenge explicitly the economic and social system which is responsible for the bulk of problems facing the French peasantry today. However, some of the *methods* tried out within this inevitably reformist structure seem potentially rich and instructive. I am familiar with only a few aspects of the work of one such unit, based in the department of Isère, but it seems worthwhile describing them here.

In an early stage – and this aspect of their work will no doubt continue alongside the others described here – the organizers commissioned, from professional directors, films meant to be shown on a national hook-up, films whose scripts dealt with such problems as *remembrement* (the regrouping of small holdings), mechanization, investment, credit, etc., and whose *mise en scène* adhered strictly to the codes of the television play. However, in order to preserve the 'authenticity' of these scripts, which it was feared might be lost through the 'filter effect' of the professional actor, it was decided to entrust as many roles as possible to non-actors; and if it was judged absolutely necessary to use a professional or two, every precaution was taken (including a long preliminary acclimation to the milieu) to ensure that their presence would not be intrusive. As was to be expected – by anyone who knows that the *reality effect* in film results from the accumulation and specific articulation of certain signs linked to certain audience expectations at a certain historical period and within a certain culture – the non-actors who were asked, not to improvise, but to *speak lines* that were the fruit of a long reflection on the correct formulation of this or that issue, instilled into their performances a strange unreality, a fortuitous 'distancing effect'. The end-product, which I had the opportunity of seeing, did not seem successful on any level, but this 'distancing effect' was to have significant repercussions at a later stage.

It is very hard to judge the impact of such films on the large audience of rural television. Moreover, one of the acknowledged weaknesses of this type of programme, which is necessarily all-purpose in character, is the absence of any strong regional specificity, since it has to offer a semblance of familiarity from Berri to Picardy, from Corsica to Alsace. On the other hand, the organization of discussion groups, with actual peasants in front of the video monitor, afforded a very different type of audience relationship.

At an early stage, the films or tapes meant for this type of use followed the model of television reportage: a series of interviews with union officials concerning the role of the farmers' unions, for example. But in practice, these officials, addressing the most controversial issues of peasant life, imposed upon themselves a kind of self-censorship. Indeed, these men and women 'wear two hats', as it were, since they themselves are small land-holders deeply involved in a tight-knit community where everybody knows everybody else. And a video tape with that kind of distribution tends to bring the two roles spectacularly close together. Addressing certain problems, then, may suddenly appear very embarrassing to the speaker, with the result that the tapes remain superficial and boring.

To avoid this kind of weakness, the people in charge adopted a very different tack, inspired by their broadcast experience, but – and this is crucial – involving far more modest equipment. They arranged to have acted out, on the basis of a schematic outline and once more by non-professionals (union officials who also worked on the outline script) twenty-minute scenes whose sole objective was to 'illustrate' this or that problem. These largely improvised scenes were recorded on half-inch video tape.

The tape which I was able to view dealt with the problem of how the sons of a deceased small-holder can reach an understanding that will avert the dismembering of the family acreage. The scene showed an ordinary family meal with five characters holding a discussion, in a style which involved a rather singular combination of 'naturalness' – these peasants were speaking from the lived experience of their class – and 'awkwardness' – they were acting out a kind of psycho-drama that was not really theirs as individuals. The scene was, moreover, staged and filmed by other non-professionals. (Those in charge of these groups are not necesarily trained film- or video-makers, their background is more often in sociology.) The result of this combination of circumstances was a product whose 'language' was only a loose approximation of the norms of the IMR and of the codes that are currently associated with it: the zooms in and back were executed in accordance with criteria that seemed largely arbitrary, unrelated to what was being said, so that the codes of shot size – derived from the codes of social distance as observed by behavioural semiologists – can hardly be said to have been respected. Similarly, a second camera, used for a few cutaway close-ups, was placed in such a way that these shots did not match with those produced by the main camera (the character on camera seemed to be looking in the wrong direction). Finally, for purely technical reasons[4], a very loud hum was heard at each pause in the conversation. More generally, the *mise en scène* displayed a spareness that is as unusual in fiction as in documentary-drama: no *surplus* 'dresses up' the scene's functionalism.

These characteristics are what a normative reading would register as the 'defects' of this product. And yet by April 1977, the organizers, having presented this tape more than fifty times, had had the opportunity of observing its remarkable effectiveness: instead of the all too common response on such occasions – a long preliminary discussion of the qualities and appropriateness of the audio-visual product itself – audiences in almost every instance immediately began to discuss the problem raised by the tape, which was of course the sole aim of the operation. Now, why was such a crude product so successful with audiences thoroughly familiar with the professional perfection of broadcast television?

The deficiencies cited above affect either the fundamental elements of the IMR (eyeline matching, shot-size coding) or such non-specific but essential codes as those of acting. Consequently, they impinge upon the normal functioning of the Institutional system and prevent the diegetic effect from 'setting in', so that spectators have at all times a clear awareness of what they are dealing with: members of peasantry (like themselves, from their own region, with an accent they recognize) acting out a psycho-drama about a problem that concerns them directly. They sense, they see, that they are not really dealing with a *mise en scène*, with actors, with a *representation of their lives which they would feel obliged to judge in terms of its fidelity to 'reality'*; they sense, they see, that they are not dealing with a film which demands that they 'immerse themselves' in it: when a close-up begins to favour 'identification', the zoom pulls back quite inappropriately, or a loud hum is heard rising on the sound-track. The culturally determined expectations of the audience *are frustrated* at one level by inadequacies which, however fortuitous, are nonetheless crucial, for they enable viewers to accept the product for what it is, to get the measure of its exact limitations from the very outset and hence *to go straight to what is essential*.

At the opposite poles to this experiment, in which, however instructive, contingency played a determinant role, is *L'Homme Sportif* ('Man as Athlete'), an hour-long film produced in conditions where the *control of meaning* was professionally ensured throughout. This film was made by Uni-Cité[5] in 1973 for La Fédération Sportive et Gymnique du Travail (FSGT).

For a number of years now, the Parisian brains trust of FSGT has been doing intensive work on the relationships between the mass practice of sport, and high-level competition, between sport as spectacle and as dominant ideology, and has been seeking to combat both the myths deliberately fostered by the ruling class to hide its dismal failures in this area (e.g. 'the French are not a sporting people') and those (complementary) ideologies which have sprung up spontaneously from a certain petit-bourgeois leftism ('spectator sport = new opium of the people', 'competitive sports develop people's warring instincts'). The Federation has also sought to extend its possibilities of pedagogy/propaganda and has made use in several instances of audio-visual media, notably by organizing itinerant athletic events which also involve film and video.

Due, no doubt, to the identity of the commissioning body – and of the chief artisans of the film, Miroslav Sebestik and Jean-André Fieschi – *L'Homme Sportif* is a milestone in the history of the pedagogy/propaganda film in France. Rejecting the magisterial and definitive discourse, rejecting the linear, closured model of the IMR, it proposes a mosaic of questions and observations, some only barely suggested, and leaves the spectator to establish his own links between them.

The film begins with a false interview presented as authentic – an ageing but very fit bicycle enthusiast, 'bumped into by accident' during his daily outing in the Bois de Vincennes, sets forth his narrowly 'gymnastic' views of sport – and ends with another false interview but this time one *designated as such*, since it is supposed to take place in a socialist France in the year 2000. Between these two scenes we see a series of authentic interviews (with an elementary school teacher, a physical education instructor, a philosopher, etc.) filmed according to the most minimal norms of television, but intercut with brief scenes that might be clips from a feature film, acted by professionals and filmed according to the norms of today's narrative cinema. So it is not in the detail of its technique that this film departs from the established mode, but in its structure, in its juxtaposition of different models in a way that ruins our expectations of unity, of linear causality, etc.

It is the film's intercut fictional scenes which are the most challenging for the spectator, it is they which break through the disquisitions of the interviewees, skewing them towards the interrogative mode. These scenes are 'slices of life' taken from the intimate life of a young working-class couple, and their only apparent connection with the general theme of the film (with its title) is that this couple seem to engage in no athletic activity whatsoever – except that the 'guy' has a motorbike on which he 'totes about' his 'other half'. However, this bike is no more than the symbol of his virility, as it were: previous prop for the seduction of the woman, object of her jealousy when the first raptures have succumbed to the tensions of the New Poverty. These images depict only the minute details of ordinary daily life: we see the rise and fall of the couple's sexual fervour; we see the husband exceptionally giving his wife a ride to work (she kisses him and says: 'If only there was a strike every day!'). No comments of any kind ever refer to these scenes and their connection with the remarks and analyses offered by the interviewees is never direct, never reduced to what linguists refer to as '*bi-univocal concatenation*' – the fundamental principle of the IMR. Rather, it is an all-encompassing, totalizing relationship, one which demands not a linear lecture, from shot to shot and sequence to sequence, with ideas following a chain of logic to a pre-determined conclusion, but a *topological reading*, as though the film were a space, not a line (linearity, we must recall, is the essential characteristic of the IMR).

Another important strategy used in this film is that the interviewees are not identified on their first appearance. Only in the course of their second or third intervention does a card appear on the screen with the name and profession of the person speaking. The television viewer in all of us is accustomed to the superimposed caption which invariably indicates (during a round-table talk show, for example) *who* is talking and *from where* (socially, professionally, politically). Consequently, in this film, our perception of what is said is profoundly modified by the temporary anonymity of people about whom, we sense, such identificational information would form a necessary complement to what they are saying. And we may well be induced to 'read' their words with greater attention than usual, seeking, unconsciously perhaps, to guess who and what they are. And when at length the identifying card does appear – resolving an essential tension – the rest of the interview acquires even greater vividness because of the itinerary that has led to that identification, because of the trace it has left in our minds.

FSGT was in charge of this film at every step, including at the circulation stage. It should be clear from the above that this is not a film that can simply be sent out by post: it is a film which must be *accompanied*; a film which must be *worked on with an audience*. And the accompanying *animateurs* (here we are at the heart of our problem) do not merely assume the issues raised by the film – the ideological soil which it tills – they also assume the mode of its discourse: they help audiences to cultivate the disruption it brings to their habits of seeing and hearing; they help them to understand that this disruption is an integral part of a continuing reflection on complex problems – a reflection which a film with a closed discourse could not set in movement, but only fix in ready-made moulds.

Perhaps it is easier to see now why I began this essay by dwelling on the Primitive lecturer swept aside by a mode of representation which demanded, for reasons both commercial and class-cultural, that a film suffice unto itself, that it tell its story in a straight line from start to finish and that before and after it there should come an implied 'nothingness'. The Primitive film, on the contrary – though it must certainly not be viewed as a lost paradise, but merely as a *site of recognition for certain 'censored' dimensions, certain buried latencies* – was anything but closed in on itself. It often dealt with famous real-life events in images understandable to the public only because the facts in the case were so well known – the lecture serving more to jog the popular memory than as a substitute for it. Or a film would often offer a digest of thick popular classics in a few elliptical tableaux, and here again, the public, with the help of the lecturer, had to fill in huge narrative gaps (see, for example, Porter's *Uncle Tom's Cabin* (1903)).

Experience has shown that, today, only when the product – film, video tape, slide show – is taken in hand at the point of delivery is it possible to create a situation that involves an audience in a radical departure from habits born of long familiarity with the IMR. And this claim is as true for the art-object as for the instrument of propaganda. In fact, it is my belief that here lies the only possible key to a future modification/extension of the relationship between the mass audience and audio-visual creation. Only when the idea has been abandoned that a film (or a tape) makes its own way, spontaneously, in the silence of our hearts and minds will any evolution be possible. Not, of course, that it is indispensable to talk during the projection, like the lecturer of old (although I am not sure that silent pictures have had their last say, so to speak, nor perhaps even the lecturer). But we must no longer consider that the work of the film begins when the lights go down and ends when they go up again – all the more so as the film itself departs from closured linearity of the IMR.

However, this work cannot be confined to the point of delivery, and this, too, is one of the great lessons of *L'Homme Sportif*[6]. In order for a film really to be taken in charge of by those who have commissioned it (by the activists of a mass organization, for example), they must be able to be at one with its creative approach, and this includes its status with respect to the 'dominant language'. In other words, having successfully resisted the temptation to imprison the 'specialists' within the strictures of the IMR, they must not, in a burst of liberalism, turn all initiative over to those specialists, however politically educated these may be, at the risk of finding themselves with a product on their hands that they don't know what to do with. This has happened more than once.

The lesson of the Soviet cinema of the 1930s and after, as I also tried to suggest at the beginning of my essay, should give us pause, above and beyond the rubric 'negative effects of Stalinism'. For members of political cadres, trade-unionists, etc., if they belong to the working class of a capitalist society, will not be spontaneously qualified to take on board novative forms of pedagogy/propaganda, precisely because of the alienation of their class with respect to cultural phenomena, that is, their inevitable dependence upon all the dominant modes of representation (they have even less time to devote to contemporary culture than the Western European worker who is not a member of a political cadre, a trade union official, etc., for example). If one believes that an enrichment of pedagogy/propaganda can and should involve a collective revision of the IMR (a collaboration which extends from the commissioning process to distribution) one must also believe that education is indispensable. This education, for reasons that the reader can perhaps imagine, is even harder to put into practice than the other.

In conclusion, I would like to cite another example, as different from the two previous ones as they were from each other. This is an experiment which comes to us from a distant socialist nation, Cuba. Its relevance to the experience of French audio-visual political militants is not, I feel, direct. In fact, no doubt it is an experiment which could be carried out only in a socialist country, and not just any socialist country at that. But it does appear to me to point to some of the prospects for an alternative mass audio-visual pedagogy/propaganda, the premises of which I am trying to outline here. It might also suggest under what conditions the old dream of

Dziga Vertov might be realized: the marriage of cultural agitation and the education of the senses of the masses, solely through the experience of film, through the reinvigoration, in a new social context, of the 'autonomous' action of film.

In order to situate this experiment, we must sum up, very schematically indeed, the history of Cuban cinema. Before the 1958 Revolution, it goes without saying, Cuban screens were massively filled by North American movies, and these were very popular with an exceptionally movie-minded population. After the Revolution, the national film production, limited to documentaries, was able to satisfy, willy-nilly, the people's hunger for cinema. But after a few years of this diet, and once the early revolutionary fever had abated, the public began to turn its back on the cinemas and to clamour for the return of the films they loved. It was decided to re-issue some of the old American movies that had been stockpiled, and to import films from the socialist countries of Europe, since the Cuban industry was not yet organized to produce features. In the years that followed, despite the growth of a significant national cinema, audiences continued to prefer foreign products, especially those of Hollywood. This is what led the film-makers of the ICAIC[7] to ask themselves questions: Would it not be interesting to take over the codes of those American films of which the public was so fond, while at the same time *fracturing* them, as it were? Would this not in itself be of pedagogical value both at the political level and at the level of that very 'education of the senses' advocated by Vertov?

Girón was directed by Tomas Guttierez Aléa[8] to mark the tenth anniversary of the defeat of the CIA supported invasion attempt at the Bay of Pigs (*Playa Girón* in Spanish). In part, the film is a full-scale reconstruction of that battle, which was so decisive for the survival of socialist Cuba. And this reconstruction, which benefited from the considerable means made available for its production, was filmed (in Cinemascope) according to the codes of the North American war film. But with a difference. A man wearing a T-shirt, filmed in the manner of *cinemá verité* (hand-held camera), stands near a car. It is daylight. He remembers: 'I heard explosions, shooting near the airport . . . I jumped into my car . . .' He gets into the car and starts the engine. *Then a change occurs*: it is night, the same man is driving the same car towards the airport and we hear the sounds of a battle in progress. As he drives, he goes on with his

Giron (Aléa, 1971)

story, still in the past tense. This opening sequence of *Girón* sets the overall pattern, perfectly simple but subject to numerous variations, upon which the film is built. Eye-witnesses re-tell, in 1971, how they took part, as members of the People's Militia or as ordinary patriotic citizens, in the events of 16-19 April 1961. On the site of a critical battle, a man tells how he was on the firing line, and we suddenly see him side by side with his comrades, indeed, in the thick of the shooting. Then, turning to the camera, he explains that a comrade at his side was hit; the camera pans to the ground and we see another participant in the reconstruction lying on the ground with a 'gaping wound' in his back. Or else, a detachment of invaders are seen in the distance, rowing in towards the beach in an inflatable raft. The defenders open fire on them, whilst a man with a loud-hailer gives the actors in the raft instructions as to the route their craft should take to comply with the reality of ten years earlier.

It is true that as the film unfolds, it tends increasingly to give precedence to the realistic war scenes, the distancing interventions which remind us that all of this is simply a *representation* of history becoming few and far between. After a certain point in the film, one can easily become immersed in the codes of the Hollywood war epic and in the 'thrilling' aspect of the spectacle. This has, incidentally, prompted some left-thinking audiences in Europe to imagine that they were dealing with a 'militaristic' film 'glorifying war'. They were forgetting that the content of that enthusiasm was inflected by both the overall structure of the film and the content of Cuban history – this was the anti-imperialist battle *par excellence*.

However, this type of misunderstanding does help us to measure the distance separating the possibilities for experimentation in this domain offered by a socialist society from the narrow range of possibilities that exist in a country still subject to monopoly domination. For when I say that it is Cuban society as a whole that inflects this film, this is not simply an image. The film was seen and presumably *understood* by most Cubans (there is nothing obscure about it, despite its deviations from certain norms implicit in the IMR). It was seen, moreover, in 'normal' viewing conditions, in cinemas, and without, to my knowledge, any special preparation. For it has connections with the lives of its audience that are not unrelated to those which existed between the Primitive Cinema and its popular audience, except that here the voice of the lecturer is that of the Cuban people, in the film, in the cinema, in the street, and everywhere. It is they who *take in charge* a film like this one.

Notes

1. Gradual changes. We must not forget that the advent of sound in the USSR – as in Western Europe – at first gave a fresh impetus to the experimentation inaugurated during the silent era.
2. Suggesting also that all of its components do not necessarily adhere to the language model, but this is an issue which lies outside the scope of this essay.
3. In the United States it was more truly popular during the Nickelodeon era (1906-1912) than during the era that was at least in part that of the vaudeville hall (pre-1900-1905), patronized chiefly by the newly urbanized white-collar masses.
4. For the technically-minded: effect of the AGC on the portable tape-recorder, amplified by successive copying for editing and distribution purposes.
5. Connected with the Propaganda Sector of the Central Committee of the French Communist Party.
6. Five years on, this film is still perfectly up to date, and is still being shown by the FSGT during the debates which it organizes up and down the country.
7. Istituto Cubano del Arte y Industria Cinematográficos, a title which is a cultural project in itself.
8. Aléa has directed at least one other film which plays upon the codes of popular cinema, *Death of a Bureaucrat*, incorporating elements of the classical North American comedy.

1987

This essay was written in 1977 for a journal published by the cultural and educational organization (Comité d'entreprise) managed by the trade-unions of the French National Electrical Company (Electricité de France). The English translation is my own. These reflections were inspired by part of my teaching experiences between 1971 and 1974 in England (at The Slade School and The Royal College of Art), where students and independent film-makers were already deeply engrossed in that search for alternative forms of radical cinema which was to play such an important role in the rebirth of the British film in the early 1980s, but which was also to determine so many false vocations and so much sterilely theoreticist film-making.

A more immediate influence, however, and politically more decisive was my intermittent collaboration with Uni-Cité – mixed media agit-prop shows, video tapes, etc. – and my regular discussions, throughout the mid-1970s, with other French Communist film-makers (Jean-Patric Lebel, Jean-André Fieschi, Jacques Bidou and Michèle Gard).

6 Film's Institutional Mode of Representation and the Soviet Response

It is tempting to regard the system of representation at work in the vast majority of films produced during cinema's earliest period (which we may situate between 1892 and 1906) as an authentically working-class system, in opposition to not only the bourgeois novel, theatre, and painting of the nineteenth century, but also an institutional mode of representation as it was to develop after 1906. In the countries where the film industry first developed, not only was the audience of this cinema largely proletarian, but in many respects the system of representation which we may identify as specifically of this period derives little from the characteristically bourgeois art forms of the eighteenth and nineteenth centuries and almost everything from popular art forms descendent from the Middle Ages and before.

However, much of the *otherness* of the films of this era is patently overdetermined, often due to the contradiction between the aspirations – conscious and unconscious – of middle-class inventors and entrepreneurs on the one hand and the influence of such plebeian or otherwise 'alien' art forms as the circus, the carnival sideshow, the picture postcard, or the lantern show on the other.[1] In any case, one must regard as highly problematic any direct intervention of the working classes, whose taste could have directly affected only the substance of the films they saw (in France and England, especially); while the deepest aspirations of the working class were sometimes catered to symbolically, these films certainly never reflected revolutionary ideology. In France this privileged relationship between an essentially populist cinema and the working classes lasted practically until the introduction of sound. In the United States, however, where even in the era of a wholly proletarian audience the substance of the films mostly reflected the lives and ideals of their petit-bourgeois makers, the industry quickly came to see that the condition for its commercial development was the creation of a mass audience, that is, one which also included the various strata of the bourgeoisie, less fragile economically and possessing more leisure time than the immigrant working classes.

It is important to realize that the extraordinary expansion of the American cinema and its rise to world dominance after the First World War were a direct consequence of the creation of that audience during the period 1905-15. In France, on the other hand, the industry remained content to exploit the early mode of representation for nearly three decades, catering to a small domestic audience which was almost exclusively working class, and counting on the skills of its cameramen and actors to continue to captivate indefinitely the huge international market which it had conquered early in the century. The corollary of this situation was that the French bourgeoisie was not to come to the cinema in any appreciable numbers until the screen finally acquired a *voice*, that crucial element of presence which would at last place it on a par with the legitimate – which is to say, bourgeois – stage.

Early cinema was marked, in the eyes of the international bourgeoisie, by the absence of the persona, of nearly all the signs of character individualization capable of satisfying expectations created by naturalistic theatre and novels, which were steeped in the primacy of the individual, in the centrality of the Subject. The lack of a voice was the biggest deficiency, hence the constant but only relatively successful efforts to invent a sync-sound system, from Edison's Kinetophonograph to the Gaumont Chronophone. However, the persona was lacking on the visual plane as well.

One of the founding visual models for the early period as a whole was the long shot as exemplified in *La Sortie des Usines Lumière* and also in a film such as *L'Assassinat de Marat*, which Hatot directed for the Lumière Company during the early months of its existence. Films like the latter – and there were many of them – illustrate in spectacular fashion the gap between early cinema and the bourgeois theatre: the coextension of proscenium arch and film frame produces an effect of distance through smallness and low definition which is very different from the effect of presence indissociable from the bourgeois stage and produced by the 'sync' voice, 'natural' colour, three-dimensionality and the eye's faculty of focusing in space, often with the aid of opera glasses. As the various socio-ideological pressures to make the cinema 'more respectable' became stronger, this long shot came to be thought of as an obstacle.

Despite legend, it certainly was not Griffith who singlehandedly solved the problem of the interpolated close-up, of facial legibility, that *sine qua non* for the institution of the persona. In fact, while Griffith, during his richly innovative career at Biograph, gradually moved the camera closer to all of his tableaux, true close-ups in his Biograph films picture objects far more often than they do people. Moreover, Griffith was one of the last directors to relent on the matter of actors' anonymity, which for a variety of reasons had been a universally respected rule during the early period. This belated adhesion to the star system – the counterpart of the close-up in the constitution of the filmic persona – was undoubtedly a cause of the paucity of true facial close-ups in the Biograph films, which were in other respects so forward-looking.

Another respect of early cinema which did not fulfil expectations created by modes of representation dominant at the turn of the century resulted from the great difficulty experienced by early film-makers in reproducing, under certain circumstances (especially for indoor scenes), the depth cues long essential in Western imagery, whether in easel painting or on the proscenium stage. A great many films during this era are characterized by the *relative perceptual flatness* of their (interior) imagery. *L'Assassinat de Marat* and other 'theatrical' films produced by the Lumière brothers at the start of their undertaking are examples of this. More significant still, perhaps, are the many remarkable instances found in what I call the mature early era.

Consider *The Life of Charles Peace*, the story of a celebrated Victorian murderer filmed by a remarkable artisan of working-class origins, William Haggar[2]. Most of the film consists of a series of single-shot, richly orchestrated tableaux, but it culminates in a multi-shot chase sequence filmed on location. All of the stylized interior scenes are shot against two-dimensional backdrops from which all illusion of haptic space seems to have been cunningly excluded, and in front of which actors play according to a strictly lateral blocking scheme. This lack of illusion of haptic space is common to nearly all scenes shot in the studio until at least 1910[3] and was brilliantly illustrated by the great Méliès, for whom the 'essence' of cinema was precisely its capacity for rendering three-dimensional space and movement in two dimensions (see in particular the trick effect in *L'Homme à la tête de caoutchouc*)[4].

This tendency continued to make itself felt in the films of Griffith and of most of his contemporaries. This was due to the persistence of two factors that had determined its presence from the start. One was filming in daylight, in studios with glass roofs or in the open air, which gave an even, 'flat' lighting that tended to place everything on the same vertical plane. The other was the stationing of the camera, still resolutely frontal, with the lens axis rigorously parallel to the floor and always at the height of a standing man. Consequently, until about 1915 or even later a character would occupy the space at the top of the screen only if he were standing in the foreground. When the actor was seated in a chair, crouching on the ground, or standing in the background, his head only reached the middle of the screen, which produced a flattening effect, familiar to graphic artists, in which the background – set or landscape – seems to be looming overhead, ready to topple into the foreground.

At the same time, however, other factors had already been working in the opposite direction. The generalization of electric lighting made it possible to obtain more subtle modelling and chiaroscuro effects. Colour had long been used by the French, including Méliès himself, to counteract the flatness of certain images (with the introduction, in particular, of artificial effects of aerial perspective). Around 1914 several directors and technicians began to avoid placing their cameras at a 90° angle to the rear wall as had been customary. Finally, there was the introduction – possibly by DeMille in *The Cheat* (1915) – of a systematic, slightly downward tilt to the camera, which meant that characters would occupy the space at the top of the screen even when they were at the back of a moderately deep set, and which furthermore accentuated the obliqueness of horizontal lines. Together, all of these procedures were gradually to bring about the creation of a full-blown haptic pictorial space 'in' which the diegetic effect would be able to reach full development.

However, the chief problem for the major pioneers, from Porter and the early British film-makers (Smith, Williamson, Hepworth, etc.) to Barker and Feuillade, was, on the one hand, what I call the linearization of the iconographic signifier and, on the other, the construction of a linearized diegetic continuum. Let us now briefly examine these two closely linked issues.

The *panoramic tableau* of the most characteristic early films offers two basic traits (which may also be seen as *complementary* – for we must not lose sight of the fact that all of these 'inadequacies' as well as the strategies which ultimately led to their reduction, interpenetrate in complex fashion). First there is the relative rareness of any of the indexes of individualization/differentation alluded to above. Secondly, there is the tendency to confront the spectator's gaze with an entire surface *to scan*. At times the gaze is directed along a relatively controlled trajectory (but one which generally took in most of the screen's surface). At other times the gaze is undirected, due to the absence of most of the ordering procedures – strategies of isolation or signalization – which when they were developed would gradually make it possible to normalize the behaviour of the spectator's eye. One very striking example of the typically 'chaotic' tableau is the opening shot of a Biograph film of 1905, *Tom Tom the Piper's Son*, known to us today through Ken Jacobs's enlightening rehandling of it. The shot shows a crowded marketplace distractedly dominated by a woman tightrope walker in white. But she has no role in the narrative (in fact, she is the only character never to be seen again). On the other hand, what is meant to be the central action – the preliminaries leading up to the theft of the pig, the theft itself, and the start of the chase as the thief escapes – is nearly invisible for the modern spectator at first viewing. For he is accustomed to having each shot in a film carefully organized around a single signifying centre and to the linearization of all the iconographic signifiers through composition, lighting, and/or editing.[5] And as we know, the first step in overcoming this 'handicap' was the dissection of the tableau into successive fragments (closer shots), each governed by a single signifier, so that each frame would be immediately decipherable (at least in accordance with certain norms of legibility) *at first viewing*.

However, in order that these successive images did not bring about the dislocation of the 'original' profilmic space – the space of the single tableau, the space, if one prefers, of the proscenium – a long evolution was necessary. Starting from the alternating shots in the work of Porter and the British film-makers, and the earliest contiguity matches (matches of direction and eyeline), this evolution, through the increasing ubiquity of the camera, was ultimately to succeed in establishing the conviction that all the successive separate shots on the screen referred to the same diegetic continuum. In other words, the time spans represented were linked together by relations of immediate succession, simultaneity, or a more distant anteriority or posteriority; the spaces pictured communicated directly or at one or more removes; and above all the whole constituted a milieu into which the spectator might penetrate as an invisible, immaterial observer, yet one who not only saw but also 'experienced' all that transpired there. The camera's ubiquity and the strategies which led to the spectator's identification with the camera's viewpoint (together with the system of orientation matches by which the right/left relationships of the spectator's own body organized his apprehension of all contiguous spatial relationships on the screen from shot to shot) reinforced the sense of spatial integrity. These two acquisitions were ultimately to converge in the figure known as the reverse-angle set-up,[6] destined to become the keystone of the entire edifice at the level of visual signification.

While the full head-on reverse-angle did not become generally used until the mid-1920s, and while of course the sync voice was not heard until the end of the 1920s, the system thus constituted as a visual entity had become fully operational in the United States before the end of the First World War and in Western Europe by the early 1920s. Fritz Lang's *Mabuse* diptych (1922) is an early example of the system mastered to a degree that has perhaps never been surpassed. And it is not without interest that Eisenstein had the opportunity of studying closely such a supreme example of the system whose emergence I have briefly sketched here, having been involved – in what capacity has not, I believe, been clearly established as yet – with the editing of the Soviet version of *Mabuse*.

Several years before the first projections at the Grand Café, Edison was already dreaming of filming and recording operas, and in this his enterprise is antithetical to that of Louis Lumière. Not only did the team working under Edison's auspices (W. K. L. Dickson and his associates) invent the first 'sound movies' with their Kinetophonograph, whose eyepiece and earphones prefigure, at the scale of the individual spectator, the dark, womblike isolation of the modern movie palace, they also shot some of the earliest close-ups. And all of this was done in the Black Maria, that precursor of the modern sound-stage. Even though the company was soon forced by the competition from Lumière to give up the attempt at sound and to copy the more typical early European models, these early experiments attest to the existence of a need, ideologically determined in part, but only in part, that would ultimately give rise to an institutional mode of representation.

We also find, as early as the first Lumière films, and throughout the early period of French cinema up to the masterpieces of Jasset, Perret, Feuillade and the émigré Gasnier, first in scenes shot on location and later in increasingly elaborate studio sets, a very thorough exploitation of the possibilities of deep-focus *mise en scène*. In fact, we are dealing here with an increasingly sharper prefiguration of that pseudo-montage within a single take (except in the work of Feuillade, intrasequential editing was still rare in France before the First World War) which would ultimately be capable of reproducing the structures of classical montage. This approach, which among French directors continued to serve as a vehicle for strictly primitive elements, such as the insistent glancing at the camera which one still finds in Feuillade as late as 1916, would reappear twenty years later in the canned theatre of the early sound years, when it was simultaneously theorized by none other than Eisenstein (the paradox is only apparent) in his classes at the Moscow Institute.[7]

The dominance of the Western mode of filmic representation was determined neither by ideological factors alone nor by sheer economic opportunism. Rather, that mode corresponds broadly to the mode of constitution of the Subject in our culture, and it developed into an ideological vehicle of unprecedented power. However massive its political and social consequences, it was the result of an overdetermined convergence and not simply a class strategy.

At the time when the civil war was receding within the young Soviet Union and the great period of artistic experimentation was beginning in that country, the system of representation developing in the film industries of the capitalist world had not yet been fully consolidated. We have already noted that the lack of sync sound constituted a serious deficiency, which, it is clear today, the intertitle never completely made good. (To the very end of the silent era, the intertitle retained – and indeed still retains – a 'distancing' potential which directors like Gance and L'Herbier had sought to exploit to aesthetic ends.) A film industry as culturally important as that of France remained very strongly dominated by early practice, with frontality still dominant as late as 1925, and with the rules of orientation still very poorly assimilated. And in all countries the various 'punctuating' opticals made possible by developments in technology were as yet scarcely encoded and were often used – and not only in avant-garde films – to contribute to a freely decorative style. This 'unfinished' state in which the system found itself, especially in Europe, played a decisive role in the orientations of the most important Soviet directors, who, with only one exception, were otherwise quite prepared to accept the system's claim to a privileged status.

It was no doubt this twofold circumstance which determined the earliest options of Lev Kuleshov and his troupe. It was this which led them to the first theorization of the system of orientation matching. Their most famous experiment consisted of a series of montage fragments linked by actors' entrances and exits, so that various parts of Petrograd were seen as contiguous, whereas anyone familiar with the city knew that they were miles apart. This experiment was in fact nothing more than the rational formulation of the contiguity match long since mastered at the practical level by D. W. Griffith. In *The Musketeers of Pig Alley* (1912), for example, a whole 'imaginary' neighbourhood is similarly constructed by laying end-to-end fragments of settings which are brought together only by the successive frame exits and entrances of the actors.

Following these laboratory experiments, the films that came out of the Kuleshov workshop attest to another concern, not unrelated to the first: studying and *appropriating* the codes governing the major genres of the capitalist film industry – the spy serial, as in *The Death Ray* (1925); the comedy, *The Extraordinary Adventures of Mr. West in the Land of the Bolsheviks* (1924); the 'Far North' adventure drama, *By the Law* (1926). The guiding principle behind all these productions was that the institutional mode of representation and the genres and other coded systems founded upon it offered ideal vehicles in the ideological struggle because of the privileged relationships which they already enjoyed with mass audiences.

After the Kuleshov group disbanded in 1925, its ambitions were no doubt best achieved in *Miss Mend* (1926), directed by an ex-disciple of Kuleshov, Boris Barnet (in collaboration with Fyodor Ozep). In this film the principle of political didacticism through pastiche is maintained, but with one fundamental difference: this monumental 'serial' (three parts and over four hours long) frequently shifts abruptly from one popular genre to another. Spy thriller, sentimental melodrama, romantic comedy, slapstick farce follow each other in quick succession. The intention is clearly to undercut the escapist and alienating absorption of the popular genres.

I have no wish to establish, in the context of this inventory, any hierarchical order whatsoever. The wide range of Soviet attitudes and opinions, which runs from Kuleshov's pastiche to Dziga Vertov's 'deconstruction', corresponded to a pluralism indispensable to the socialist ethic. It also reflected the very concrete and highly diversified needs of Soviet society, coming into existence under notoriously complex and difficult conditions. Kuleshov's undertaking thus appears doubly justified. The urban masses were already quite familiar with the then current mode of representation and forms of expression, and it was obvious that one important way of reaching them consisted in acquiring the theoretical mastery of that mode and in appropriating its forms of expression. Furthermore, although the bulk of the peasantry did not come to know the cinema until after the revolution, it takes the optimism of a Vertov to become convinced that linear expectations with regard to the cinema would only be produced by previous film-going experience, and that these peasant masses were consequently 'unspoiled'.

V. I. Pudovkin also came out of the Kuleshov workshop. His approach was not fundamentally different from that of his mentor, although his methodology – and, of course, his stylistics, which are not the subject of this essay – is quite different and his ambition, in a sense, far greater. Pudovkin was striving principally to extend the possibilities of the existing system, while maintaining its essential principles. This undertaking has undeniably enriched our cultural heritage, with such remarkable films as *The End of Saint Petersburg* (1927) or *The Deserter* (1933), but it was certainly not devoid of contradictions. Significantly enough, these actually repeated, at a higher level of elaboration, the contradictions experienced by the pioneers of the early and formative periods.

The Extraordinary Adventures of Mr West in the Land of the Bolsheviks (Kuleshov, 1924)

The Death Ray (Kuleshov, 1925)

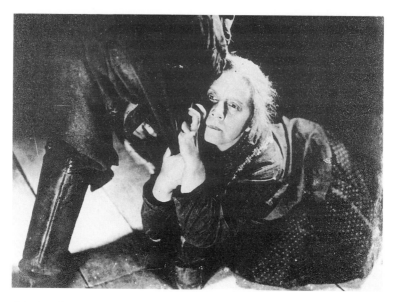

Mother (Pudovkin, 1926)

Earth (Dovzhenko, 1930)

124 IN AND OUT OF SYNCH

Some years ago, in a programmic essay which has not surprisingly fallen into neglect, two British critics, Michael Orrom and Raymond Williams, voiced a number of criticisms concerning the Pudovkin method in connection with a sequence from *Storm Over Asia* (1928).[8] They argued that the director disrupted too radically the cohesion of the spatio-temporal continuum, that essential guarantee of verisimilitude, of, in other words, the full-blown diegetic effect. And they went on to compare this outmoded, disjunctive style, too analytic for their taste, with the techniques of modern cinema, illustrated by a sequence from George Stevens' *Shane*. Here, they demonstrate, continuity is ensured by the juxtaposition in long shots of all the signifiers present to the scene, their ordering being assured by picture composition instead of their being linked together only by eyeline and screen-direction matching, as was so often the case in Pudovkin's films. Despite the ingenuous character of their demonstration, these writers pointed to a fundamental contradiction, one which is of considerable interest to basic research in this field.

Pudovkin's writings and his polemic with Eisenstein clearly bear out the evidence of his films that his chief concern was to draw the ultimate consequences from that historical process of linearization of the iconographic signifiers to which I have already referred. Let us consider the sequence at the beginning of *The Mother* in which the father, trying to take the household clock down from the wall to exchange it for vodka, is confronted by his son and wife. He accidentally breaks the clock and leaves the house carrying off the laundry iron which served as the clock's counterweight. This scene is a perfect illustration of Pudovkin's method. The scene is broken down into a series of key fragments, big close-ups whose meaning is wholly unequivocal and which, while respecting and rendering quite satisfactorily the continuity of the action, primarily serve *to spell out* that action in a series of elementary, carefully differentiated signs, in a simple, causal chain. A face grows tense, an arm is raised, a wheel of the clockwork rolls across the floor. There is no room for the gaze to roam unguided (or even guided) about the image for so much as an instant. The director's constant concern is, on the contrary, to regulate the 'flow of signs' as closely as possible. Moreover, in a sequence such as this one – and it is here that Pudovkin adds a new dimension to an approach which is otherwise fundamentally Griffithian – acceleration of tempo and strong rhythmic patterns in certain editing fragments generate the *pathos* of the close-up, to use an Eisensteinian term which seems perfectly apt in this context. The fragmentary scansion of the signifiers no longer has as its sole aim the conferring of order on denotative signs. It also serves to control the underlying production of meaning, the connotative dimension of the filmic discourse – what has often been called the 'emotion' of the scene – by means of the dynamics of the succession of the montage fragments. Moreover, the connotative production is also used by Pudovkin in a reiterative manner, in particular to suggest sound effects. One thinks of the bar scene in *The Mother*, which immediately follows the one described above. The lively atmosphere and the throb of the music are suggested by the very dynamics of the succession of details, no longer subject to causal order but rather swirling about in an impressionist description, a vertical equivalent to the horizontal transparency of Griffithian linearization.

It is a fact, however, that in many passages, especially those involving confrontations beween more than two characters – here I have in mind a scene involving the mother, the son, and the tsarist soldiers, or another in which 'The Heir to Genghis Khan' confronts the English fur traders – Pudovkin's analytical penchant, his concern to make each picture into a 'brick' as elementary as possible in a chain of signification which he can control as closely as possible, does indeed lead him *to weaken the verisimilitude of the diegetic spatial continuum*. And yet this verisimilitude was a founding historical condition of the system which subtends his whole endeavour. Wishing to carry to its extreme consequences the logic of linearization through editing, Pudovkin comes up against the same obstacle encountered by the pioneers when they were casting about for methods capable of overcoming the unfortunate 'dissociative' effect which the first interpolated close-ups had upon the unity of films that still depended almost exclusively on the layout of the primitive tableau. In both cases, this disintegration was the price that had to be paid for an increase in 'expressiveness', in other words, a greater control over the production of meaning. Striving to remain within the bounds of fundamental linearity and to strengthen that linearity, Pudovkin fails to see that the enunciation characteristic of the system is not simply a succession of signs, as decomposed as possible, but is founded on a dialetic between such 'stripped-down' images and a more complex spatiality offering complementary guarantees.

The close-up, as integrated into filmic discourse by Griffith, Barker, the Ince brothers, etc., drew an important share of its signification from the wider shots that preceded and followed it and from which it was in a sense *excerpted*. It was through this alternation of long-shot and close-up that the strongly diegetic cinema was to attain maximum effect (and in this sense a film like *Shane* is certainly an example). Intoxicated, as it were, by the possibilities revealed in the new-found mastery of orientational matching procedures (and in particular the eyeline match), Pudovkin sought to reconstitute a given profilmic space in its entirety solely through the successive presentation of its details. He attempted to render the full presence of characters, objects and indeed the diegesis itself solely through this 'near-sighted' approach. Yet in so doing he set his work at odds with a whole dimension of the system he was seeking to improve, since in many sequences of his silent films diegetic space is reduced to such an abstraction that important effects, such as the illusion of the presence of characters *to each other*, are considerably weakened.

Paradoxically, one of the finest moments in *The Mother* is that at which the method described above is abandoned completely and Pudovkin returns, for reasons of stylistic and dramatic contrast, to a space which is much closer to that of the films of Louis Lumière. The first part of the admirable scene showing the confrontation between revolutionary workers and strikebreakers in the factory yard is filmed in fixed, wide-angle shots which remind us how aptly suited is the primitive tableau to scenes of mass struggle. This demonstration will be confirmed again and again throughout the Soviet cinema's silent period and well beyond it.

It was Dreyer, in *The Passion of Joan of Arc* (1928), who went on to derive from what we might call the Pudovkin contradiction a coherent dialectic based precisely upon that diegetic dissolution, *assumed as such*, of profilmic topography. However, it was the Ukrainian master Alexander Dovzhenko, in the opening sequence of his greatest film, *Earth* (1930), who went furthest in putting that contradiction to work, designating it as such and showing how it was possible to construct, with classical spatiality, an ambiguous diegetic space, in the sense that it is essentially and disturbingly *uncertain*.

This celebrated sequence deals with an old man dying and a dialogue between him and friends and relatives standing or sitting around him. But is it so certain that they are actually around him? Some shots, especially those of the baby playing, seem to involve a relationship which has nothing to do with the ordinary contiguity; they seem more like elements of 'attraction' in the manner of Eisenstein. The characters are never seen together in the same shot; they are linked only by their eyeline exchanges. A close reading of this sequence shows a whole series of discrepancies which actually render impossible a reading of diegetic space in keeping with the traditional system of orientation: 'in the place where' the orientation of a glance from the old man had enabled us to situate this or that character, we now encounter another; in the course of another series of apparent reverse-angle shots, we encounter still another character 'in the same place', and yet, as far as we are able to judge, the hieratic stillness of the scene has been preserved throughout. At other moments a shot of a field of wheat seems to be located in an 'impossible' space with respect to the eyeline directions of those who see it. And this opening scene offers only one of various strategies employed by Dovzhenko: often an articulation between sequences will leave fundamental doubts about the precise moment when the spatial or temporal hiatus actually occurred. Along other axes, certain shots, though more closely related to an 'emblematic' space-time than to the diegetic space-time proper, nevertheless continue to entertain subsidiary links with the latter (witness the series of shots indicating the passing of the seasons, the quasi-symbolic sequence of 'the lovers' night', or the shots of a young woman standing by a sunflower). Conversely, other moments which are firmly anchored in the primary diegesis (such as Vassili's famous dance-and-death and his father's night of mourning) seem to partake in turn of the quality of those emblematic shots, tending to suspend the movement of the diegesis. It is through such ambiguities as these, such derogations from the seamlessness of the representational fabric, such attacks on the integrity of the diegesis by the introduction of fragments of a metaphoric discourse, that Dovzhenko comes closest to an important aspect of Eisenstein's great adventure. But in fact this type of construction in one way or another was a major concern of nearly all the important Soviet directors. Yet while it has often been identified with them exclusively, it should be pointed out that these techniques grew out of an objective encounter between crosscutting of the type perfected by Griffith in *Intolerance* (1916) and the metaphoric cutaway of Gance, procedures which in turn are merely extrapolations of the earliest inserts and crosscutting.

The final sequence of Eisenstein's *Strike* (1924-5), consisting of an alternation between shots of butchers at work in a slaughterhouse (shots which absolutely do not belong to the principal diegetic space-time) and images of the persecution of the striking workers by mounted Cossacks, provides the earliest example of this type of figure in narrative Soviet cinema. Here the relationship between diegetic and metaphoric space-time (which in this instance involves its own strongly diegetic effect) still derives from a linear concept which is perfectly compatible with the Griffith approach. In fact, one might cite several mainstream films of the sound era which have incorporated this technique of parallel and extended metaphor (Walter Graumann's *Lady in a Cage* comes to mind, and do not the shots of buildings and city streets in *Muriel* function in a similar way?). On the other hand, Eisenstein's developments of this strategy in *The General Line* (1926-9) and above all in *October* (1927-8) may be said to be fundamentally at odds with this linearity.

The mechanical peacock in *October*, which appears fragmentarily within the montage piece associated with the opening of the door as Kerensky enters the great room which is to shelter his precarious power, is of course a symbol of Kerensky's fatuous character. But it is so tightly meshed into the movement of the door itself that it resists any reduction to a single signifying function. A naïve reading, predicated on the inviolability of diegetic space-time, might conclude that this is an automaton set in motion by machinery which connects it with the door. This is but one (perfectly 'legitimate') aspect of a complex production of meaning irreducible to any linear model.

I cannot draw here a complete picture of Eisenstein's contribution to the far-reaching investigation of the established representational mode – an investigation undertaken in fact by all the most advanced members of the Soviet school. One would have to discuss typage, that important reconsideration of the cinematic persona, and the complex relations which it entertained with the stereotyped casting of the capitalist cinema. One would have to discuss as well the concept of the mass-as-hero and the revaluing of the long-shot associated with it, the mixtures of style and genre in *Strike, October* and *The General Line*, and of course such ambitious attempts to extend the director's range as 'tonal montage' and 'intellectual montage'.

However, it seems to me that Eisenstein presents the most stimulating challenge when, first in his films and later in his teaching, he strives to found a dialectics of orientational matching which, though he saw it as a complement to the representational system, also tends to undermine the very foundations of that system.

I have already implied that it was precisely because of the unfinished status of the representational system that Eisenstein and his fellow Soviet film-makers found themselves in a relatively privileged situation for a rethinking of film practice. At that time in Europe, eyeline and direction matching, for want of any universally accepted codification, for want of a 'continuity girl', was no more than a working hypothesis, one which seems to have enjoyed favour, it is true, but which remained only one possible option among others (witness all the mismatched eyelines in French and German films of every category as late as the mid-1920s).[9]

In this connection *Strike* contains an extremely significant sequence. The spying foreman is knocked off his feet by a clout from a huge steel wheel swinging on a crane driven by a group of mischievous revolutionary workers. In this sequence, perhaps for the first time in film history, we see illustrated the proposition that 'correct' direction matching, the logic of which corresponds to that of the right/left orientations of a real or imaginary 'establishing shot', could very well coexist with other systems, and that although the latter might contradict the logic of the former, together they could constitute a single *composite space-time* characterized by its unnaturalness (i.e., its rejection of left/right body logic). For indeed, in the successive shots showing the foreman being knocked over, the swinging wheel changes screen direction at each shot change, and yet all the diegetic evidence (and our own common sense) tells us that in reality the direction of the wheel remains constant.

Of course the object of the intention here, and, at one level, the effect produced, is an exteriorization, through this 'violation' of representation, of the latent class violence behind this relatively harmless incident. In his account of Eisenstein's teachings, Vladimir Nizhny tells how the master theorized his doctrine of the 'montage unit', which advocates dividing up a given sequence into sub-sequences defined by successive crossings of the 180° line. These 'bad' position/direction matches are of course meant to emphasize privileged moments of tension in the narrative flow. Indeed, whenever Eisenstein provoked a rationale for his innovations – invariably after the fact – he invoked criteria derived from the ideology of representation. And the dramaturgy at work in the sequences that are most representative of his dialectics of matching provides confirmation of this 'expressionist' outlook and of the correlation between such experiments as these and Eisenstein's quest for the effect which he called 'pathos'. However, it seems to me no less true that there is a precious parallel statement in this strategy, for it also involves a jeopardizing of the system's greatest 'secret': the fact that a film is made up of fragments of montage, that it is not by nature but by artifice that the classical *découpage* produces an effect of continuity.

We find one particularly vivid illustration of this in the Odessa steps sequence in *Potemkin* (1925). Here the extreme discontinuity produced by the editing goes far beyond mere impressionistic subjectivism, and the principle of montage units intervenes spectacularly to organize the climax of the episode. In this instance the expressive intention is accompanied by a programmatic statement of no small importance: that a secondary organization of the signifiers, endowed with relative autonomy, can give filmic discourse an entirely new dimension, irreducible to linear expressiveness. The sequence is constructed around two broad montage units, of which the sound intervenes only when the nurse first appears with her baby carriage and is then associated with the carriage as it rolls alone down the steps. However, the images of this dramatic trajectory are intercut with shots of the continuing massacre, and these are filmed from angles which belong to the first montage unit. Finally, the carriage seems, toward the end of its run, to 'fall back' into the first unit (in other words, into the initial right/left relationship), and after this 'dissonant' period consisting of cuts back and forth between the two units, the sequence ends entirely in the first. It is through such constructions as these – one might also cite the second section of *Potemkin*, 'Drama on the Quarterdeck', the cream-separator sequence in *The General Line*, or the raising of the bridge in *October* – that Eisenstein became the first to succeed in relativizing certain fundamental norms of the institutional mode of representation. This mode would, of course, reintegrate them into a subsystem which was derived from it, but which at the same time contained the premises of a more fundamental contestation. One may, I believe, sum up both the progressive and the contradictory nature of this work with the following well-known observation taken from *Notes of a Film Director*:

> The strength of montage lies in the fact that the emotions and minds of the spectators are included in the creative process. The spectator not only sees those elements of the work which are capable of being seen but also experiences the dynamic process of the emergence and formation of the image just as it was experienced by the author. This probably is the highest possible degree of approximation to visually conveying the author's sensations and conception in the greatest possible completeness, to conveying them with 'that almost physical tangibility' with which they arose before the author during the creative process, at the moments of his creative vision.[10]

Under close scrutiny, this text may be seen to reveal with great precision Eisenstein's complex attitude. On the one hand, he rejects everything in the representational system which causes the spectator to see only 'those elements capable of being seen', in other words, he rejects transparency. This is the credo that underlies his 'dialecticization' of the matching system and all the other 'illusionist' strategies; his goal is to make the work of the signifier visible. Yet at the same time this work is reintegrated into a spectacle of the classical type, one which is certainly on a 'higher plane' than the other, but one which nevertheless must in the last analysis submit to the same linear, we might even say totalitarian, model: what the spectator is supposed to grasp at the end of the process, whatever work he may have been called upon to perform, is assumed to be what the author put into it. We find ourselves face to face with the old illusion that holds the work of art to be a mediator, a means of communication between two sensibilities. This will perhaps also help us to understand why Eisenstein never sought (not even in *Strike*, despite all claims to the contrary) to oppose the system by then established with any notion of a *tabula rasa*. In spite of their differences, in spite of their disputes, he shared with Pudovkin and Kuleshov the deep conviction that the 'language' with which the name of Griffith was then so closely associated was tantamount to a basic language whose fundamental components were intangible. Even a film-maker who proclaimed his attachment to dialectical and historical materialism and who felt his task was to enrich that system through critical reappraisal was bound to remain within the conceptual framework which it defined. This is the nerve centre of his polemic with Vertov. Needless to say, it would in my estimation be foolish to reproach him for this.

Among the Soviet masters, Dziga Vertov alone advocated uncompromising *tabula rasa*. In the USSR of the 1920s, such a position also involved contradictions which are far from negligible. The fact remains, however, that Vertov was the first film-maker and theoretician to produce – in ways that were at times crude, at others deceptively polemical – a critical definition of the nature of cinematic representation, and to undertake, in his masterwork *The Man with a Movie Camera*, a practical critique of it.

Reading certain Vertov texts overly literally, commentators have often made of him the irrepressible champion of documentary against the fiction film. However, what this reading of his career fails to reveal is that the reason Vertov seemed to be combating fiction *per se* was that he perceived in the fiction film of that era the hegemony of a deeply alienating system of representation. This was in part because of the ideological substance which in capitalist countries it almost invariably purveyed – explicitly or implicitly – and in part because of the passive attitude that it required of the spectator. And if he attacked Eisenstein, seeming to confuse him with the masters of Hollywood, it was because he felt that in the revolutionary context a *tabula rasa* strategy was indispensible to clean the eyes of the masses, as he might have put it. Reading his texts, seeing his films, it is hard to believe that he did not realize that *The Man with a Movie Camera* (or *Kino-Glaz*, for that matter) was as much, or as little, a fiction as *Potemkin* or *The Mother*.

We know that Vertov's project did not merely concern the perception and reading of images. Vertov had a deep political commitment, and he even had the presentiment that exercises in the decoding of images could provide training for the decoding of reality. This project still holds promise today, and we have had, in the films of socialist Cuba, a glimmer of its fulfilment. In the Soviet Union of the 1920s, however, such an amalgamation could easily lead to serious political illusions. It is also true that in Vertov's case, it produced masterpieces. Through recent literature we are beginning to have a better appreciation of the true breadth of *The Man with a Movie Camera*, long regarded as a simple display of cinematic fireworks.[11] This classical response, so common among viewers even today, is indicative of the almost total illegibility of this film for several decades, and is both a symptom of the veritable crisis which the film causes within filmic representation as a whole – and an occlusion of all the light which, at a second level, it sheds upon it. I can only sketch the broad outlines of the work accomplished in this immense film, and I must start with the observation that its chief target is the fundamental linearity of filmic representation, a linearity contested in all its aspects, and no longer simply in that of syntax, as was chiefly the case with Eisenstein.

The Man with a Movie Camera is not made to be viewed only once. It is impossible for anyone to assimilate its work in a single viewing. Far more than any film by Eisenstein, it demands that the spectator take an active role as *decipherer* of its images. To refuse that role is to leave the theatre or escape into reverie. For the relationships proposed between these images are seldom self-evident; often the logic of successive significations moves backwards, denying our usual sense of chronology, and even more often it will take us along an axis which is no longer syntagmatic, but paradigmatic of the film's very production (frozen frames, photograms, editing scenes, shooting scenes, screening of the film before an audience). Here again, however, the trajectory followed is not determined by any simple chronology of production but is the result of the multiple interaction of other structures – the cycle of the working day, the cycle of life and death, a reflection on the new society, on the changing situations of women within it, on the vestiges of bourgeois life, on poverty under socialism, and so on. Further associated with all this is a reflection on filmic representation itself, on the constitution of haptic space, the illusion of movement, and so on. One may safely say that there is not a single shot in this entire film whose place in the editing scheme is not overdetermined by a whole set of intertwined chains of signification, and that it is impossible to decipher fully the film's discourse until one has a completely topological grasp of the film as a whole, in other words, after several viewings.[12] Resolutely reflexive, this film was the most radical gesture that the silent cinema had known – in the Soviet Union or elsewhere.

Vertov was, however, a communist; as long as he was permitted to do so, he strove to involve his work in the concrete construction of socialism. At the same time, his analyses – written and filmic – were some thirty or forty years ahead of their time. Not until the 1950s did the young Stan Brakhage produce a critique as penetrating, albeit written from the opposite ideological position; not until the mid-1960s did European Marxist critics reintegrate Vertov into Left aesthetics. Small wonder, then, that Vertov should have fallen prey to the pedagogical illusion, that he should have imagined that films which have probably only become legible in the past ten years or so (and even then only through much hard work) could spontaneously 'educate the senses' of the illiterate peasant masses or, for that matter, of the urban masses, whose expectations, however highly developed their political consciousness, had long since been programmed by their experience of the dominant film practice.

Nothing will ever erase or justify the persecutions to which this great master was subjected during the latter part of his life, when he was given practically no opportunity to work. Nevertheless, we must make no mistake about it: even if the work of Vertov still contains an immense theoretical potential, even if it helps us to understand the system which still governs 99% of the world's film and television production, and even if it helps us to reflect on the possibilities of eventually developing – within a political and social context comparable, *at the very least*, to Vertov's methods of audio-visual education and propaganda which might depart significantly from the basic norms of cinematic representation, he invented no magic recipes. In particular, it is clearly a delusion to imagine that reflexiveness has automatic pedagogical value. The key to educating the senses of the masses, an education that would enable them to read the filmic system – to read themselves inside it rather than simply being written into it again and again – lies in changes a good deal more far-reaching. Even at the strictly audio-visual level, the education of the senses must pass through the schools of Kuleshov and Eisenstein before that of Vertov, must move, in other words, in an ascending order of contradiction.

Notes

1. More recent research has shown that other contradictions, economic and psychological, played a major role in this process of overdetermination.
2. This film is a fine example of the populist tradition in the early British cinema. Peace is treated as a kind of folk hero.
3. I should exclude the very precocious Danish cinema from this statement, however.
4. In this film a magician-scientist pumps his head up to huge proportions with a bellows. As is shown in Franju's film *Le Grand Méliès*, the effect was obtained by pulling Méliès up an inclined plane on an invisible trolley towards the camera. For Méliès, close-ups were always 'giant faces': the screen, he felt, was the only plane a film could contain.
5. It should be noted that as often as not a contemporary presentation of this or any other film would have been accompanied by a 'lecture', the task of which was to centre these a-centric images. Independently of the *alienating* nature of this typically primitive splitting of the narrative signifier, it is my contention that an audience may well have been sufficiently 'on its toes', even without the help of a lecturer, to conduct spontaneously a slightly more topological reading than we are normally capable of today.
6. Also called 'shot-reverse-shot' or 'shot-countershot' in tribute to the French '*champ-contre-champ*'.
7. See Vladimir Nizhny, *Lessons with Eisenstein*, trans. and ed. Jay Leyda and Ivor Montagu (New York, Hill and Wang, 1962).
8. Raymond Williams and Michael Orrom, *Preface to Film* (London, Film Drama, 1954).
9. In Lang's *Metropolis*, L'Herbier's *L'Argent* and Raymond Bernard's *Le Miracle des loups*. We are clearly not talking about the mistakes of amateurs.
10. S. M. Eisenstein, *Notes of a Film Director* (New York, Dover Press, 1970) pp. 77-8.
11. See for example Annette Michelson, '"The Man with the Movie Camera": From Magician to Epistemologist', *Artforum*, vol. 10, no. 7, March 1972, pp. 60-72.
12. In my work, the concept of the univocality of the institutional mode of representation refers of course to a relationship between the films and the spectators – most spectators – who have been written into the institution by society. The others – a few scholars, critics and film-makers – will often perceive the very real polysemic dimension of just about any film text. However, not only is this reading conducted from outside the institution (whose vocation, as Christian Metz reminds us, is 'to fill theatres, not to empty them'), it is also ultimately irrelevant to our understanding of the institution as a single text.

1987

This essay was first given as a lecture, in French, at the annual congress of the FIAF Fédération Internationale des Archives du Film held at Varna, Bulgaria, in the Spring of 1977. The present English translation, which is my own, first appeared, in *October*, 12-13, October 1979.

Like the two pieces that follow, this essay was a spin-off of work then in progress on a new book, *La Lucarne de l'infini* (published in an English Translation as *Life to Those Shadows* (1990)), devoted largely to an exploration of the primitive cinema, with an eye to evolving a theory of the genesis of institutional film 'language'. That lecture was my first serious attempt to distance myself, on the terrain of film history as such, from a thitherto exclusive commitment to the values of a certain modernism, to what a perceptive member of the Cinéthique group had termed, in 1969, my *'structuralisme fantasmatique'*. Nonetheless, it was probably with some justification that a Yugoslav admirer at Varna was able to jump up and claim that this lecture had demonstrated once and for all that Dziga Vertov was the only truly revolutionary Soviet director of the 1920s, that all the others had been 'bourgeois'. And although I hastened to agree with a young Soviet semiologist who remarked that I 'had not said anything of the sort', re-reading the piece today makes it clear that the formalists were still viewed as *Good Object*, and that the salute to Kuleshov remained very perfunctory. For another take on the Kuleshov school, see Chapter 11.

7 Porter, or Ambivalence

The work of Edwin S. Porter – in so far as it is known to me, at least[1] – is a locus of contradictions which informed the development of the cinema in its beginnings. Among professional historians, circumscribed as they are, no matter what their orientation in other respects, by the linear view which has hitherto proved such a serious hindrance to any attempt to evolve a materialist theory of the history of the cinema, Porter's films have aroused entirely contradictory attitudes. Three may be distinguished, each corresponding to one of the main ideological positions which turn by turn have hindered any systematic examination of this period.

First there is the prevailing thesis concerning these beginnings, according to which a language gradually emerged out of a sort of primordial chaos generally described as 'theatrical': *the* language, the cinema's *natural language*, innate in the camera from the outset, and only brought into the light of day as the result of determined efforts by certain 'pioneers of genius'. From which it follows that the prescribed approach for anyone wishing to study this period is the enumeration of 'firsts': 'the first close-up', 'the first match cut', 'the first parallel montage', and so on *ad nauseum*. And although the deliberate falsification of documents in support of some film-maker or other's claims to priority is not entirely proven, what is certain is that the proper thoroughness has not been displayed in the examination of certain documents, as I mention below. It was under the criterion of this pursuit of 'firsts' that many historians felt, like Lewis Jacobs,[2] that they could establish Porter as the 'inventor of cinematic language'. No such assertion, of course, in no matter what area, is admissible today.

Without departing from this linear and teleological view, other historians who stress the 'popular charms' of the primitive cinema, and who feel no obligation to argue precedence for Porter, fall into the opposite extreme: they see in Porter only a common plagiarist (I shall return to the ideological ramifications of this interesting accusation), largely outstripped as an 'artist' by the French film-makers and as a 'pioneer' by the English. This is the attitude of Deslandes and Richard, but also, to a certain extend of their *bête noire*, Georges Sadoul.[3]

Lastly, another attitude seems to have been emerging over the past few years, linked more or less to the notion that the primitive cinema was a sort of Paradise Lost, 'regained' today thanks to the various avant-garde movements. As early as 1962 Professor Gessner[4] felt he could trace the seeds for *L'Année dernière à Marienbad* in the unusual montage of *The Life of an American Fireman*, while other writers like to contrast the 'avant-gardism' of Méliès with the 'conformism' of Porter, Griffith et al.

To understand why the adherents of a linear history – and as one sees, their ideological horizons can be very different – seem unable to *read* Porter's films, a brief examination of the forces working on the cinema at this period is necessary. Also relevant would be an analysis, not of the spontaneous emergence of some 'natural' language, but the establishment of a mode of representation, historically and culturally determined, and of the conditions which enabled it to continue exercising an almost absolute hegemony over Western film production down to the present day. Such an analysis lies outside the scope of the present article, but my examination of some of Porter's films, which expose the first stages of the process, will provide some clues towards its explanation. First, however, a consideration of the contradictory forces that were working on the emergent cinema even before 1895 is necessary before I go on to describe how these forces were to exercise contradictory influences on these films of Porters.

As the investigations I am conducting stand at present, I distinguish three forces or historical and cultural trends which moulded the cinema during its first two decades.[5] Chief among these, obviously, was the aggregate of folk art kept alive by the urban working classes in Europe and the United States at the turn of the century. These comprise both modes of representation and narrative or gestural material deriving from melodrama, vaudeville, pantomime (in England), conjuring, music hall and circus; from caricatures, the 'penny plain, tuppence coloured' sheets and strip cartoons; from magic lantern shows in the home,[6] the street and the theatre; and from street entertainers, fairground acts[7] and waxwork shows. The corollary to these circumstances was that in its early days the cinema addressed itself exclusively to the urban 'lower classes', and that its practitioners were for the most part still 'of humble origin'. It is therefore not surprising that for at least ten years the more affluent turned up their noses at the cinema, and that the middle classes contented themselves with sending their children (naturally) and the latter's nurses or, sometimes (it came to the same thing), their mothers and grandmothers to these dubious places where all one saw were pictures reflecting, 'in form and content', *the infantilism of the working classes.*

The cinema, however, was developing within a society governed by certain specific production relationships. It would have been unthinkable that it might be 'immunized', that it might escape the underlying pressures[8] exercised by the specifically bourgeois modes of representation – this being my second 'force' – from literature, painting, and especially the theatre, which were then in their heyday. Moreover, although a film might very occasionally mirror the aspirations and struggles of the popular masses, the substance of the great majority of films at this period reflects, directly or indirectly, the viewpoint imposed by the ruling classes. But this had been true of the English melodrama, for instance, since its birth: only one or two 'factory melodramas' at the beginning of the nineteenth century took up positions of class struggle (and, as with the primitive cinema, this was usually a matter of opportunism on the part of the lower-middle-class playwrights addressing themselves to a working-class audience). Nevertheless, the melodrama undoubtedly constituted a theatrical form quite distinct form those of the bourgeois theatre. So for the first ten years of the cinema's existence, linearity, haptic scene space and the individualization of characters are features to be found only incidentally here and there. They figure largely as elements dominated, in particular, by others of popular origin. But between 1908 and 1915 this relationship was to undergo a gradual reversal, principally because of the economic development of the cinema and the resulting need to attract an audience with more money and leisure at its disposal.

A third force, which I shall call 'scientistic', also presided over this first period of development; and for a while its role, *in conjunction with the modes of popular representation*, was wholly determinative.

This 'scientism' certainly figured as an element of dominant ideology, but it was also linked to genuinely scientific practices; and it was in this respect that it was to influence the early cinema in a way directly opposed to the impetus given by those arts on which the bourgeois era had already left its immutable mark. On a strictly technological level, the first moving pictures came most directly out of experiments by Muybridge, Marey and other researchers whose goal was almost certainly not the restitution or representation of movement, but simply its *analysis*. The physiologist Marey considered himself satisfied when, by means of the varied ingenious instruments and apparatuses he had constructed for the purpose, he had succeeded in *breaking down* human and animal movement into successive photographic images. Yet only a small further step remained, still from a strictly technological point of view, for engineers like Auguste and Louis Lumière, or Edison and Dickson, to complete these experiments by synthesising the movement that had been thus decomposed.

Already adumbrated between these two first steps towards the entertainment cinema, however – by the Lumières and by the Edison team – are the terms of the contradiction which was to govern this whole first period. Edison, for whom the recording and reproduction of moving images was merely – and this is significant – an extension of his earlier (and very profitable) invention of the phonograph, had set as the goal of his first experiments in this new area the recording and mass distribution of *opera* (an echo of the ideology of the *Gesamtkunstwerk*). And one of the 'cinema' devices which emerged from his laboratories, the Kinetophonograph – whose lone spectator, in the sensory isolation of its twin eye-pieces and headphones, received more or less synchronous images and sounds – provided a striking configuration of the conditions of cushioned darkness to be met with in the picture palaces of the 1930s. At the opposite extreme of the production line, it was Edison's collaborators who also constructed a studio foreshadowing the first real moving picture close-up: *Fred Ott's Sneeze* (1895). It seems to me indicative of the profound nature of the forces which were thus already at work on the emergent cinema that the stipulation from the journalist who initiated this film was that the close-up should show *a pretty girl sneezing*. It was purely for reasons of expediency, it appears, that Dickson happened to use his assistant, Fred Ott, thus frustrating his 'client' of the orgasmic image of his desires. But Raff and Gammon, sub-contractors of the Edison/Dickson processes, were soon to make the erotic vocation of the close-up[9] explicit in another way with their premonitory film *The Kiss* (1896), a brief tableau borrowed from a successful Broadway play (in other words, from the bourgeois theatre). Edison himself, it seems, lost all interest in the cinema when he realized that his dream of 'reproducing life' was impracticable in the short term (as president of a vast trust he would, of course, soon display a keenly renewed interest). Nonetheless, through his vision of the cinema and in the drift of the early experiments made under his direction, his name stands for the presence, during the cinema's beginnings, of forces stemming directly from the bourgeois ideology of representation; forces which were, before too long, to exercise an overwhelming influence on the future of the film industry.

But the 'invention of the cinema' did not take place solely in Orange, New Jersey.

Georges Sadoul is correct in stressing that the first programme at the Grand Café offered *themes whose class content was perfectly evident* to a clientele recruited on the *Grands Boulevards* of Paris: they saw that distinguished representatives of the solid citizenry of Lyons were showing off *their* wives, *their* children, *their* pastimes – in short, *their* property. Yet these films also possess another dimension. Although the class content of a film like *La Sortie des Usines Lumière* is identical to the rest at an iconographic level – the Lumières show *their* workers just as they show *their* private harbour at La Ciotat – it presents (along with *L'Entrée d'un Train en Gare, Recréation à la Marinière, Lancement d'un Navire à la Ciotat*, and innumerable other films from the first Lumière catalogue) a *representational approach* diametrically opposed to the one in *The Kiss*, or for that matter in *Le Déjeuner de Bébé*. And this approach, which consisted in setting up a camera outside the factory gates and cranking the handle as soon as they opened in order to record an event which was certainly predictable in general outline but totally unrehearsed in detail, is akin to the 'scientificness' of Muybridge photographing a galloping horse, or Marey birds in flight.[10] These 'documentary' images, on the one hand, and the 'narrative tableau' of *L'Arroseur arrosé*,[11] on the other, were to give birth to a sort of *panoramic view* – an acentric, 'non-directive' image leaving the eye more or less 'free' to roam over the entire frame, and to organize the signifiers as it will (as best it can); an image, moreover, in which the presence of the characters never predominates over their environment,[12] but is invariably inscribed within it.[13] And it was *this view*, to be seen in both the films of Méliès and Edwin S. Porter's work for the Edison company, which was to dominate cinema the world over for more than ten years.

Of the four vitally important Porter films of 1903 that are known to me, *Uncle Tom's Cabin* is the most purely primitive; that is to say, it epitomizes and strikingly illuminates some of the principal features of the cinema of the period. It also shows that the primitive mode of representation was not simply an 'obstacle'; despite the opprobrium habitually levelled against the primitive 'theatricality' in terms of which this film is entirely conceived – and which I shall attempt to reconsider – it is a remarkable piece of work. Made following the popular success of a stage version of Harriet Beecher Stowe's celebrated novel, *Uncle Tom's Cabin* is an admirable example of the relationship which apparently existed between the primitive cinema and its audience. In the context of the system prevalent today (and this has been true for more than sixty years now), a screen adaptation of even a very well-known work must 'make as though' that work had no previous existence outside the film. The 'digest' that is made of it must hold water on its own: a typical Hollywood adaptation, even of the Bible, will identify and establish all its characters and situations *as though introducing them for the first time*, in accordance with the canons of the enclosed, autarchic world of the bourgeois novel, where the story (and history, for that matter) exists only in so far as it is invented by the text. A film like *Uncle Tom's Cabin*, which 'tells' a novel several hundred pages long in some twenty tableaux and in ten minutes, was predicated upon the knowledge of the audience, who were left to fill in enormous narrative gaps for themselves (possibly with the aid on occasion of a lecturer – whose role, however, was to jog the audience's memory rather than to take its place). Each tableau is preceded by a title, such as 'Eliza asks Tom to Go Away with Her'. Apart from their obvious reliance on the spectator's prevous knowledge of the novel (the title just quoted is the first in the film), these succinct titles always refer to the climax of the tableau, often still some time away. For example, 'Eva and Tom in the Garden' introduces a tableau which begins with a long dance number performed by black servants before Eva and Tom make their entry. There is therefore *no direct causal link between title and image* of the kind which was, of course, to become the rule after 1915 (and which would find its equivalent in the word/image relationship after 1929). Each tableau is thus programmed in advance, each *coup de théâtre* is 'given away' in advance, which obviates all effect of suspense and induces, with the complicity of the audience, an expectation quite different from the kind of expectation involved in the bourgeois theatre and novel, for instance. Actually, the notion of suspense is entirely irrelevant here, since the audience, knowing the story already, ultimately did not come to discover its twists and turns, but to look at the pictures, to enjoy the concatenation of a series of spectacularly presented archetypes – to browse through an album of sumptuous photographs illustrating a text which was to be found elsewhere: it came to participate in a ritual of confirmation.[14] One thinks of the medieval Japanese courtesans contemplating the scrolls which illustrated familiar stories handed down over the centuries. And this is only one of the ways in which the primitive cinema more closely resembles the arts of the Orient than those of the bourgeois West.[15]

Uncle Tom's Cabin, according to the historians of linearity, is a 'retrograde' film. And the montage model it presents is indeed the first and the most elementary produced by the cinema (around 1896): a succession of tableaux without continuity links, either spatial or temporal, undoubtedly 'modelled' on the theatre, but – and the qualification is important – the *popular* theatre: we are a long way from the 'three unities' which the bourgeois theatre borrowed from the classical breviary. And one has to be completely blinded by the ideology of 'progress' in the cinema not to realize that within the framework fixed by this mode, no matter how elementary, remarkable films were produced: Haggar's *Life of Charles Peace* (1904), for instance, or Billy Bitzer's *Kentucky Feud* (1905), not to mention films which have, admittedly, been more universally recognized, like Zecca's *L'Histoire d'un Crime* (1901) or Méliès' *Le Voyage dans la Lune* (1902). These films, deriving from popular entertainments and bearing no real relationship to the theatre of Shaw, Feydeau, Antoine or Belasco, constitute a cinematic 'specificity' whose *legitimacy* we should, after Warhol and Godard, be in a position to recognize. We can, in other words, no longer impugn the plebian origins of the cinema, taxed with 'theatricality', as a sort of original sin expiated by the 'great Griffith'. In fact Griffith and his more innovatory contemporaries were to endow the cinema with the essential characteristics of another theatricality – that of 'the grown-ups', of the bourgeois theatre – through a number of contributions which were undoubtedly constituent of a second 'specificity'. The failure of the attempts to make a pure and simple transposition of the bourgeois theatre to the screen (*Films d'Art*), a failure due precisely to the basic incompatibility between the primitive mode of representation and the codes of the bourgeois theatre, had shown that only the establishment of a thoroughly haptic screen space, the linearization of the visual signifiers (through montage, 'centering' and lighting), the constitution of an *enveloping* diegetic space-time, and so on, could in fact 'render' what was essential to this theatre (as well as the novels and paintings) prized by the middle classes, the *lack* of which was being increasingly sharply felt by film-makers, producers and the more perspicacious critics, notably in America.

But no history of the cinema claiming to be informed by historical and dialectical materialism can any longer give absolute precedence to this second 'specificity' – the institutional mode of representation – over the first, from either a heuristic or even an aesthetic point of view.

The first manifestations of a narrativity through montage (the juxtaposition of several shots temporally and spatially disjoined, and linked principally by a knowledge of the story to which they refer: a system of which *Uncle Tom's Cabin* is a belated and fully achieved example) were the innumerable versions of The Passion which flourished in both Europe and America after 1896. Without the aid of a single intertitle,[16] sometimes presumably without even a narrator, these sequences of visually autonomous tableaux nevertheless formed an easily recognizable narrative progression, where everyone knew what had gone before and what was coming next, and where everyone spontaneously furnished all the necessary mental 'articulations'.

Next came a more elaborate form, which held sway for a good ten years: *the chase film*, thought to have been conceived in England around 1900. The trend of this evolution is obvious: at each stage, the concern was to weave closer and closer *and more and more significant* links between the successive tableaux. To start with, lacking the more sophisticated liaisons which were not long in appearing (match-cutting systems, alternate montage, and so on), film-makers contented themselves with launching a narrative course, clearly constructed from one tableau to the next, which would forge a chain of spatio-temporal sequentiality *no matter what*. No matter that the screen direction (and/or entries and exits from the frame) comprised 'bad matches' (according to criteria formulated much later, of course); the simple situation of the chase, bi-univocally concatenated from one shot to the next by its very nature, sufficed to make the narrative movement *legible*. This was the first decisive step towards closure, towards the linearity of the institutional mode.

With *The Life of an American Cowboy* – also 1903 – it becomes evident why Porter is the 'Janus' of this period. With this film he had – to talk like a traditional historian – one foot effectively 'in the past' and one 'in the future'. Admittedly phrases like this do relate to a very real trend in history; but for my part I shall simply say that this film has some of the characteristics of two modes of representation, one of which was to succeed the other, but cannot be said to embody the future all on its own.[17] And it is precisely the coexistence of these two modes within the same 'text' – and above all the manner of this coexistence – that makes Porter's films so arresting and, from a heuristic point of view, so important. *The Life of an American Cowboy* opens with a series of tableaux showing 'scenes from daily life' in a settlement in the Far West (and one cannot stress too highly the fact that at this time the term still referred to a living reality; hence, perhaps, in part, the extremely realistic effect of some of the tableaux in this film – and in *Kentucky Feud*). Nothing seems to bind these tableaux together, unless (possibly) the continuing presence of the same characters. These characters, however, are still so dwarfed within the frame, and their dress is so similar,[18] that to distinguish one from another is difficult, to say the least. One would be hard put to it, for instance, to assert that the characters seen in the saloon (where a somewhat intemperate cowboy rides in on horseback, and where a citizen is persuaded to 'dance' by six-gun bullets) are the same as the ones subsequently seen in front of the hotel (the arrival of a stagecoach full of tourists, an exhibition of lassooing). This latter shot, which is exemplary in its 'primitivism', with a small crowd moving about and several actions going on at once, lasts for several minutes. Then, about two-thirds of the way through the film, there is a radical change in narrative method: bandits attack the stagecoach, and in a series of shots which instantly arouse a sense of recognition in the spectator today,[19] a 'thrilling chase' begins, still in long shot of course, but with the connection between the shots (both temporal and spatial) very clearly defined as being one of *proximity* (if not of actual contiguity). Here we are at the opposite extreme from the loose autarchy of the earlier tableaux which 'led' nowhere, and whose busy, acentric composition has been replaced by a determined effort towards simplification and 'centering' which greatly facilitates the establishment, link by link, of the chain of signification.

The Great Train Robbery, Porter's most celebrated film, made at the end of this crucial year, 1903, after *The Life of an American Cowboy*, extends this concatenatory structure to the whole film (with the exception, as we shall see, of one shot). Each tableau therefore now brings its 'brick' to the narrative edifice (Pudovkin's terms are already apt here), and we pass from one décor to the next with inexorable logic. The shots showing the robbery itself arouse a very strong impression of continuity and proximity, and certain articulations even come remarkably close to an effect of contiguity (which was undoubtedly anticipatory for the period). The final pursuit, notably with its crossing of a river followed by a relatively mobile camera, is a model of the genre already explored in England. Yet almost all the shots show the action from 'far away', so that it still remains just as difficult to distinguish between the characters. There is even one moment at which the modern viewer, attuned to certain codes which developed in symbiosis with the institutional mode, invariably assumes the horsemen riding towards the camera to be the lawmen, whereas they are in fact the outlaws, as one realizes only when the pursuing lawmen appear in frame from behind them.

Given the course that Porter had taken, this remote

impersonality, with its lack of *presence* and individualization, could not but be felt as a deficiency – just as it was by the bourgeois 'non-audience' which turned up its nose at Porter's films along with the rest.[20] No doubt that was why he added (and this may have been a 'first') a close shot of a man (the Edison catalogue states that it is 'Barnes, leader of the outlaw band') aiming his gun at the camera 'and firing point-blank at each individual in the audience'. But the most remarkable thing is that this shot was originally delivered to the American nickelodeons and the fairground cinemas of Europe in the form of a separate reel; *it was up to the exhibitors to decide whether to stick it on at the beginning or the end of the film.*

This shot is rich in its implications. In the first place, in addition to being what was no doubt an excellent publicity gag aimed not at the audience but at the exhibitors (at a time when they were beginning to clamour for novelty), the gesture of allowing exhibitors to choose where to place the shot suggests that the production executives, even though they may have realized what it introduced into the Lilliputian world of the remaining tableaux in terms of an *individualized presence*, had absolutely no idea what to do with it. Not only did they feel it impossible (they were in fact not yet in possession of the necessary syntactical means) to introduce this shot during the course of the film – would it not break up just this effect of continuity which had been so hardly won? – but they were very probably unable to settle the problem of whether it should go at the beginning or the end. Placed at the beginning, of course, the 'frightening' effect of this unaccustomed image might soften the spectators up emotionally; but would they not then be disappointed by the subsequent return to and maintenance of separation from the spectator and the codes of acting that entailed?Placed at the end of the film, the shot might have a surprise effect (by contrast with the preceding ones) and leave the spectator with a pleasant memory; but in that case, would the shot 'colour' the whole film as one might hope?[21] Because, of course, this strategy, however prophetic it may seem to have been, also remains a 'step backwards' as our advocates of linear interpretations would say, because it in fact undermines the narrative closure which was beginning to establish itself at this time. The shot is not an element in the film; it simply purports to establish a new kind of link between the spectator and the screen (and the metaphor of an outlaw firing

The Great Train Robbery (Porter, 1903)

The Life of an American Fireman (Porter, 1902)

straight at the camera indicates clearly enough the sort of relationship – fascinated aspiration and forcible rape – it was to be). But it does so from 'outside' the diegesis: this outlaw is in fact the lecturer in a new form. What we have here is therefore a device that is essentially primitive in character, both in its quality of 'openness' and in its quality of paradoxical 'distancing' (at one level the gesture annihilates the distance, and at another, re-establishes it). Interestingly enough, this device of the 'emblematic' close shot soon became common practice and remained so for several years. Lubin's *Bold Bank Robbery* (1907) begins and ends with a group portrait (in close shot) of the three main characters,[22] and it was not uncommon for a film to end with a close shot of the pretty heroine, whose charms had hitherto been revealed only in ensemble shots, smiling at the camera. One can imagine the reactions of a predominantly male audience to this sudden 'intimacy'.

By pointing to the existence of an earlier film, called *Fire!* (1901), by the important English pioneer Williamson, some historians have sought to diminish the interest of *The Life of an American Fireman*, which is both the most impressive and most problematic of the films made in this key year in Porter's career. It is in fact true that these two films are very much alike, in both subject-matter and narrative profile. But quite apart from the fact that Porter's film comprises very specific experiments which make it of exceptional interest to the historian, such attempts to project into the world of primitive cinema our conceptions of originality and plagiarism (deriving from bourgeois notions of private property) – in actual fact our repression of intertextuality – are merely another manifestation of the determination to linearize a phenomenon which is basically resistant. To take this attitude is to ignore the fact (while acknowledging it as an 'exotic' item) that for several years cinematographic pictures simply did not belong to anyone, either by law or by right (just as still photographs, for several decades, belonged to no one),[23] and that there was a free circulation of ideas and images such as we can only guess at today. The notion of plagiarism is all the more irrelevant here in that most films borrowed both form and subject from elsewhere anyway – from the popular arts which composed the last real 'public domain' – and that far from degrading 'original ideas', the films which 'copied' others frequently improved on them. (Sigmund Lubin's reputation for being a mere plagiariest does not always seem to me to stand up to a viewing of the films themselves, which are often very much above average in quality.)

At all events, among the major contradictions of this period, as illustrated by Porter's films, the one that implies the deepest disruption is undoubtedly that which is illustrated in *The Life of an American Fireman*. The film opens with a montage often comprising ellipses so startling that one wonders how audiences could follow the story without a lecturer's help (in his office, the chief fireman dreams of a woman and child in danger – they are seen in vignette; in close-up, a hand breaks the glass and activates a fire alarm; in their dormitory, the firemen get out of bed and rush to the pole that leads to the engine-house, the fire engines start up; the doors open, and the engines leave). Next, a series of shots corresponding directly to the 'cops and robbers' or Western chase: the engines hurry to the scene of the fire. Finally a long shot shows the burning house and the engines arriving. We pass inside the house (a rudimentary studio set): the woman makes an agitated appeal in front of the window, then collapses onto the bed. A ladder appears, then a fireman. He carries the woman to safety in his arms, returns, carries off the child, returns, and puts out the fire (the whole comprising lengthy intervals during which the frame remains empty between the successive disappearances and reappearances by the characters). The next shot shows the façade of the burning house. The woman appears at the window, makes an agitated appeal and disappears. The firemen set up a ladder – and we see, obviously occupying the same length of time, the same action that we previously witnessed from inside the house.

Seeing this curious document in the form in which I have described it – that is to say, as it was deposited at the Library of Congress in 1903 – any historian worthy of the name ought to find the process of its 'dialetical' gestation obvious enough: sensing the as yet still distant possibility of absolute ubiquity in the camera – the possibility, that is to say, that the spectator might accept a series of shots as being different points of view of a single continuous action, rather than simply variants of 'what he might see from his seat' (here I am simplifying problems that are more complex) – Porter in fact films one action twice, from two different 'points of view' (actually the two were several miles apart, which also implies an extra-ordinary intuition of the possibilities offered by montage in the area of fictitious connections, theorized by Kuleshov some twenty years later). But at the same time Porter felt, probably with reason, that the audience was not yet ready to accept this sort of transportation in space-time, and he (or someone else, it doesn't really matter) decided to show the two actions successively – which obviously has the effect of undermining the already remarkably controlled sequential linearization of the preceding scenes. So once again one of Porter's 'steps forward' in fact ends by accentuating some features of the primitive cinema even more strongly than before: its non-homogeneity in *The Life of an American Cowboy*, its non-occlusion in *The Great Train Robbery*, and here its non-linearity.

But the historiography of this film provides another lesson. Around 1940, it seems, on the strength of an entry in an Edison catalogue which appeared to suggest that this double sequence had been put together *in 1903* in accordance with the rules of modern continuity, someone (who?) simply re-edited the film, leaving out parts that quite obviously originally belonged, and Porter was turned into the modest inventor of one of the basic syntagms of the institutional mode – some ten years before any such figure began to appear in the standard syntax. What is unfortunate is that a number of historians, including Georges Sadoul, continued to give credence to this myth, following Lewis Jacobs, who appears to have been the first to take this catalogue into account. More interesting, however, is the question as to the authenticity or otherwise of the description. For if it should prove to be authentic (and for the moment I have no real evidence to the contrary), it might mean that the aspiration to this linear ubiquity which was to become characteristic of the institutional mode had reached a level where it could be written down but not yet realized on film – not because of some technical obstacle, but because of an enormous *blind spot* difficult for us to analyse. However, the fact that, once these two shots were filmed, it was decided to connect them in a manner implying an obvious non-linearity rather than disturb the unity of the spatial viewpoint, seems to me to say a good deal about the *alterity* of the relationship these early films entertained with the spectators who watched them. Does it not suggest that the feeling of being seated in a theatre in front of a screen had, for spectators then, a sort of priority over the feeling of being carried away by an imaginary time-flow, modelled on the semblance of linearity which *ordinary time* has for us? But any such hypothesis is extremely hazardous, and would require the backing of a good deal more evidence before it could be seriously entertained.

Visionary, plagiarist, 'auteur': none of these clichés can really help in situating Porter's work. It is the readiness to confine his films within these terms which leads so often to the obvious being bypassed: the fact that these films are the loci of contradictions, that their contradictions are also those of an era of cinema, and that neither Porter's films nor the rest of those of the era can be deciphered except by way of this twin perspective. But once this decipherment has been achieved (and I can only claim to have prepared the way here: among other things, access to a far wider corpus of work is essential), it will enable us to determine absolutely basic matters concerning the genealogy of the institutional mode as well as the nature of the primitive modes; and it is probably in this respect that Porter's films will ultimately occupy a privileged place in the history of the cinema.

Translated by Tom Milne

Postscript

The Fédération Internationale des Archives du Film (FIAF) symposium in Brighton (May 1978) gave me an opportunity of seeing most of the remaining Porter films that have survived. These confirm the theses set forth here on the basis of what turn out to be, indeed, his most important films (to which, however, I would now add *The Life of an American Policeman* (1905). American scholars have now definitive confirmation of what has been for some years the prevailing hypothesis concerning *The Life of an American Fireman* (a distribution copy found in Maine is identical with copyright version), and while it was pointed out to me that 1903 is an incorrect date for *The Life of an American Cowboy*, the fact that this film actually dates from 1906 merely confirms that 'progress' in Porter's work, as in primitive cinema as a whole, was anything but linear.

Notes

1. Eight films out of the fifty-odd which have survived: *The Life of an American Cowboy, The Life of an American Fireman, Uncle Tom's Cabin, The Great Train Robbery, Romance of the Rails* (all 1903); *Rounding Up the Yeggmen* (1904); *Dream of a Welsh Rarebit Fiend* (1906); *Rescued from an Eagle's Nest* (1907). *Romance of the Rails,* one of the earliest advertising films I have seen, is remarkable chiefly for a long tracking shot behind a train; *The Dream of a Welsh Rarebit Fiend* is a pleasant trick film in the Pathé manner; *Rescued from an Eagle's Nest* is absolutely typical of the general advance of the American cinema in 1907, but is otherwise unremarkable. I limit myself to a closer analysis of the four major films of 1903.
2. *The Rise of the American Film* (New York, 1939, reprinted, New York, 1968).
3. Jacques Deslandes, *Histoire comparée du cinéma*: vol. 1, *De la cinématique au cinématographe, 1826–1896* (Tournai 1966) vol. 2, with Jacques Richard, *De la cinématographie au cinéma, 1896–1906* (Tournai, 1968). Georges Sadoul, *Histoire générale du cinéma*, 3rd ed. (Paris, 1973–   ).
4. Robert Gessner, 'Porter and the Creation of Cinematic Motion', *Journal of the Society of Cinematologists*, vol. II, 1962.
5. The present article has been produced in connection with a wider study with Jorge Dana relating ot the genealogy of the mode of representation characteristic of the institution of cinema.
6. Aimed, it should be stressed, at the *children* of the bourgeoisie, like all scientific toys such as the zoetrope or the praxinoscope which foreshadowed the projection of moving pictures. A fascinating study could be made of the relationship between the popular *presentational* arts (circus, puppets, etc.) and an audience of middle-class children not yet broken into the codes of the *representational* arts of their class.
7. One of the most important features of the early fairground cinema in England and France was the lecturer, a barker who lured passers-by into the booth, then delivered a commentary during the screening whose 'distancing' effect became literally unbearable around 1910 with the development of 'absorbing' techniques in the dominant narrativity. The American lecturer, whose social implications were quite different, derived from the tradition of the slide-show lecture.
8. Transmitted, in particular, through the medium of a specialized press which, in America at least, developed rapidly after 1905. Cf. Kauffman and Henstall (eds.), *American film criticism from the beginnings to 'Citizen Kane'* (New York, 1972).
9. A vocation deriving in our cultures from the codes of social distance as classified by the semiological discipline know as *proxemics*, whereby the close-up corresponds to the 'intimate distance' associated with bodily contact (sexual intercourse or wrestling); cf. Edward T. Hall, *The Hidden Dimension* (London, 1969).
10. The etymology of the name given by the Lumières to their invention (*Cinématographe*: 'inscription of movement') as against the Edison–Dickson *Vitascope* ('image of life') neatly summarises the distance separating their respective ideological approaches.

11. Possibly derived from a contemporary strip cartoon.
12. The contrast with the black background in Dickson's interiors is striking.
13. This is the great paradox involved in the literal transposition to the screen of the proscenium frame: the characters are suddenly 'crushed' by sets which they would have dominated in the theatre through their voices and their 'presence' in relief, as well as the use of lighting . . . and opera-glasses.
14. It is of course difficult to imagine how recent immigrants, said to form the main clientele of the nickelodeons (in order to perfect their English, according to Billy Bitzer) reacted to a film like this.
15. In Japan, the cinema retained its 'lecturer' (the *benshi*, derived in particular from the doll theatres) until 1937.
16. These do not seem to have been incorporated into films prior to 1900; the magic lanterns with which the more prosperous fairground booths were equipped were apparently used only to project the opening titles. Since each tableau of the Passion films was sold separately, each had its own opening title.
17. The future was also *The Cabinet of Dr Caligari*, much closer to the primitives (or to us) than to Griffith or DeMille.
18. No doubt the zealous attempts to make films in colour, which very soon resulted in a number of ingenious processes, were largely due to a premonition that this problem of differentiation might be resolved by colour.
19. Which doubtless also explains why our impression of 'hyper-realism' vanishes too: for us montage, contrasted with 'non-montage', is an undeniable sign of 'fiction'.
20. With the exception, it seems, of travel films and other documentaries, though these were still made 'in the Lumière manner'.
21. It goes without saying that I do not claim, here or elsewhere, to be reconstituting the thoughts of people long since dead; I am simply trying to open out, in a graphic way, the area of speculation suggested by this shot.
22. The effect here is even more 'progressive' than in Porter's case, since the characters, instead of being filmed against a black background, are in the setting shown in the following or preceding tableau. The match cut was not very far away – in fact the English, it seems, were employing it already: cf. Cecil Hepworth's *Rescued by Rover* (1904).
23. cf. Maurice Edelman, *Le Droit saisi par la photographie* (Paris, Maspero, 1972).

1987

This essay was written in French for Raymond Bellour's anthology *Le Cinéma Americain* (1980) and first appeared in this English translation by Tom Milne in *Screen* (No. 11). Most of the substance of the piece was incorporated into *La Lucarne de l'infini (Life to Those Shadows* (1990)). What I soon came to regard as outdated here was the implication that the primitive period, and particularly the relationship of the primitive audience with the films that addressed it, was some kind of lost paradise, was somehow superior to what followed.

From a strictly historiographical point of view, this essay also projects onto the history of the American film-going audience the experience of France, where in fact the bulk of a very small film-going public did belong, until at least the end of the First World War, to the urban working and craftsman classes. In the USA, however, this was true only for the brief period of the nickelodeon, when most film-goers seem indeed to have been immigrant workers (see above, Chapter 5, note 2).

8 Primitivism and the Avant-gardes: a Dialectical Approach

In 1899, Jules-Etienne Marey, physiologist and inventor of what had potentially been the first motion picture camera, wrote in a preface to a book on 'animated photographs':

> What such pictures show, after all, our eye could have seen directly. They add nothing to our ocular powers, they remove none of our illusions. Now the true character of scientific method is to remedy the inadequacies of our senses or correct their errors. In order to achieve this, chronophotography must renounce showing things as they really are.

And Marey concluded this veritable credo of anti-illusionism by asserting that the only techniques of motion synthesis that could possibly interest science were those which enabled us to slow down or speed up the appearance of reality.[1]

Twenty-five years later, Dziga Vertov wrote:

> What am I to do with my camera? What is its role in the offensive I am launching against the visible world?
>
> I think of the Camera Eye . . . I abolish the customary sixteen frames-per-second . . . high speed cinematography, . . . frame-by-frame animation and many other techniques . . . become commonplace.
>
> The Camera Eye must be understood as 'that which cannot be seen by the human eye', as the microscope and telescope of time . . .
>
> The Camera Eye is the possibility of making visible the invisible, of bringing light into darkness, of revealing what is hidden . . . of turning the lie into truth.[2]

And now here is another pair of quotations, spanning, this time, a period of over sixty years. In 1904, future pioneer producer Fred J.

Balshofer was working for the Shields Lantern Slide Company in New York City. In his memoirs, he recalls the following anecdote:

> I timidly suggested to Shields the possibility of making moving pictures as well as lantern slides. Shields was a stubborn, pompous man and in his typical sarcastic manner, said: 'Make moving pictures? Why those flickering things hurt your eyes. They're just a passing fancy.'[3]

In 1966, Jonas Mekas interviewed Tony Conrad, maker of *The Flicker*:

> CONRAD: . . . The patterns that I selected to use in *The Flicker* are an extension of the usual stroboscope techniques into a much more complex system. *The Flicker* employs harmonic relations, speeds, pulses and patterns different from those used until now.
> (At this point in our conversation, James Mullins, the manager of the Cinemathèque, where *The Flicker* was screened, walked in.)
> JONAS MEKAS: What was the effect of the film on you? You saw it twice.
> JAMES MULLINS: It gave me headaches.[4]

What these two pairs of quotations have in common is their ambivalence. Neither pair can be said to express a true equivalence – either between the thinking of a conservative, middle-class scientist whose mechanistic materialism goes straight back to Descartes and that of a Communist film-maker deeply committed to dialectical and historical materialism, or between the effect of scintillation due to a technological 'blindspot' of the early cinema (the failure to discover that flicker could be eliminated by the simple expedient of the double-action shutter) and that which was deliberately produced by a sophisticated film-maker using single-frame exposures of a kind unthinkable until at least the 1920s.

Yet at the same time, there is no doubt in my mind that such encounters – and there have been many – are meaningful, that they can clarify our thinking, not only about the Primitive Cinema – and pre-cinema – but also about the various avant-gardes, provided we avoid simplistic conflations, and are careful to hold onto both ends of the chain – as the French working-class colloquially expresses its grasp of Marx's dialectics.

It is no exaggeration to say that Marey, on the brink of inventing the cinema, and despite his belated and half-hearted attempt to emulate Edison, actually did refuse to accomplish the decisive step. The attitude behind this behaviour, expressed in the above quotation and shared implicitly by Muybridge and explicitly by Albert Londe, derived from a scientistic functionalism which inclined him to see the synthesis of movement as a gross redundancy from his cognitive point of view. Yet Marey's science was far from innocent: he himself advocated applying the results of his studies of human locomotion to the rationalization of the burdensome load of Monsieur Thiers' foot-soldiers, and his analyses of work motion may be seen as one source of Taylorism (that technology by which Capital sought and still seeks to make the worker an appendage to his machine). Vertov, of course, made no pretence of being a scientist in the usual sense; yet, perhaps because Marxism is also a rationalism, his project does have that one point of tangency with Marey's; the pre-eminence of the cognitive over the analogical model.

What, however, can possibly link these two other facts: that, on the one hand, in the 1960s a handful of middle-class connoisseurs successfully combated headache and eyestrain to achieve, no doubt, an 'expanded vision', an attentiveness to the marginal functionings of their own optic systems under unusual stimulation and that, on the other, the large plebeian audience of the first ten years of motion pictures put up with a flicker that their social 'betters' regarded as so intolerable a discomfort that it contributed to their overwhelming absence from the places where films were shown – those smoke-filled, rowdy places frequented exclusively in those days by a class of people for whom motion pictures were cheaper than an evening at the gin mill and certainly less uncomfortable than a day spent in the racket and stench of the factory or sweat-shop?

In any but a purely contingent sense, there appears to be no link at all here, and in fact any attempt to establish one might seem at best ahistoric, at worst grotesque. Yet I have come to regard this encounter as an emblem of the contradictory relationships between the cinema of the Primitive Era and the avant-gardes of later periods. For the elimination of flicker and the trembling image, fairly complete after 1909 was, it seems, a crucial moment in the achieving of the preconditions for the emergence of a system of representation which conformed to the norms of the bourgeois novel, painting and theatre, and for the recruitment of an audience which would include various strata of the bourgeoisie. When the successive modernist movements set about extending, whether pragmatically or systematically, their 'de-constructive' critiques of those representational norms to the realm of film, it was inevitable that sooner or later the flicker should reappear, valued now for its synesthetic and 'self-reflexive' potential.

While such links, then, are not entirely arbitrary, we must, it seems to me, consider them with the greatest caution. For while it is no doubt the experience of the avant-gardes – and particularly those of the 1960s, in both Europe and the United States – which has enabled us today simply to *read* many of the phenomena encountered in the earliest films, that experience has also led, for want of an understanding of the historical context, for want, too, of any coherent theoretical framework, to highly tendentious assumptions of many kinds. I will cite only two, sufficiently remote for their mention not to be too embarrassing to their authors. Early in the 1960s, a well-known scholar of the American film had the naïvety to suggest that the celebrated narrative anomaly found in Porter's *Life of an American Fireman* – the same action shown twice, from different angles – was in some way a prefiguration of the labyrinthian textuality of *Last Year at Marienbad*. And, later in the 1960s, a distinguished archivist, who should have known better, authenticated what appears to be the prodigiously 'modern' editing of a 1907 bicycle farce included in the Paper Print Collection of the Library of Congress. Yet a perusal of other films deposited by the same firm (the Selig Polyscope Company) clearly shows that those daringly elliptical match-cuts, worthy of Eisenstein at the very least, are due simply to the fact that the producers considered it necessary for copyright purposes to supply only fragments of their films.

Such confusions should make us very wary whenever we encounter an effect of familiarity in an historical context which is, in fact, only deceptively close: these seventy-five years of cinema history are to be equated, in my view, with seven hundred years of literary or theatrical history, and the 'logic' which governed the productions of Pathé and Biograph before 1905 is in many respects more contemporary with that of *The Romance of the Rose* or *le Jeu de Robin et de Marion* than that of *Major Barbara* or *l'Assommoir*.

The otherness of the Primitive Cinema – and I am referring precisely to *a quality which is recognized* by a generation of critics, historians and film-makers suckled on the radical modernism of the last three decades – is, in fact, two-fold. Let us first consider the Primitive Mode of Representation proper, derived without question from a number of models that were socially important at the turn of the century – the picture postcard, the vaudeville and melodrama stages, the circus, the Wild West show, the comic strip, etc. – but which cannot be said to be a literal or wholesale transposition of any of these. By the time it reached maturity, by the time it began gradually to give way to the Institutional Mode of Representation that was to supersede it, the Primitive Mode had become undeniably *stabilized*, having acquired a degree of specificity as advanced as that which the Institutional Mode itself was one day to achieve. The Primitive Mode was initiated as much by W. K. L. Dickson as by Louis Lumière, and was kept alive in its purest form until 1912 by Georges Méliès. It continued to haunt the cinema of France until the end of the silent era and left visible traces in many American films until at least 1920.

In its most characteristic guise, the Primitive Mode has, I believe, four primary traits. The first is well known: the *autarchy* and *unicity* of each frame. Any given tableau will remain unchanged in its framing throughout its passage on the screen, and from one appearance to the next (in the event of a recurring set or location); it is complete unto itself and never 'communicates' with any other. In other words, the successive spaces depicted are presumed to occupy a common diegetic framework, but that is all: their spatio-temporal connections remain fundamentally unspecified.

The second primary trait which I distinguish may be called the '*non-centred quality*' of the image, and it must be considered under two separate heads: first, the entire frame is a possible playing area. The areas close to the edges of the frame are as likely to be the site of vital action as those more centrally located. Secondly, it is often difficult for the eye – at least for our eye – to locate the narratively significant centre of the diegetic action – and there are times when none actually exists at all, when the entire image is being offered simultaneously to our gaze. The most famous films of Louis

Lumière come to mind here, of course (*Workers Leaving a Factory, Arrival of a Train at La Ciotat*), but also countless tableaux of narrative films as well.

Next, there is the crucial matter of camera distance. In the great majority of films made before 1906 (though not in all – and I shall return to this point), shot-size approximated to what we today would call 'medium long shot'. That is to say, a standing character seldom occupied more than two-thirds of the height of the screen and often much less. The consequences of this were several, but they may, I believe, be summed up as the production of an overall effect of *exteriority*: the third primary trait of the Primitive Mode. The lack of any significant facial detail in such shots inevitably renders the characters' presence solely *behavioural*: one sees what they *did*, but there is absolutely no sense of that psychological interiority characteristic, for example, of the classical novel, except when such interiority is grossly exteriorized through a markedly calligraphic pantomime, which deprives it of any 'naturalness'. The Primitive Cinema at its most characteristic is apsychological. Characters lack that internal 'presence' which was guaranteed on the bourgeois stage by the voice (with the help, from a gallery seat, of a strong pair of opera-glasses), and in the bourgeois novel by such strategies as the omniscience of a demiurgical narrator. Moreover, their external presence is comparatively weak as well: spectators remained far more *apart* from those tiny silhouettes than from the characters on any stage, whose actual, physical presence could be verified by countless details addressing nearly all the senses (besides the visual perception of colour and depth, we may mention the sounds of footsteps on the planks or of swirling gowns, the odour of grease-paint, tobacco or perfume).

Maxim Gorky, in an article written upon first seeing the Lumière Cinématographe at the Nizhni-Novgorod fair in 1896, expressed eloquently the alienation which the spectator, accustomed to the bourgeois stage and novel, almost certainly must have experienced to some degree when confronted with those images:

> Before you a life is surging, a life deprived of words and shorn of the living spectrum of colours – the grey, the soundless, the bleak and dismal life.
>
> It is terrifying to see, but it is the movement of shadows, only of

shadows . . . you feel as though Merlin's vicious trick is being enacted before you. As though he had bewitched the entire street, had compressed its many-storied buildings from roof-tops to foundations to yard-like size. He dwarfed the people in corresponding proportions, robbing them of the power of speech and scraping together all the pigment of earth and sky into a monotonous grey colour.[5]

Significantly, the film from that first Lumière programme which seemed most 'alive' to the great naturalist writer was *Baby's Breakfast*. And while he not unexpectedly addresses his remarks solely to the iconography of the film – the couple 'are so charming, gay and happy and the baby is so amusing' – we cannot fail to note that this film was the only close shot on the programme. And in this connection, I wish to stress that *Baby's Breakfast* was not to remain an isolated instance in the Primitive Cinema. Contrary to popular belief, this shot – and similar ones, produced by Dickson – inaugurated an important minor genre which was to last for nearly ten years, that is a presentational medium close-up – or close-up – of one or two (generally well known) actors mugging into the camera, or even – in the Gaumont *Phonoscènes*, for example – singing or reciting comic monologues in very approximate synchronism with a tinny cylinder phonograph. These shots, which undoubtedly introduced *the presence of the persona* into the Primitive Cinema programme and later, through the related practice of the emblematic close-up, into individual films, may be said to have fulfilled a role prefiguring that of the interpolated close-up in the nascent Institutional Mode of Representation after around 1910.

The fourth major trait of the Primitive Mode may be designated by the somewhat barbarous term '*non-closure*'. Consider one of the latest and most accomplished examples I know in the American cinema of the purely Primitive film: the 1905 Biograph *Kentucky Feud*, thought to have been directed by Billy Bitzer, soon to become Griffith's precious collaborator. This film refers to an actual feud which took place in Kentucky and which has come down to us through a celebrated ballad. However, the film's mode of fictionalization has little to do with that of, let us say, *All the President's Men*. Instead, it is assumed that the audience is familiar with the broad lines of the events described, and the successive tableaux seem conceived more like *hors-textes* or tabloid newspaper engravings. They are illustrations for a narrative which is elsewhere: that is, they are not self-contained scenes in the usual sense. Moreover, the function of the intertitles deserves careful consideration here, exemplifying as it does the fundamental non-linearity of many Primitive narrative procedures. Indeed, in *Kentucky Feud*, as in so many films of the period (and the films which Griffith directed six or seven years later for that same Biograph Company still retain this trait), the titles pre-empt, as it were, the strictly narrative dimension of the images, destroying any sense of suspense, baulking for the moment any formation of the bi-univocally concatenated narrative chain that ultimately was to characterize the Institutional Mode.

Of course, in one sense, this description of the narrative process at work here is incomplete, as was my description – and as also in one's experience – of the topologically a-centric Primitive tableau. For we must never forget that in what may have been by this time a majority, or at least a large number, of cases, the presentation of a film was accompanied by some sort of oral commentary in the theatre, delivered by the 'lecturer'. And however much these 'lectures' varied in quality and effectiveness, it seems fairly certain that their chief aim was to linearize the visual signifiers – to tell the audience where to look and when – and to operate some sort of closure – in this case, to give the audience background material they might not have known. Yet while the lecturer represented a concerted attempt to overcome certain inadequacies of the Primitive Mode, and to help new middle-class patrons decipher a medium to which they were unaccustomed, that lecturer was also part of a general exhibition situation which continued to stress the priority of the actual spectatorial space-time over the illusory space-time of the film. We know that besides the lecturer's comments, off-colour jokes, etc., there were always the more or less irrelevant piano accompaniment, and the constant comings and goings among the patrons, and in New York City, at least, it seems that the nickelodeon doors were generally left open during the performance. Clearly this was a far cry from the rapt attention devoted to silent films in film societies and Cinémathéques today, but was strangely close to the atmosphere that reigns in a 42nd

Street flea-house during a kung-fu movie.

Before going on to describe a very different aspect of the 'otherness' of Primitive Cinema, I would like to open a brief parenthesis concerning terminology. It seems to me that the films of the Primitive Era suggest why the category 'narrative film' is powerless to define in any essential way the films produced within the Institution. *Kentucky Feud* can hardly be described as 'non-narrative', yet I am sure most modern viewers of it would agree that the experience of watching it is about as far removed from that of watching a fully-fledged Institutional film as is that of watching, say, Ernie Gehr's *Reverberation*. Not, I hasten to add, that I regard these equally removed experiences as equivalent; however, they do help us to define the boundaries of a centred, linear, closured, Institutional experience which is not at all co-extensive with the 'space' of narrative (most classical documentaries are less 'narrative' than *Kentucky Feud*, and yet are an integral part of the Institution). The very meaning of the term 'narrative' seems clouded indeed in the minds of those who adopt a critical stance towards narrative. A well-known American film artist recently presented one of his works to a London audience with the warning that it contained 'narrative elements'. These turned out to be a strip of film (apparently slipping past the camera lens) on which there were dark, blurred photograms showing what might have been a woman's face. 'Figurative' had come to equal 'narrative'. The use of the term 'Institutional Mode of Representation' to designate the basic framework within which mainstream cinema has evolved during the last fifty years has the advantage, even if it has no other merit, of avoiding such tendentious confusions.[6]

The pressures – economic, ideological and cultural – that were eventually to create, first in the United States, then throughout the Western world, the conditions for the triumph of the Institutional Mode exerted themselves on the cinema as soon as it was born. The Primitive Mode, as a consequence, never existed in a vacuum. It was challenged from the outset by that aspiration to analogue representation that is so deep-rooted in Western culture, that throughout the nineteenth century was so closely associated with the development of photography, and that further manifested itself in such peripheral but significant phenomena as the Diorama, the stereoscope and the British temperance movement's photographic lantern-shows known as 'Life Models'. The Primitive Era was essentially contradictory; it was the scene of a constant confrontation. On the one hand we have the analogue aspiration, exemplified in Edison's sensationalist declarations about the canned operas of the future, and in the couplets about 'man's victory over death' intoned by French newspapers after the première of Lumière's films at the Grand Café. On the other hand are the attitudes about representation which stemmed both from certain popular art-forms and from the scientist ideology upheld by a number of pioneers. Marey's out-and-out anti-illusionism is one instance of this attitude and Louis Lumière's personal commitment to the 'raw document' – his indifference to *mise en scène* – is another.

Actually, the most spectacular and most 'obvious' evidence of the drive towards the perfect analogue is to be found in the constant presence on the motion picture market between 1894 and the First World War of systems designed to endow those silent pictures with the Logos – with a Soul, as some have put it – in other words, with lip-synch sound. In the period between the Edison Company's Kinetophonograph of 1894 (whose earphones and eye-piece prefigure, over and beyond the clatter of the penny arcade and the nickelodeon, the sensorial isolation of the picture palace of the 1930s) and the vastly improved machine bearing the same name that was placed on the market in 1911 (but which failed, like all its rivals, for want of adequate amplification) an impressive number of synch sound systems appeared and disappeared. The Gaumont Chronophone had a considerable commercial success, and the several hundred *Phonoscènes* directed by Alice Guy figured on the programmes of theatres in France and elsewhere for over half a decade, in alternation with silent films. It is significant, of course, that all these efforts (as well as those which involved the 'dubbing' of films during the projection by actors hidden behind the screen) had ceased completely by the eve of the First World War, when the Institutional Mode, with its interpolated close-ups and spoken titles, was beginning to assert itself in the films of Reginald Barker, the Ince brothers, DeMille and others.

Far more exotic, however, are the traces left by attempts to transform films *visually* in such a way as to overcome the exteriority – the lack of presence – from which the Primitive Cinema, judged by the criteria of late nineteenth-century naturalism, was felt to suffer so severely. One of the most spectacular of these was the Cinéorama, presented by the French engineer Grimoin-Sanson at the 1900 Paris Exhibition. This was a technically successful attempt to create a single, unbroken, circular image, filmed by twelve synchronized cameras and projected onto the inside of a dome-like screen by twelve projectors placed beneath a platform which held the audience. This ingenious attempt to *surround* the audience, to *enfold* them in an image which still otherwise cleaved to the distant exteriority of the Lumière model, can, of course, only have heightened the topological dispersion of the Primitive tableau (where were you supposed to look now?), so that this experiment objectively retarded the historical movement towards spectatorial identification with a ubiquitous camera, that linch-pin of the Institutional Mode.

The American equivalent of the Cinéorama was Hales' Tours. Here we are no longer dealing with an eccentric parapraxis – a term which can aptly describe many of the contradictory experiments of the age – but with an astute commercial venture, however extravagant it may appear today. Hales' Tours were permanent cinemas which flourished in the United States between 1904 and 1912 and which were more or less elaborately fitted out inside to resemble pullman coaches. Sitting in the seats as if they were passengers in a moving train, patrons watched films that had been taken from the cow-catchers of moving trains or trolley-cars. This *strategy of penetration* no doubt conferred upon the Lumière model an effect of presence which it hitherto had lacked, but such exhibitions were necessarily limited to documents of a very particular sort, and the only immediate impact of Hales' Tours was to establish the need for fixed exhibition centres for films. Yet for me, Hales' Tours are above all emblematic of a tendency which marked the first decade of cinema and which consisted in interventions from outside the film – interventions in the realm of spectatorial space – designed to achieve a goal which history was to show could, on the contrary, only be achieved by blotting out spectatorial space.

The director whose work perhaps best embodies the contradictory 'otherness' of the Primitive Era is Edwin S. Porter. The anomalous character of so many of the major experiments (and here I use the word 'experiments' advisedly) that he produced for the Edison Company between 1900 and 1906 was always due to the conflict between the Primitive Mode as I have described and illustrated it and the drive to overcome its 'shortcomings', to achieve the interiorized presence of the future Institution.

I shall cite only two examples of these experiments, chosen for their direct relevance to our subject. Porter's celebrated *The Great Train Robbery* was taxed by Sidney Peterson[7], among other spokesmen of the American avant-garde, with embodying the Original Sin of the motion picture, of incarnating the precise moment when the Primitive Paradise was lost, when that evil object 'narrative film' reared its ugly head. Paradoxically, this view was also shared by narrowly chauvinistic historians of mainstream film, such as Lewis Jacobs, for whom Porter was indeed the inventor of all the basic elements of 'motion picture grammar'. However, when the smoke of such special pleading has cleared, the film can be seen for what it is: a significant moment in the continuing, historically inevitable process of the expansion of diegetic space–time beyond the confines of the Primitive tableau. It was certainly not the first film to attempt what semiology has dubbed the 'alternating syntagma', and its famous chase sequence was only one among the first of its kind – both had appeared earlier, in the work of the British pioneers. However, it was certainly one of the earliest attempts in the USA at a *developed form* using these linearizing figures, key harbingers of the future Institutional Mode.

At the same time, however, this film remains wholly within the Primitive Mode in at least one essential respect: for every tableau, the camera is still placed at a considerable distance from the action, and the lens used is such that the characters are often no taller than a quarter of the height of the screen, with their faces only barely visible and hence unreadable. Despite, then, the extension and linearization of diegetic space–time, perceptual exteriority is maintained throughout and character presence is still minimal. However, this film – and in this respect it may have been a 'first' – also displays a peculiarly acute awareness of this lack, an awareness expressed in the famous medium close-up showing Barnes, the outlaw chief, shooting into the camera. This shot, as is well known, was not actually incorporated into the film itself but was delivered to exhibitors as a separate roll which they could splice onto the beginning or the end of the film, whichever they chose.

Now, at this simple factual statement, our minds begin to form connections. We think of rare and relatively recent experiments in the film-mobile, such as *Chelsea Girls*, we think of aleatoric music, etc. But before indulging in such extrapolation, it is important to understand exactly what sort of object we are dealing with here. At a time when spectatorial identification with the camera, and hence the possibility of camera ubiquity within the pro-filmic space of the primary tableau, was still far in the future (despite isolated experiments in England and even the USA, including one by Porter himself, oddly enough), this shot is a particular kind of anaphora of the interpolated close-up. It brings to the film as a whole the dimension of individual presence, but cannot as yet 'penetrate' the diegesis proper and must be content to wander about at the periphery, to be placed indiscriminately at the beginning or end of the film, at the discretion of exhibitors, that is to say, at random. Excluded from the film by the taboo still surrounding unicity of viewpoint, this 'emblematic' close-up not only introduces the dimension of presence in this overall manner, but also provides an example of an early attempt to encapsulate the 'essence' of the film – to provide a 'treasure' which each spectator could carry home. Here is another anaphora of an Institutional strategy *par excellence*, essential to the constitution of the film as a consumer product. In this double capacity, the emblematic close-up became quite widespread over the next five or six years, chiefly in the USA but also in Europe.

The mobility of the close-up appended to *The Great Train Robbery* is thus seen not to be simply an instance of Primitive 'freedom' (though it is true that similar 'editorial responsibilities' were sometimes left to the exhibitors). It was also the contradictory symptom of an historical blind spot and of a relentless ideological undercurrent. And while this instance of the 'openness' of the Primitive film clearly finds an objective echo in the occasional film-mobile of our time, one wonders whether reflection on the organic relationship of this 'wandering close-up' to the history of the Institution might not give rise to a more consequential exploration of aleatoric film forms.

The most celebrated anomaly in the work of Porter occurs in his film *The Life of an American Fireman* (1903). In the form in which the film was deposited at the Library of Congress in 1903, the rescue of the woman and child by a fireman is shown *twice*, from two different 'points of view' – one (diegetically) inside the room where the victims are trapped, and one from outside. We see the same action twice, in succession.

I know of no example in Primitive Cinema where 'time repetition' as radical as this occurs again. However, other, shorter repetitions do occur in a few American films and in those of Méliès, for instance. Moreover, a film like *The Story the Biograph Told* (1905) admirably dramatizes the taboo surrounding camera ubiquity with an elaborate narrative apparatus whose sole purpose is to accomplish a 90° shot change – a figure which as far as I can judge was not to become widespread until the end of the First World War. And the existence of this taboo is what authorizes me, I feel, to speak of the 'price' that Porter paid for challenging it in his *Fireman* as a kind of parapraxis or failed act in the Freudian sense, in which a 'collective unconscious' replaces the individual.

Porter's *Life of an American Fireman* also gives us a further clue to the underlying nature of the many encounters between strategies employed by this or that modernist movement and certain of these Primitive parapraxes. Let us consider the overlap match-cutting in certain films of Eisenstein. The most famous example here would no doubt be the raising of the bridges in *October*. It is clear that this has nothing in common, contextually or conceptually, with the time repetition in *The Life of an American Fireman* (or those in such little-known films as *Next!*, from 1903, and *The Policemen's Little Run*, from 1907, in which the repetitions are of a much smaller extent). Yet the Eisensteinian strategy is, at one level, the *negative* of the Primitive parapraxis. The latter is a contradiction characteristic of an era we may regard as 'pre-seamless', whilst Eisenstein's dialectic between the visual expression of a temporal 'impossibility' and the commonsense notion of the linear flow of time is, among other things, a critique, implicit at least, of *that same seamlessness*. Moreover, if my reading of the narrative anomaly in *The Life of an American Fireman* is an historically relevant hypothesis (it can never be more than that, since even if the producers' or director's rationale was conscious, it is no doubt buried with them forever), then there is also an encounter implicit in the two procedures at the level of the 'positioning of the audience'. The resolution of the Eisensteinian conflict – the acceptance of the time repetitions by the spectators of *October* is a specifically cultural act today (once it may also have been a political act), and it is hard to believe that the Primitive spectators, to the extent that they were following *The Fireman* at all, did not also need to make some kind of conscious mental adjustment to seeing the same narrative fragment twice. Here, however, I am treading on dangerous ground, which can lead so easily to such myths as that of the Lost Paradise of the Primitive Cinema. I must stress immediately that a parallel such as this is of theoretical interest only. It says little about film history as it was lived by those who made it (behind the cameras or sitting in halls before screens). It is in fact only from the point of view of a working theory of the Institutional Mode and its genealogy that any meaningful correlation can be established between processes which to all intents and purposes might have taken place on different planets. And I should add that to my knowledge, none of these parapractic anomalies was ever consciously emulated. However, in the history of what has been called 'avant-garde' or, perhaps, 'radical' film-making, there have been a number of more or less concerted 'revivals' of this or that aspect of the Primitive Mode, proper.

Without doubt, the first of these efforts was *The Cabinet of Doctor Caligari*. Although it has not been fashionable in avant-garde circles in the USA to do so, I continue to regard *Caligari* as a film of considerable importance, and in particular as the first significant modernist film.

It seems to me not at all accidental that the epithet which certain modernist critics have used to dismiss *Caligari* from the Pantheon of the avant-garde is 'theatrical'. This, after all, is the same epithet with which classical film history has dismissed the Primitive Cinema: motion pictures 'begin' with Smith, Porter and Griffith – with the premises of the Institutional Mode – while the Primitive Cinema is merely an 'imitation' of the theatre; the history of the early cinema equals the history of the 'shaking off' of the theatrical influence, etc. What such pronouncements have always failed to reflect is the fact that the theatre which, indeed, had a deep impact on the earliest cinema was not the legitimate stage of the middle classes, but melodrama, vaudeville, Grand Guignol and other plebeian forms; and that when cinema at last 'became a language and an art', as the saying usually goes, it was through the constitution of a mode of representation which reproduced, albeit with specific, original means, the underlying project of the bourgeois ('legitimate') stage.

Nor was it by accident that it was a film issuing directly from the Expressionist movement which was the first to effect a deliberate, sweeping 'return' to some of the major gestures of the Primitive Mode. Expressionism, after all, in its critique of all the manifestations of Naturalism, had for nearly two decades been keenly attentive to 'primitive' art of all kinds: the sculptures of Africa, the folk woodcuts of Germany, as well as the creations of mental patients and children. I have no evidence that the collective effort which produced *Caligari* was actually informed by any awareness (or remembrance) of the forms of the Primitive Era. However, here I feel we can all agree that the encounter is striking in its scope. Let me simply point up its chief traits.

Caligari was produced in 1919, at a time when Institutional editing had become a universal aspiration, although mastery of it varied from country to country. Yet here we are dealing with a film consisting almost solely of a series of frontally shot, autonomous tableaux from which intra-sequential editing is almost excluded. The autonomy of the successive tableaux is stressed by articulations that are strongly disjunctive, either through sharp graphic contrasts or through elaborately hesitant irises. Moreover, on the occasional instances when there is a shot change within a tableau, disjunctiveness is similarly stressed – by graphic contrast, notably through the use of vignettes – to a point where we usually feel these 'match-cuts' to be as ragged as those in, say, the films Sigmund Lubin was making around 1906.

However, it seems to me that *Caligari* engages most resolutely with the historical process of the constitution of the Institutional Mode in the matter of the homogenization of pictorial space. Until around 1912, and even afterwards in France, the cinema was characterized by a sharp division between two types of pictorial space. One type, exemplified by so many Lumière films, derived most immediately, I believe, from the scenic picture postcard, so much in vogue in the late nineteenth century. It is a model associated in the cinema for over a decade with outdoor shots almost exclusively, and involves a very strong emphasis on linear perspective and the rendering of haptic space in accordance with the model provided by the painting of the Renaissance. However, and contrary to a rather persistent myth (albeit of relatively recent origin), there coexisted with this model, and often within the same film, as soon as these began to contain both interior and exterior scenes, a pictorial approach which, on the contrary, emphasizes the picture plane. This is done through a number of strategies, some of which seem due to contingency (e.g. small studios, low budgets), while others seem quite deliberate. The role of contingency – massive at this time and never, I feel, historically meaningless – is illustrated by an anecdote recorded by Georges Sadoul. One of Ferdinand Zecca's many tasks when he became the principal director for Pathé was to paint scenery. He was not good at it. One day, having set out to paint a backdrop meant to represent a cobbled street in perspective, he wound up with what looked like nothing so much as a pile of rocks. Always able to cope with an emergency, Zecca hung a sign over the canvas flat: 'Men working: detour'.[8]

A British film by a populist film-maker, himself of plebeian origins, the remarkable William Haggar, demonstrates vividly the contrast between the two modes of pictorial representation which characterized the era. *The Life of Charles Peace* depicts with bold, simple strokes the career of a famous robber and murderer of the mid-nineteenth century. During the early sequences, shot mostly in a studio, each autonomous tableau is filmed against a backdrop that is blatantly and schematically flat, with, for example, wall-beams merely outlined with white paint on a canvas flat. In the latter part of the film, a chase, that typically Primitive mode of narrative concatenation, is shown in a series of shots which, on the contrary, make systematic and equally typical use of deep space (in fact, one of them reproduces the, by then, archetypical frame of Lumière's *Arrival of a Train*).

It has not, I believe, been widely recognized that in this matter of the pictorial representation of space on the screen, those whose historical mission was the constitution of the Institutional Mode, had a double task to perform. First, they had to bring depth and volume to the interior scenes of the Primitive Cinema (and to overcome the tendency, very evident with Griffith in particular, to flatten even exterior images through a rigidly level camera attitude and frames decentred towards their lower edge). This transformation was achieved through innovations in camera attitude and set design, as well as the development of electric lighting, all of which made it possible to introduce the codes of classical painting into cinematography. Secondly, through a variety of means, which also included camera placement along with the choice and handling of lenses and, of course, the development of editing, they had to reduce that depth of field which, in the Lumière model, produced such a strongly dispersed, de-centred image. This homogenization of pictorial screen space, conferring on close-ups and long-shots alike a similar look of controlled haptic depth, was not fully achieved in the United States until the end of the First World War, and in France until a few years later.

Here, *Caligari*'s relationship to the cinema of previous years is not simply at the level of mimesis, conscious or unconscious. Here the film actually puts the elements of an historical process to work within its own singular system. We are dealing with a precocious example of 'epistemological creation' in the film medium.

The imagery in *Caligari* continually plays upon a carefully contrived ambiguity. The film's famous graphic style presents each shot as a stylized, flat rendition of deep space, with dramatic obliques so avowedly plastic, so artificially 'depth-producing', that they immediately conjure up the tactile surface of the engraver's page, somewhat in the manner of Méliès. Yet at the same time, the movement of the actors within these frames is systematically perpendicular to the picture plane, in a way reminiscent of Primitive deep-field blocking. The same images thus seem simultaneously to produce two historical types of pictorial space, superimposed one upon the other.

This issue of haptic space has, of course, been at the centre of many important films of recent years – those of Godard and Snow, as well as Dreyer's *Gertrud*, come immediately to mind. But what seems to me so striking about *Caligari* is that through these multiple references to the issue as it historically evolved, it offers an almost unique commentary on the constitution of the Institutional Mode as a visual system.

It is clear from much modern critical work, however, that no purely visual model can satisfactorily account for the Institutional Mode. The issues involved can be indicated by juxtaposing Cocteau's *Blood of a Poet* and a 1902 Biograph called *A Search for*

Evidence, in which a woman and a private detective peer through a series of hotel-room keyholes, affording the audience a suggestion of picturesque scenes, until the unfaithful husband and his mistress are confounded at last.

A Search for Evidence was by no means an unusual film for its day. We know that during the Primitive Era, when copyright was either non-existent or virtually impossible to enforce, especially from one country to another, there was an extraordinarily free *circulation of signs*. It is no exaggeration to say that for a time film images were, in effect, public property. This is a situation difficult to imagine today and it invariably arouses the righteous indignation of classical historians, always quick to denounce plagiarism. In fact, they are peering into a kind of historical enclave in which, for a combination of ideological and economic reasons, the bourgeois concept of property took several years to establish the hegemony which it exerted over every other human endeavour throughout the Western world.

Here I might point out that while I personally know of no such avowed intertextuality among avant-garde artists in the USA or Western Europe – these tend on the contrary to safeguard, jealously, the principles of artistic property – I did see in London in 1979 an example from Yugoslavia which deserves mention and reflection on. Ivan Ladislav Galeta's *Two Times in One Space* (1972) is a two-projector, single-screen performance of an interesting single-shot, slice-of-life exercise, directed three years earlier by a main-stream director. A ten-second lag between the superimposed pictures and the sound-tracks heard through separate speakers, adds a new dimension to the original film without ever impinging decisively on its visual and narrative impact. I am not sure that it is completely by accident that such an experiment should come to us from a socialist country, where the concept of property in general is under reconsideration.

I have no idea which was the first version of the archetypal keyhole film, actually more developed in *A Search for Evidence* than in the standard model, which was totally devoid of narrative structure and simply showed scenes viewed through a keyhole by a peeping maid or bath-boy. I am not even sure where the genre originated, though I suspect that it was in France.

It is my contention that the Primitive Cinema acted out, in naïve,

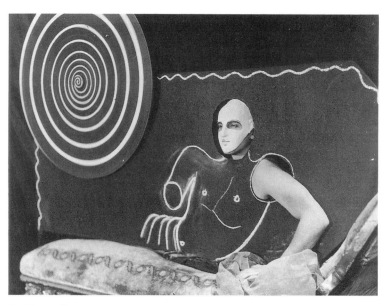

Le Sang d'un Poète (Cocteau, 1930)

The Cabinet of Dr Caligari (Wiene, 1920)

176 IN AND OUT OF SYNCH

overt fashion, many essential gestures which would eventually become consubstantial with the very morphology of the Institutional Mode, which would become submerged to such an extent in what we call 'film language' as to be completely interiorized by makers and spectators alike. The gesture of voyeurism is indubitably one of these.

The earliest voyeur scenes, however, do not follow the model of *A Search for Evidence*, but rather that of Léar's famous film *The Bride Retires* (1897). In that purely Primitive model, the voyeur is at all times co-present on the screen with the object of his gaze – invariably a woman undressing. The shift from this first type of representation to the keyhole type involves a curious change of emphasis, for while overt voyeurism is still at the forefront of the action, curiously enough it is the *process* of voyeuristic desire, rather than its object, which is exhibited. Destined, it seems, for a larger audience, these films rarely show women undressing, but rather a series of incongruous vignettes such as those seen in *A Search for Evidence*. More important, however, this evolution clearly introduces the earliest mode of spectatorial identification with the camera, a phenomenon which was to be at the centre of the diegetic process of Institutional Cinema. The keyhole film, I should add, was not the only manifestation of the new voyeurism: there also appeared films with telescopes (and these, it is true, were often pointed at women), magnifying glasses and even microscopes, but the principle was always the same. Through the alternation of views of the watcher and the watched, spectators were given their first, very simple lesson in camera ubiquity, in identifying with the camera, since the voyeur on the screen is the spectator's obvious surrogate.

It has been pointed out (by Tom Gunning, I believe) that the spectators of the earliest keyhole films were often peering through a hole themselves, since they were patrons of the Kinetoscope or, later, the Mutoscope. But of course this technology was itself by no means 'innocent', especially if we remember the analogical dreams that haunted the West Orange Laboratory where the Kinetoscope was born. The fulfilment of the ideal of analogue representation through moving photographs would absolutely require a certain positioning, a certain centring of the spectatorial subject. The peephole film was the first step in this process.

What has this to do with Cocteau's work? In a lecture which Jean Cocteau delivered in 1932 on the occasion of a presentation of *Blood of a Poet*, he said: 'I used to think that . . . films weary us with shots taken from below or above. I wanted to shoot my film from the front, artlessly.[9] This is already enough to indicate that to some degree Cocteau was consciously thinking of the early cinema when he devised his pioneering film. I believe he may have been the first modernist film-maker to have turned deliberately to Primitive strategies as an 'antidote' to those of the Institution. After all, did he not say elsewhere that the slowness of *Blood of a Poet* was a reaction to the rapid-fire editing of American films?

I have little doubt that when Cocteau conceived the sequence of l'Hôtel des Folies Dramatiques in *Blood of a Poet* he was remembering, consciously or unconsciously, the many keyhole films he must have seen as a child (for many years, the children of the French bourgeoisie, along with their grandmothers and nannies, were, almost, the French cinema's only middle-class spectators). When one reflects on the crucial articulation which the keyhole film represents in the genealogy of the Institutional Mode and on the central role the voyeuristic position was to play in the established Mode itself, it becomes difficult to dismiss this as a chance remembrance. Especially when one further observes that this sequence, which aligns apparently disconnected fantasies in the best Primitive manner, also contains an explicit allusion to a type of Primitive trick-film which, though perhaps not as commonplace as the peep-hole film, was in its way equally significant.

In a Pathé film from around 1902, an 'ingenious Soubrette' hangs pictures on a wall by apparently crawling up it. The trick – hardly one at all for the modern eye, accustomed as it is to camera ubiquity – merely consisted in placing the camera perpendicular to a horizontal set, which therefore looked as if it must be perpendicular to the ground. The overwhelming dominance of frontality and unicity of viewpoint in the Primitive Era must have made such tricks totally effective illusions, even when there was only a black backdrop lying beneath an actor rolling about on the studio floor (as in another Pathé film *The Devil's Dance* (1903)).

Cocteau uses the same device twice in the l'Hôtel des Folies Dramatiques sequence, first in the shots of the poet in the hallway, where the effect is to show the actor struggling against invisible forces, and again, in more elaborate form, in the shots inside the room marked 'Flying Lessons', when the little girl is seen inching her way up the wall and across the ceiling. It is difficult not to be impressed by this association in a single sequence of two overt allusions to such central – and ultimately related – issues of early cinema development: the historical resistance to the abandoning of frontality in favour of camera ubiquity, and spectatorial identification with the camera.

It will perhaps appear incongruous that I have chosen to dwell for so long on two modernist films that were made over fifty years ago, when it is clear that these instances are singularly isolated in their period and that there appear to be numerous and widespread correlations with the Primitive Cinema among modernist films of Europe and the USA made since the late 1950s. However, it seemed important in this context to provide a perspective on these matters – to stress that the otherness of pre-Institutional cinema was a natural pole of attraction for even the earliest modernist challenges to the Institution. And perhaps it is also useful to have thus reminded ourselves that until 1930 the impact of Primitive Cinema could still be direct (through personal memory and through traces still found in the cinema – and in that of France in particular), while today we are dealing with apparently fortuitous encounters or with the consciously assumed shock of rediscovery and recognition. It is also true, however – and this is of great significance – that the aspect of the Primitive Cinema which may be said to have had the most 'success' among modernist film-makers of this later generation (and I say this even of those who may never have seen a film made before 1920) is one which never remotely interested any film-maker at all, I believe until the painter Andy Warhol turned to film (although I am, of course, confining my frame of reference to the cinema of the West: Japanese films from the 1930s would belie this statement). I am referring to what I will call here the Primitive camera stare, epitomized in the films of Lumière and his cameramen but apparent in the fictional Primitive film as well (in, for example, *Kentucky Feud*).

To what extent is P. Adams Sitney's recognition of Lumière as a distant 'precursor' of the so-called 'structural film'[10] – from Warhol to Gehr, let us say – actually the recognition of a larger affiliation, between the Primitive Mode proper and what is still today, I take it, the dominant attitude in the avant-garde film?

It was the successive effacement of the major traits of the Primitive Mode – the autarchy and the a-centric quality of its image, the exteriority of the spectatorial Subject and the non-closure of the filmic commodity – which in my view made possible the constitution of an Institutional Mode founded on an indefinitely extensible diegetic space-time, on the centred organization of the image (and later of sound), on camera identification and the presence of the filmic persona and on the closure of the film as a consumable, throw-away product. And it is not difficult to demonstrate, in the light of these mutually exclusive models, that many of the major gestures of today's modernist cinema – and I do mean the gestures, not necessarily the work – have been objectively aimed at *reversing* the changes that took place after 1905.

The Warhol camera which in *Chelsea Girls* typically remains staring into space, unable or unwilling to move, when a character goes out of shot is behaving after all like the camera of Méliès, which Georges Sadoul likened to the eye of 'that gentleman in the stalls who never once thought of getting a closer look at the leading lady's smile or following her into the dining room when she left the parlour'.[11]

When Barry Gerson says of his own films 'one part of the image is no more important than another part – the forms operate together – what is occurring on the left edge of the screen lives because of what occurs on the right edge, top edge, middle, etc.',[12] how can we not be reminded of the a-centric Primitive image and the topological reading which it required?

And here is a very choice example: Michael Snow's *A Casing Shelved* is actually a single colour-slide with an hour-long magnetic tape, but I share the view that in our context it is equivalent to a film performance, with 'the artist's voice, taped . . . cataloguing the objects, bringing them into our view, directing the spectator's eye in a reading of the image',[13] as Annette Michelson has described it. Here, the encounter with the Primitive model is spectacular, since the projected image of objects on shelves forcefully inscribes – though using very different means, of course – the Primitive exteriority of the spectatorial Subject, while the artist's voice on tape, reading that image and organizing those apparently disparate, 'meaningless' objects into an autobiographical narrative, recapitulates almost literally the Primitive lecturer's contradictory gesture, both linearizing and distancing.

However, having marked this clear affinity with the Primitive Mode, what, I wonder, have I actually said about these films? Have I not simply said what they are not and discovered that what they are *not*, the Primitive Cinema also was *not*, and said nothing, for example, about the elaborate and comprehensive work of testing the limits of diegesis that is to be found in the work of Michael Snow, or about the contradictory ideological implications of role-playing in Warhol, or about the significant role of the new drug culture in the emergence of an audience for these films, if not in the films themselves? Or have I not, rather, simply defined in the most general (or rather, pertinent) terms possible the conceptual framework which so much of the recent avant-garde has laid out for itself, a framework which not too surprisingly is definable, it appears, in terms of the 'interface' between the Primitive and Institutional Modes. For, the films mentioned here are limit instances. Their chief privative traits serve to define a 'space' within which has evolved much of the significant modernist film-making in the USA and Europe over the past fifteen or twenty years. But the limitations of this 'discovery' must be clearly perceived, in order for the usefulness of such an insight, to theoreticians and film-makers, to grow.

I know of only three modernist films which, in recognition of this affinity, have explicitly engaged with Primitive Cinema. In *After Lumière*, Malcolm LeGrice stages a series of black-and-white variations on *l'Arroseur Arrosé*, seemingly stressing the mechanical, exterior nature of narrative in that archetypal film-gag. The ensuing shift to a colour shot of a woman playing the piano music which has accompanied the previous variations opens up an interesting reflection on the role of music in bridging the gap between spectatorial and diegetic space in early film history.

Both Ken Jacobs and Ernie Gehr have engaged directly with Primitive films as 'found objects' which can be said to have stimulated the sense of recognition in question here. Jacobs's choice of *Tom Tom the Piper's Son* (1905), a film from the mature Primitive Era, is of considerable interest from my heuristic viewpoint. The film's rigorous respect of the 'rule' that all characters must enter and leave a shot before it may end, originally a sign of the chase film's attachment to the autarchy of the Lumière tableau, was ambivalent at this late date, and verged, I believe, on parody. The film's stiff frontality, and highly mechanized gags, appear almost as a last, half-sophisticated, indulgence in the 'child's play' of the Primitive Era before Biograph was to get down to the serious business that began with Griffith. It is of course with the future course of film history that Ken Jacobs's work on this film engages directly, through his re-filming procedures. The opening shot of the film, so typically Primitive in that its narrative substance is totally unreadable for the modern eye at first viewing, is analysed in a way that is evocative – though only evocative – of the linearizing editing procedures of the Institution, so that it becomes readable on second viewing. Here, I feel, is a wonderful example of a combination of work and play on the materials of a crucial historical process.

In contrast to the complexity of Jacobs's film – addressed as much, I realize, to the synchronic paradigm of film production as to the diachronic – Ernie Gehr's more recent *Eureka*, by its very simplicity, points up admirably the ambivalence, and indeed certain illusory aspects, of the parallel between the Primitive and the modernist. This film, which Gehr painstakingly stretched to many times its original length, again by a process of re-filming, was, in all likelihood, made to be shown in the mock Pullman coaches of Hales' Tours, already described. It was shot from the front of a Market Street cable car in San Francisco and shows the long approach to the Ferry Building. As I have indicated, its existence corresponds to a need felt at the time to create conditions for *penetration* into the motion picture image a good ten years before this could be achieved by editing and camera placement, and by the establishment of theatres which were dark, quiet and comfortable enough to create the conditions for a symbolical voyage, rather than a simulated one.

Gehr extracts the main visual component – the film – from a context which can be described as a form of synesthetic illusionism – in some instances, fans blew air and even smoke through coaches which swayed and creaked like those of a real train. In his appropriation, he takes images which, though they follow the Lumière model, were no longer viewed as were the original Lumière films, but were experienced as part of a physical environment – and proceeds, indeed, to reverse an historical process, restoring to those images that alienness which Gorky had felt ten years earlier. In fact, as one watches, or tries to watch, that swarming, uncentred, 'unreadable' frame, one seems to hear Gorky's voice: 'This is not life, but its shadow, this is not movement but its soundless spectre.'[14] And of course, for modern anti-illusionism such a statement is not a lament.

Now, as Peter Wollen had occasion to point out a number of years ago,[15] there have been, in the 1960s and 1970s, two avant-gardes, one resolutely placing itself outside the Institution – and largely outside history – in an 'anti-narrative' perspective, the other working on the fringes of the Institution, in both the aesthetic and economic sense, addressing itself to the Institution explicitly – and often, as well, to the social system which fostered the Institution's growth and maintains its power. This latter avant-garde, mainly European, has incorporated into its critical arsenal strategies which clearly hark back to the Primitive Era. In my opinion, these strategies, on the whole, reflect a much higher degree of historical responsibility than any such in the former of the two avant-gardes, wholly American, where the work, with all its enormous artistic importance, usually seems to have taken place somewhere in the Platonic firmament of Form and Perception.

Jean-Luc Godard's use of frontality – in the sense both of setting his camera up perpendicularly to a wall, for example, and of having his actors play to the camera – has been much discussed. I simply wish to stress here that this encounter with the Primitive Mode is far from being historically uninformed, as is evidenced by the scene in one of his most radically frontal films, *La Chinoise*, where the characters discuss the respective roles in film history of Méliès and Lumière.

But I would like to mention three other, lesser-known instances, from France, Spain and Belgium, where the issues implicit in the confrontation between the Primitive and Institutional Modes play a central role. Jackie Raynal's *Deux Fois*, which has been extensively analysed by the Camera Obscura Collective,[16] is in my view an important meditation on several important aspects of Institutional representation. Its almost literal use of the Lumière model (long, uncentred Barcelona street scenes, in particular, all the more panoramic as they are filmed in Cinemascope) provides a kind of point zero from which such elementary but primary issues as the extension of diegetic space-time and the exchanges of the gaze can be explored.

In the Spanish film-maker Paulino Viota's still little-known *Contactos*, which I continue to regard as one of the most important European films of the past decade, Primitive stare is conscripted into a representational and narrative system based upon a radical de-centring. For example, an exchange of a few words between two revolutionary activists working in a restaurant is buried, as it were, in the comings and goings of waiters and waitresses through the kitchen door, as the camera stares at this uncentred work activity for several minutes on end.

Chantal Ackerman's masterful meditation on a woman's alienation, *Jeanne Dieleman*, may be said to be an almost systematic tribute to the Primitive stare, reproduced often with extraordinary fidelity under its two major aspects: the medium long shot, filmed from a position rigorously perpendicular to a wall; and the frontal medium close-up of a person seated behind a table, facing the camera, 'doing something' (whether it was the Lumières' baby eating breakfast or Dranhem kneading dough and reciting his monologue, *The Baker*.) Furthermore, direct matching – inconceivable in the Primitive Cinema and indispensable to the principle of camera ubiquity in the Institution – is studiously avoided. The association of these attitudes produces one of the most distanced narrative films of recent years – re-creating to a large extent the conditions of exteriority of the Primitive Mode (the sparseness of speech seems to be a further contributing factor here) – positioning the spectator once again in his seat, hardly able because hardly enabled to embark upon that imaginary journey through diegetic space-time to which we are so accustomed and obliged ultimately to reflect on what is seen rather than merely experience it.

It may have seemed at times that my presentation here was over-polemical. This is because I feel that there has been a tendency in the past – and perhaps not only in the past – to oversimplify the significance of our responses to those strange objects which are happily encountered in some archive and which are 'signed' 'Lumière', 'Méliès' or 'Zecca' (though never, perhaps, was the concept of authorship so irrelevant to an understanding of films than with those of the Primitive Era). A tendency in particular to regard the Primitive Cinema as a Lost Paradise wherein 'our' values thrived before being subverted by the Demon Narrative has helped at times to reinforce a dichotomous, indeed Manichaean, view of film history and film aesthetics which has only served to cloud our understanding of the filmic experience in our society, determined essentially, after all, by fifty years experience of the Institutional Mode of Representation. The Institution is in us and we are in it, and it has been the scene of practices of immense importance, both artistic and societal.

This dichotomous ideology – the Institution as Bad Object, primitivism and modernism as Good Objects – has also given rise to the idea that film history might have been – that is, should have been – different somehow, and that the Muses were only waiting for the New American Cinema to come along and set cinema back on the path of adventure from which it had veered when the shadow of Griffith fell upon it. I am afraid I can only describe such a viewpoint as childish.

As for the theoretician wishing to elucidate the Institutional experience – to clarify its origins, its growth and its transformations, and the relationships of all these to the contest for social control in our societies – it appears necessary for him to deal with early cinema not only as a meta-discourse about filmic process – and here the perspective offered by modernism is of value – but also in terms of its actual insertion into history, no matter how many unanswered, and perhaps unanswerable, questions such an approach may raise. As I said earlier, it is essential to try at least to hold onto both ends of the chain.

Notes

1. Marey, preface to Trutat, *Les photographies animée* (Paris, 1899).
2. Vertov, *Articles, journaux, projets* (Paris, U.G.E., 1972), pp. 61-62.
3. Fred J. Balshofer and Arthur C. Miller, *One Reel a Week* (Berkeley, University of California Press, 1967), p. 3.
4. Jonas Mekas, *Movie Journal, The Rise of the New American Cinema 1959-1971* (New York, MacMillan, 1972), p. 230.
5. Quoted in Jay Leyda, *Kino* (London, Allen and Unwin, 1973), p. 408.
6. A comprehensive survey of even the visual dimension of the Institutional Mode and its development over the thirty-five years that preceded the coming of sound lies outside the scope of this paper, although I will be led to mention certain aspects of it. See my book *La Lucarne de l'Infini* (*Life to Those Shadows*).
7. P. Adams Sitney (ed.), *Film Culture Reader* (New York, Praeger, 1970), p. 402.

8. Georges Sadoul, *Histoire Générale du Cinéma*, vol. II (Paris, Ed. Denoël, 1973), p. 187.
9. *The Blood of a Poet, a film by Jean Cocteau*, trans. Lily Pons (New York, Bodley Press, 1949), p. 52.
10. P. Adams Sitney, 'Structured Film', *Film Culture*, ed. P. Adams Sitney (London, Secker & Warburg, 1971), p. 329.
11. Sadoul, *op. cit.*, p. 141.
12. *Film Culture* No. 63-64, 1977, p. 115.
13. Annette Michelson, 'Towards Snow', *Artforum*, July 1971.
14. Leyda, *op. cit.*, p. 407.
15. 'Godard and Counter-Cinema: *Vent d'est*', *Afterimage*, no. 4, 1972. See also Peter Wollen, 'The Two Avant-Gardes', *Studio International*, December 1975. Both these essays have been reprinted in the collection of Peter Wollen's writings, *Readings and Writing: Semiotic Counter-Strategies* (London, New Left Books and Verso, 1982).
16. *Camera Obscura*, no. 1, Autumn 1976.

1987

This essay, the only one in this collection to have been originally written in English, was first given, in a slightly modified form, as a lecture at the Whitney Museum, New York City, in November 1979 as part of a series on primitive cinema and the avant-garde. It was later published in an anthology of criticism edited by Philip Rosen entitled *Narrative, Apparatus, Ideology*.

I had been engaged in a desultory flirtation with the so-called 'New American Cinema' for over fifteen years, under the guiding auspices of P. Adams Sitney and Annette Michelson. The adepts of New York modernism were no doubt distressed to find that the only piece of writing ever to emanate from those hours of privately arranged screenings of the films they championed so fervently took the latter merely as illustrations for a metalinguistic, historiographic approach to the institutional cinema which most of them so heartily despised.

Now that the 1960s, when the most exciting work of Brakhage, Warhol, Snow and others was accomplished, are far behind us, it seems clear that very little is left of that attempt to conscript film into the modernist logic except precisely what those films tell us about the nature of the real institution, and about the isolation of the American community of artists from their society and from the world at large.

9 A Dissentient Cinema?

At a time when the audio-visual industries of Western Europe are obliged to carry on a desperate struggle to preserve their individual identities against the invasion of North American models, it is important to recall that this struggle has a distinguished antecedent which left an indelible mark on a major national cinema: that of Japan.

Cinema as we know it was the end-product of an evolution in the realm of both the technological and the imaginary that took place in countries whose colonial expansion was, at the very moment of cinema's birth, in full swing. The new invention immediately spread to what was not yet called the 'Third World'. The bringing back of exotic images to Europe, both to impress the popular masses who would never visit those climes and to entice potential immigrants (and wealthy globe-trotters), was a prime concern of the Lumière Company. And indeed, it was through one of Lumière's cameramen-projectionists that cinema first came to Japan, in 1897.

All the great nations of the East are rightfully proud of the longevity of their motion picture traditions, which go back to 1908 in China, 1913 in India and 1918 in Egypt. However, these countries were all more or less subject to European domination, and their film industries developed under the aegis of Western investors and technicians. Japan, at the beginning of this century, was the only major non-Western country never to have known the yoke of imperialism, thanks to a shrewd policy of selective opening/assimilation practised for half a century by the rulers of a populous, warlike nation, whose conquest would have been difficult and whose commerce was highly desirable.

While each national cinema of the East developed from the very outset themes, genres and subject matter derived from its own cultural traditions, the exceptional situation of Japan among the non-Western nations had unique consequences at the most basic level of film 'language', allowing Japan to develop, in the long run, forms and styles that were peculiarly her own.

Cinema's classical system for representing 'narrative space-time' – with its match-cuts, its elisions, its dialectics of continuity and discontinuity, of the part and the whole – is today an integral component of what Christian Metz was the first to designate the 'Cinema Institution', in the East as well as the West. This system has been hegemonic in the West ever since the film was first endowed with lip-synch sound – the keystone of an edifice that had been thirty-five years in the building. There is good reason to believe that for those non-Western cinemas whose films, during those same decades, were made largely by European and North American technicians, or by native technicians trained in Western methods, the system of representation dominant in the West came to impose itself simultaneously as it grew to perfection in our own studios.

Yet nothing of the sort occurred in Japan. In keeping with the method employed throughout the period of assimilation of Western industrial technology, the Japanese sent the foreign specialists home as soon as they had learnt how to operate the cameras and to develop and print film. Soon the aspiration towards autonomy was carried to the point of manufacturing film-stock (and even cameras). Thus the Japanese cinema soon became the only non-Western film industry to function quite independently of the Euro-American powers, and continued to do so for nearly half a century. To what has been said, one needs to add an important historical reminder: thanks to the long, 'conservational' isolationism associated with the reign of the Tokugawas (1663–1867) and to the nature of the compromise between the aristocracy and the rising bourgeoisie which averted any revolutionary rupture and resulted in a certain opening up of the country and a degree of modernization under the Emperor Meiji (1867–1912), Japan kept alive, down to the most minute details of everyday life, systems of representation and an aesthetics which had remained remarkably unified and remarkably unchanged for over a thousand years.

As far as it is possible to judge from the few surviving examples, the 'language' of the primitive Japanese cinema (1897–1910) was approximately that of the West for the same time-frame: eye-level camera placement, a fairly wide angle shot with the camera motionless and the action taking place originally in a single shot and subsequently – but already a bit later than in the West – in a succession of autarchic tableaux. In France, in England, and in the United States especially, there began around 1908-10 a process of replacing this *primitive mode of representation*, all traces of which were to have disappeared by around the mid-1920s. By contrast, it is no exaggeration to say that in Japan this system was to remain dominant throughout the 1920s and that important traces of it were to subsist until at least the end of the Second World War.

Besides its specific visual traits – frontality, shot-size and separateness of the successive tableaux – the primitive cinema of the West share a trait with the silent cinema of Japan as a whole which was, as it were, the nerve-centre of a mode of representation specific to the films of that country, at least until the imposition of bourgeois democracy in 1945. I refer to the use of a *lecturer*, whose presence beside the screen, more or less frequent from year to year and from one country to another, could have been observed practically everywhere in the West until around 1912. This lecturer took the form in Japan of the *benshi*, who was *universally* present in Japanese cinemas from the beginnings of the Japanese film, and who was not relegated to film museums and societies[1] until the final 'Westernization' of the Japanese cinema under the US occupation.[2]

The *benshi* descends directly from a number of recitational arts that were still popular in Japan at the turn of the last century, among them *heike biwa* – vocalized narratives accompanied on a sort of lute – and *gidayu bushi* – the 'expressionist' chanting which accompanies the solemn gesticulations of the giant *bunraku* dolls. It is therefore not surprising that the institution of the *benshi* rapidly acquired such great importance and that around 1920 the stars of the screen were far less popular than these 'stars of the hall'.

Is it not obvious that the presence – for more than thirty years – of that voice in front of the screen which narrated and commented upon the film with artfulness and authority could not have failed to have had a decisive impact on the very nature of the film performance in Japan? And is it not obvious that this holdover from the *presentational* arts of a feudal society within an art whose occidental, bourgeois vocation was to attain the summits of *representationalism* could not have helped but divert for a time the Japanese cinema from that Western path? In other words, is it not obvious that it was this presence of the *benshi* – and through him of a long cultural tradition – which 'retarded the development' of the Japanese cinema, to use the kind of phrase found under the pen of many a historian – retarded, that is, the naturalization in Japan of the techniques of *découpage* developed in the West? Indeed, a cinema whose narrative dimension *resides outside the film* has no need to subordinate the discourse of the images to the discourse of narrativity: it has no need to impose upon the audience a univocal reading of the moving pictures.

The gradual development in Europe and the United States of the classical language of editing – with its matches of continuity and orientation, with its condensation of real time into narrative time – corresponds to a search both for a certain linearization of the image and of the narrative and for a certain *centring* of the spectator, whom the classical film addresses *as an individual only*. Totally different is the approach of *kabuki, bunraku* and the other theatre arts which, in Japan, presided over the cradle of cinema and which addressed themselves to a public *that was conscious of itself as a collectivity*, in images which were anything but linear. Now, the linearization of the Western cinema – in particular through the fragmentation of the primitive tableau into montage pieces and the successive presentation of signifiers previously seen only in a simultaneous confusion – as well as through the imaginary centring of the spectator – were the corner-stones of an 'illusionism' which originated in Renaissance painting and in the drama and novel of the bourgeoisie. This fundamentally Western approach is at the opposite pole to all of the theatre arts of the Orient, Japan included, which are basically non-linear and anti-illusionist. These were the arts wherein Brecht encountered distancing effects in a 'natural' state, so to speak; where Eisenstein found examples of materialist montage.

Those who view the slow, belated accession of Japanese cinema to classical editing as an example of cultural backwardness display, even in the case of Japanese historians, a crude occidento-centrism. Rather, one needs to realize that for some three decades, traditional Japanese society sought, with considerable success on the whole, to *conscript* cinema into the nation's array of traditional arts, which by that time had entered into their historic decline. And it was this effort that was to give rise for over a decade (1930–1943) to the richest and most original national cinema of its day.

However, we must hasten to add that traditional Japanese society in that first third of the twentieth century consisted by and large of the country's most reactionary forces. And that this effort of conscription, which was actually quite paralysing during the 1920s because overly mechanistic, and which was to bear such splendid fruits during the 1930s and early 1940s, was nonetheless directed, to a large extent, *against* the nation's most progressive elements.

It was no accident that the first concerted effort to Westernize the Japanese cinema took place at the end of the First World War, in which Japan had scarcely played any role at all, but whose aftermath she was to experience in much the same way as war-torn Europe: economic crisis and the intensification of the class struggle. Nor was it accidental that this effort was made by liberals and progressives for whom Western 'film language' carried the essential message of a democratic and enlightened West. It is no exaggeration to say that the defeat of this artistic tendency prefigured that bloody débâcle, a few years later, of the social and political forces whose representative it was. And it is important to underline here the rigour with which the North American occupation from 1945 to 1950 was to root out, in the name of democratization, everything which ressembled, however remotely, 'feudal' culture. Even today, one will often encounter, among Japanese liberals and progressives, an immense distrust of that pre-war cinema, in which feudal values weighed so heavily on both form and content.

There is no doubt whatsoever that the first Japanese film-makers carefully observed the advances made by 'film language' in the West. When they began to adopt certain Western techniques – close-up, cut-in/cut-back, shot-reverse-shot (more as privileged stylistic elements than as figures of 'ordinary speech'[3]) – the Japanese displayed perfect mastery of them. But when, following the success in Japan of *Intolerance* in 1919, American and European films began to be imported in large numbers, the same audiences which gave them a warm welcome were very reticent towards the Westernized films made in Japan. It would also appear that such films were only marginal to the bulk of production until the end of the 1920's. It is true that they often evoked social realities that might have appeared embarrassing to some and irksome to many others. But it is also certain that the persistence of an 'archaic' mode of expression – with the *benshi* and with an acting style, make-up, narratives, and genres which derived more or less directly from the various traditional forms of theatre (*shimpa, shin-kabuki* and even *kabuki* itself) – was overdetermined by mass cultural preferences which embraced a conception of representation at the opposite poles to that which reached its ultimate form in the Western film.

Of the two samples of a Westernized cinema that have come down to us from the early 1920s, neither can be said to be a carbon copy. *Souls on the Road* (Murata and Osanai, 1921) makes use of the system of cross-cutting popularized by Griffith, but in a spirit of *excess* which conjures up the Japanese approach to Westernness in general, characterized by a tendency to aestheticize that which in the West was of a purely functional order. In a cinema where the intertitle was still rare, the makers of this film introduced a plethora of titles which carry over onto the screen the *benshi*'s verbiage (interestingly enough, it resembles an exaggerated version of Western titling between 1905 and 1914 or so, which itself derived from the practice of lecturing). We are no doubt dealing here with an attempt to steal the *benshi*'s thunder and reduce him to silence.

    Winter Camellias (Inoue, 1921) on the contrary, relied almost entirely on the *benshi*, with rudimentary editing and a few intertitles, often with a purely phatic function. Here, the Westernness lay in the fact that a woman played the main role (at a time when the *oyama* or female impersonator was still the rule, just as he was in *kabuki* and *shimpa*), as well as in the theme of class conflict.

    A few years later, the two masterpieces of Kinugasa in the Western manner – *Kurutta Ippeiji* (*Page of Madness*, 1926) and *Jujiro* (*Crossroads*, 1928) – formalized even further their approach to the Western system, coming (fortuitously?) close to certain experiments carried out in France, Germany and the Soviet Union on the fringes of the Institution and little or not at all known in Japan at the time. If we are to judge by the small number of films or fragments of films that have survived, it was by around 1928 that a number of directors – Makino Shozo, Futugawa Montabe and also no doubt Ozu and Mizoguchi – acquired a credible mastery of the Western system. And it was soon afterwards that there took place the decisive encounter between the frozen Japanese tradition and a Western mode of representation which, after the creative explosion

Kurutta Ippeiji (Page of Madness, Kinugasa, 1926)

Jujiro (Crossroads, Kinugasa, 1926)

of the 1920s, was becoming frozen in its own turn. This encounter was to produce, in Japan, a creative revolution as impressive in many respects as that which had just taken place in Europe.

It is quite deliberately that I refer here to an encounter between two modes of representation. True, a few directors active after 1930 – and they were by no means minor talents – immediately opted in favour of a thoroughly Western approach to film 'language' (Gosho, Shimazu, Inagaki, etc.). Others, however – often the same men who had precociously introduced the Western approach into Japan (Ozu, Shimizu, Naruse, Mizoguchi) – began to take increasingly crucial liberties with the Western norms. And these would ultimately come to constitute at once a carry-over and a renewal of Japanese 'primitivism' rather than a mere stylistic variant on the Western system, such as was the case with German Expressionism and French 'Impressionism'.[4]

Let us first try to identify the most basic (and perhaps the most prevalent) traits of the Japanese films of the 1930s. For while Ozu, Mizoguchi, Naruse, Shimizu, Yamanaka and Ishida must certainly be recognized for the great 'auteurs' which they were, their work must also be understood in terms of what it owed to their period and to their shared culture. It is in this sense that, however individual the stylistics of each, taken separately, all of these directors' work adheres, at a certain level, to the approach which underlies a film like Toyoda's *Iguisu* (*The Nightingale*, 1939) and is fundamentally at odds with, say, Uchida's *Keisatsukan* (*Police*, 1932), whose language conforms in every way to that which was current in the West at the time.

The main traits of the Japanese cinema of the 1930s derive, then, quite directly, from the 'neo-primitive' cinema of the previous decade, but also[5] from literary, artistic and ceremonial traditions that go back much further, and in which the 'primitivism' of the earliest Japanese cinema might be said to be ultimately grounded.

The formal trait that was most commonly shared by the film's of this Golden Age, both 'serious' and 'standard-commercial', is the inordinate length of shots, both temporally and spatially. It reflects the relative reluctance of directors to resort to editing in general and to the close-up in particular. It is almost as if these film-makers, whose images had for so long been relieved of the burden of storytelling by the *benshi*, did not feel themselves under any greater obligation to resort to editing now that the actors had the power of speech, now that the Word had climbed onto the screen, so to speak: for them, words were still part of the off-screen world, they were independent of the imagery. Nor must we forget that neither Ozu nor Naruse made talking pictures until 1936, when their neo-traditionalist visual styles had reached maturity, whilst Mizoguchi and Gosho, having tried out the new medium around 1930, returned to the silent film for several years.

Of course, it must be granted that the principle, inherited from the previous era, of showing a substantial dialogue scene in a single long take, with little or no camera movement, quickly verges on academicism – the historical tendency of oriental art. And in contrast with the plodders of traditionalism, it is clear that the directors who opted uncompromisingly for the Western style of *découpage* often brought to their films an exceptional social, psychologial or poetic dimension (one thinks of Gosho or Shimazu). However, neo-traditionalism bore far more spectacular fruit, especially when it was fertilized, as in the case of the above-mentioned masters, by experience of the Western system. When Mizoguchi, for example, began to abandon Western-style *découpage* – around 1933, and in any case, between *Tokyo koshin kyoku* (*Tokyo March*, 1929) and *Taki no shiraito* (*White Threads of the Waterfall*, 1933) – he developed an approach to the single-shot sequence which did have certain affinities with the practices, during the same period, of Pabst or Renoir, but which *denaturalized* this technique through the recomposition and the stylization of the successive movements and framings.

Japanese critics habitually characterize their two greatest pre-war masters, Ozu and Mizoguchi, as being the exponents of editing and of 'non-editing' (which they call '*photogénie*') respectively. And it it patent that Ozu, when he developed, around 1933, the system of *découpage* which in essence was to be his until his death in 1962, absorbed elements of Western editing, in particular shot-reverse-shot. However, at the same time, he began systematically to use the 'incorrect' eyeline match, denaturalizing that standard procedure which, in the classical system, ensured the biological and imaginary centring of the spectator-as-individual.[6]

In addition, Ozu adopted a strategy of frontality and pictorial flatness which was equally remote from the norms of Western cinema, and this in spite of his experience as an occidentalist and his lasting attachment to the work of certain Euro-American directors (Ophuls and Lubitsch, for example). However, the distance that separates Ozu from the classical cinema of the West – indicated by the fact that his films were not known to us at all until the 1960s – is not a narrowly visual matter. It is overdetermined by the ceremonial implications of his very low camera placement and by his elimination (total from 1936 until after the war) of camera movement, both of which suggest the famous *cha no yu* or tea ceremony. It is due also to the celebrated emblematic cutaways, which are reminiscent of a technique used in classical poetry (the pillow-word or *makura kotoba*) and which tend to suspend the diegetic process itself; to those tenuously poetic narratives which call to mind texts as old as the *Genji Monogatari*; and to that strange divorce which the director achieves between the dialogue narration and the flow of images which in themselves tell no tale whatsoever – a divorce which evokes the *bunraku*, and the cinema of the *benshi*.

What further places a great many Japanese directors of that era, including some of the most Westernized (for example, Gosho), at odds with Western norms is their constant harking back to the mood of traditional Japanese literature. The *shomin-geki*, a film genre which deals with the urban petty bourgeoisie, was generally of a quotidian naturalism that would have thoroughly bored the vast majority of Western audiences (and if the minority of sympathetic *cognoscenti* among us has grown larger today, it still remains an extremely small one).

In the work of Shimizu, one of the most austere of the neo-traditionalists, this naturalism is sometimes accompanied by a formalization of the narrative that evokes Saikaku's extraordinary story-chains, with their *haiku*-like structures. And one could continue for many pages enumerating the beauties of these films which set them so firmly apart from the films of the West – a task which I have carried further elsewhere.[7]

Yet however splendid this renewal of artistic traditions which often date back to a time before the Tokugawa era, we cannot ignore its ideological resonances.

In 1931, Japan invaded and conquered Manchuria. In answer to

Gonin no Sekkohei (Five Scouts, Tasaka, 1938)

Tsuchi to heitai (Earth and Soldiers, Tasaka, 1939)

a chorus of international protest, she withdrew from the League of Nations. The country was swept by a wave of national-chauvinism, and the democratic façade that had been adopted for a time by a ruling class with an age-old authoritarian tradition was beginning to show ugly cracks. This was reflected in neo-traditionalist film-making. True enough, Ozu, for example, in his youth, had had progressive leanings. In 1933 and 1934 he made films which dealt quite unambiguously with such themes as the oppression of women or the tragedy of unemployment – *Tokyo no onna* (*Women of Tokyo*), *Tokyo no yado* (*An Inn in Tokyo*). But in these same films, he also inaugurated his aesthetic system which can already be seen to carry within it the seeds of a certain backward looking passivism. And after 1936, in films that were increasingly accomplished, he became the champion of the traditional family, that pillar of the militarist, proto-fascist regime that was tightening its grip on Japanese society.

As for Mizoguchi, his remarkably progressive views on women,[8] especially prominent in *Taki no shiraito* (1933), *Gion no Kyodai* (*The Gion Sisters*, 1936) and *The Naniwa Elegy* (1936) did not prevent him from participating directly in the imperialist effort as early as 1932 (*Mam-Mo kenkoku no reimei* (*The Dawn of the Foundation of Manchukuo and Mongolia*)) or from contributing brilliantly, albeit ineffectually, to the official propaganda campaign during the Pacific War, with that splendid celebration of every traditional value *Genroku Chushingura* (1943), known in the West as *The Forty-Seven Ronin*.

Another neo-traditional master, Shimizu, had placed his poetic naturalism at the service of the regime's propaganda as early as 1939, with a film on the pre-military training of high-school students which takes the form of a 'chain-poem' very much in the manner of Saikaku.

But the most spectacular locus of convergence between the neo-traditionalist school and the reactionary regime of the period is to be found in the war-films that crowned the career of Tasaka Tomotaka between 1938 and 1943 (*Five Scouts, Earth and Soldiers*, etc.)[9]. These films display an ultra-documentary, objectivist spareness which excludes dramatization and, to a considerable extent, editing itself (witness the slow destruction, in long shot, of a Chinese farmhouse in *Earth and Soldiers* or the long, static views of the fort at night in *Five Scouts*). These films are like a condensed run-down of the most prevalent traits of the films of the preceding decade, in the service of a subtle ideology which presents war as dirty work that one has to slog through, for Emperor and Nation.[10]

Here, finally then, is a confirmation *a contrario* of the thesis – shared by many progressive Japanese critics – of an obejctive collusion between the most creative tendency of the cinema of the 1930s and the regime which was rising to hegemony. The works of the most politically conscious film-makers, even when they did contain traditional elements (see especially those of Naruse around 1936), all tended towards a Westernized stylistics, sometimes in lieu of an active political involvement and sometimes in conjunction with one (for example, Itami and, above all, Yamanaka, who paid for his political commitment with his life). As with the occidentalists of the early 1920s, it was understood by these film-makers with democratic aspirations that the analytic language of Western editing was a better vehicle for ideas of social change and criticism than the traditionally formalized pictorialism.

The end of the war marked the decline, if not the demise, of neo-traditional cinema. It is true that when Ozu returned to the studios in 1946, after a silence of several years, he remained faithful to the letter of his system, making absolutely no concessions to the new norms which the occupying power sought to impose and with which most younger directors were prepared to comply. And Naruse, although he had already for some time abandoned such neo-traditional idiosyncrasies as the eyeline mismatch and the Ozu-like cutaway (see *Tsuma yo bara no yo ni – Wife Be Like a Rose*, 1936), continued to cling to the naturalistic intimism of *shomin-geki*, spurning Western narrative models. Mizoguchi, however, whilst preserving the principle of the pictorial single-take sequence in his *jidai geki* (costume dramas), considerably relaxed the rigours of his technique, which became more organic and less formal. By his own admission, he was seeking to prove that he could vie with Wyler and Welles, whose prowess with the long take was known in Japan soon after the end of the war, thanks to the 'cultural' effort of the occupation authorities, eager to provide the Japanese masses with 'democratic' (that is, American) models. Furthermore, the contemporary melodramas which he shot during that period all defer, in more or less classical ways, to the canon of Western editing.

It is, moreover, no accident that around 1950 Japanese films (*Rashomon, The Gate of Hell*, et al.) began to win awards in international festivals – awards which their predecessors no doubt deserved more. Indeed, Japanese directors had at last learned to make films whose Japanese character could be perceived in the West as exotic rather than as a 'thing' from outer space.

Indeed, with the exception of a few back-sliders, all Japanese directors fell pretty much into step with Europe and the USA, from out-and-out progressives, like Imai, Yamamoto Satsuo and Yamamura So, to conservatives like the veteran specialist of *chambera* (sword-fight films) Ito Daisuke, and including such middle-of-the-roaders as Kinoshita and Gosho. Editing was finally granted its 'normal' status, the long take fell out of fashion, and a certain static, elegant pictorialism, while still present often enough in *jidai geki*, was replaced in modern-dress films by a dynamism imitated from Hollywood or occasionally from Soviet formalism during its heyday.

Of course, it would be foolish to claim that the greatest post-war master, Kurosawa, even during his 'neo-realist' period (1945-49), did no more than copy the Hollywood codes. Within the framework of the 'classical language', he developed a system which was extraordinarily Japanese in its 'artificiality', in the way in which it took on board, unabashed, a certain *stylistic visibility*, foregrounding the 'work of the signifier'. We find a similar approach in the work of a lesser talent like Ichikawa Kon. And it was through the examples of these two and of a few others that the sensibilities of the next generation of directors were to be fashioned – those of Oshima, Teshigahara, Hani, Yoshida and Matsumoto, who called upon even more violent traditions to create a 'baroque radicalism' which was as specifically Japanese, in its way, as had been the stylistics of Ozu.

Of course, the theories that underpinned the work of the 1960s rebels were often of European origin – derived from Freud, Sartre, Artaud, Brecht. But the de-centred, eccentric pictorialness and the privileged role of the wide-angle shot refer back to the pre-war *jidai geki*, often quite 'wild' in their own right, in a spirit which derives, I believe, from certain aspects of *kabuki* (and perhaps from the comic interludes known as '*kyogen*'). And when Oshima or Yoshida carried out experiments in eccentric editing, it was less, perhaps, by reference to Eisenstein than to the sword-play films (*chambera*) of the 1920s.

Today, it seems, the tendency is towards a greater and greater convergence. The only responses to the growing domination of Western (Hollywood) models offered by young Japanese directors seem to be those suggested by the most cosmopolitan modernism or mannerism. Does the future hold in store any reaction of a different kind? Let us hope that the price to pay will not be a rebirth of the exacerbated nationalism that produced the great films of the 1930s. And yet, sometimes the pride of a people can provide fertile soil indeed.

Notes

1. It is perhaps significant that the Japanese still today regard the *benshi* as a natural accompaniment to silent films, whereas in the West, any attempt to revive the lecturer for a presentation of *La Mort du Duc de Guise* at the Cinémathèque Française or of *The New York Hat* at The Museum of Modern Art would most certainly result in a riot.
2. In the years that followed the 1945 defeat, the penury of films, but also no doubt genuine cultural pressures from the social strata that were seeking diversion from the horrors of the present in the contemplation of a happier past, prompted the re-issue of silent films with the addition of a narration not unrelated to that of the *benshi*.
3. Makino's 1917 version of *Chushingura* involves the use of a single shot-reverse-shot figure at the moment of the crucial confrontation between Asano and Kira.
4. Insofar as these are *schools*: individual films like *Caligari* (Wiene, 1919) and *Rose-France* (L'Herbier, 1919) do involve fundamental departures of this sort, I believe.
5. As was recognized, fifty years ago, by the celebrated critic Katumoto Seiitiro (*Japan Film Yearbook* (1937)). Needless to say, this progressive writer deplored the fact.
6. Indeed, the Institutional Mode of Representation organizes the montage fragments in accordance with a right-left logic homologous with that of the spectator's body as the centre of convergency of its unity.
7. Noël Burch, *To the Distant Observer*, Scolar Press and University of California Press, London and Berkeley, 1979.
8. A similar feminism characterized many intellectuals of the period. It was associated with a certain male masochism, a kind of chauvinism in reverse. The regime also propounded its own feminism. The militarist leaders were anxious to prepare women to abandon their domestic slavery and participate in the war effort.

9. The same Tasaka had developed, before 1930, a style close to one which was to appear in the work of Ozu only a few years later.
10. Margaret Mead was astonished by the contrast between these films, viewed in prints captured during the war, and the Western war films, with their melodramatic, sensationalist portrayal of war heroics.

1987

This essay, written five years after the publication of my book *To the Distant Observer* (1979) for a collective history of Japanese cinema to be published in Japan, was a welcome opportunity both to address a Japanese public still unfamiliar with my work on their national film history and to correct a few of what I now regard as the very serious distortions which my formalist bias left in a text that had taken up nearly seven years of my life. While it was impossible to correct the serious neglect in *To the Distant Observer* of the rich post-war years, when the establishment of bourgeois democracy in Japan was the occasion for young film-makers to explore themes that had previously been inaccessible to them, it was possible to suggest that the Japanese cinema of the 1930s did not exist in a complete vacuum and that the film-makers who sought to follow Western language models were not necessarily to be thrown onto the scrap heap of history.

This essay was originally written in French; the English translation here is my own.

Part III
Forward . . . and Not Forgetting

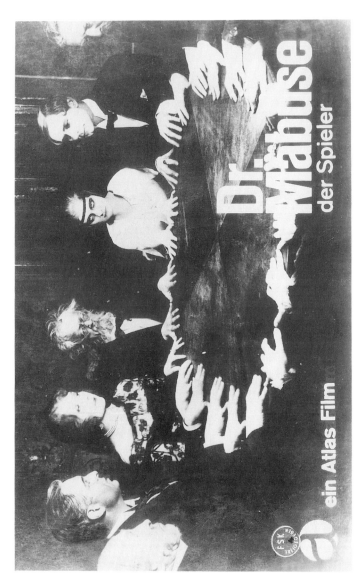

Doktor Mabuse der Spieler (Dr Mabuse the Gambler, Lang, 1922)

10 Notes on Fritz Lang's First *Mabuse*

'Surely,' I said to Hitch, 'we'll have to explain *somehow* why she's dumb, or the audience won't stand for it.' 'They'll stand for anything,' said Hitch, 'as long as you don't give them time to think.'   Rodney Ackland, *The Celluloid Mistress*

Fritz Lang's first great achievement, *Mabuse der Spieler*,[1] dates from 1922. It is a film which has always seemed to me to occupy a strategic position in film history. This impression originally stemmed from a very simple observation: in all of silent cinema, this film seems to have been the first to address itself directly to 'us' today, insofar as we are all 'average spectators'. I am referring to a phenomenon which is difficult to analyse, but which has been confirmed time and time again on the occasion of student screenings in both Europe and America. Whereas other key films of the period, signed 'Griffith' (*Broken Blossoms*), 'DeMille' (*Male and Female*), 'Murnau' (*Nosferatu*), or even 'Stroheim' (*Foolish Wives*), appear to almost anyone today as fundamentally *archaic*, *Mabuse*, though it may not seem as stylistically modern as L'Herbier's *L'Argent*, for example,[2] does seem amazingly close to our own *cine-dramaturgical space*, owing to the precision of its dramatizations, the subtlety of its characterizations and the multi-layered density of its script. It was to take several years, I should say, until this type of *presence* was to become a general phenomenon in Europe and the USA. In fact I am inclined to think that it did not become absolutely commonplace until the coming of synch sound, that every silent film – including, in this sense, the film we are concerned with here – keeps a certain distance from us, a distance inherent in the muteness of their images. However, it is also clear that this film reduces that distance by at least as much as any other silent film.

It might then seem a logical step to assert that this was the first film to conjugate all of the pertinent founding traits of the Cinema Institution qua system of representation – all except for those, of course, which are wholly determined by synch sound. But if, at one point in the past, I did not hesitate to take that step,[3] I have greater scruples today. Yet even if we are not dealing with a 'first' – at best a trivial notion, in my view – it appears to me increasingly evident that the undeniable precociousness of this achievement makes it a precious field of investigation for anyone seeking to understand the origins and the nature of *Institutional efficacy*.

This, however, is a considerable task, one which will yield all its implications only within the context of a broader undertaking, which I have been engaged upon for several years now with my friend Jorge Dana. The goal of this project is to lay bare the *genealogy* of film 'language' as instanced in classical cinema (I prefer to speak of an 'Institutional mode of representation').

The notes that follow, then, constitute only a preliminary attempt to inscribe *Mabuse* as 'end-result' – a temporary one, of course, in view of the decisive contribution of synch sound – but end-result all the same, given the relative historical autonomy of the silent cinema.

These notes are actually a re-writing of notes taken during an umpteenth viewing of the film's first part only. To have extended my note-taking to the second part – to which I do refer when necessary – would no doubt have been to add weight to these observations. However, I doubt that it would have basically affected the conclusions reached thus far.

Some of these observations and conclusions may also appear to belong rather to the category of codes peculiar to this film, rather than to the system upon which Institutional practice has rested for over fifty years. It seems to me, however, that while Lang's characteristic *clock-work* – for example, the sequence-changes through 'question-and-answer' as described below – may be more visible, more 'self-designating' than the equivalent articulations in, say, Hollywood *film noir* (which was to engulf Lang the exile), the distinction is solely quantative. True, such a statement as this remains to be demonstrated, as does the assertion that 'deceptive appearances', as discussed below, are central to the Institution as a whole. In speaking of the classical film in general, is it really legitimate to suggest that the symbolic mechanisms and underlying ideological gestics actually take precedence over the manifest content of the narrative, the surface logic of the plot?

Still, I invite anyone who grasped all the cogs of a plot such as that of Howard Hawks' film *The Big Sleep* at first viewing to please step forward. And I here refer to a film which was a box-office success in its time and still delights many an unsophisticated audience in film societies and repertoire houses. True, it is an extreme instance – as was *Mabuse* in its way – but I continue to believe that such instances merely make the general method more visible; they do not contradict it at any time.[4]

It should already be clear that I am trying to come to grips with this film at every level – here, in a somewhat random order, owing to my decision to publish these notes as they stand. I am attempting to shed light on symptomological traits at the levels of syntax and narrative construction, as well of those of ideology and of 'film language' history. The articulation between those levels will, I hope, belong to a future stage of the work in progress. For the moment, I will leave that task to my readers.

1. The set of photographs that Mabuse spreads out before him at the very beginning of the film has an emblematic density. We see the disguises which this master-gambler – or rather *games master*, for Mabuse gambles only when he is sure to win – will put on in the course of the film. Mabuse shuffles the photographs and chooses at random a disguise for that day's performance. But this is the only instance when the Doctor actually does invoke chance: it is partly for this reason that this moment is *outside the film*. The images that constitute this short prologue descend from techniques which date back prior to 1910: vignettes at the beginning or at the end of a film for the presentation of actors and the characters they portray. Here, in *Mabuse*, there is a reversal and even a subtle parody of this technique. Even if the spectator is unaware of the fact at that moment, the man who looks at the photographs and the man portrayed in them are one and the same, while the other major characters of the film are presented abruptly, 'naturally', without any of the 'oratorical' precautions of post-primitive cinema. Hence, from the outset, *Mabuse* is located at the most advanced point of classical narration in 1922 by *perverse allusion*.

2. The introductory shot of Mabuse merits consideration. Seated,

enthroned, he faces the camera in medium shot. Contrary to popular opinion, this type of image was one of the earliest known to cinema: it was the 'close-up' of primitive cinema, and was 'invented' by Louis Lumière in *Le Déjeuner de Bébé* (1896). But there is a difference: before 1905-6, the one or two actors portrayed in such an image usually looked directly at the camera, while Mabuse's look just misses it. (More on this later.) Frontality is nonetheless strongly predominant in this first part of the sequence. Then, when the Doctor turns towards his secretary/factotum Spoerri (located off-screen), he opens up a *space* behind and around him, where there seemed to be nothing more than the neutral background of the primitive equivalent. Thus, in a single shot, Lang 'says' where cinema has come from and what it has come to: the shot-reverse-shot that will follow between Spoerri and Mabuse is an admirable conclusion to such a 'demonstration'.

3. The exchange of dialogue-titles between Mabuse ('You've taken cocaine again') and Spoerri ('If you dismiss me, I'll blow out my brains') is an extraordinary example of semantic condensation. A master-slave relationship is established, whose homosexual dimensions are suggested also (thus Spoerri, by conventional standards, is a slave three times over, to Mabuse and to his two vices). In addition, as a subsidiary connotation of drugs, especially in that era, we know for certain now that we are inside the world of crime. The force of this emblem – for, like the photographs on the desk, this exchange too is an emblem, if not in exactly the same way – consists in an accumulation of bourgeois taboos (suicide constituting a third) and their condensation in a brief exchange of dialogue. Nowhere do these themes ever reappear explicitly, but this single moment is enough to establish their constant underlying presence.

4. Until Mabuse takes out his watch, we have seen only the enthronement of the puppet master or, better, of the dealer. The game begins when Mabuse glances at his watch (although what follows is still in a sense a prologue): an iris (the circular form of which rhymes with the shape of the watch) opens onto a train that rushes by below us (Mabuse looks down at the watch-face and the train): watch in hand, he dominates and

governs the world, not unlike the film director who directs shooting and montage with his chronometer. Indeed, until the appearance of von Wenck, Mabuse does rule 'the world'. Since nothing transpires independently of his desires, this part of the film objectifies the fantasy of Mabuse, and the fantasy that is Mabuse.

5. The various components of the machinery of the theft are enunciated before the fact (the assassin and his victim alone in the train compartment; the driver next to his car; the line-man at the top of his pole; and Mabuse himself). On another level, this is yet another prologue: the placing of the pawns. But these introductory devices, continuing throughout the first part of the film are *naturalized* – lose their mechanicalness – as they are embedded within a narrative. (Tiny irregularities cunningly inserted into the machinery contribute to this naturalization, e.g., the 'hesitation' in the montage pace between the cut from the assassin looking at his watch to the driver looking at his, or, on a different plane, George's hurting his hand as he leaps from the train after his crime.)

6. 'Bravo George', Mabuse's congratulations to his assistant, is the fourth title of the film. Each title has possessed great narrative density (the 'Banco' with which the man on the pole signals the success of the operation to Mabuse continues, of course, the metaphor of gambling, but also signals that the challenge has been made, that another game – the film – begins). Of the four titles seen so far, this 'Bravo George' is the most important. First, the title marks a contrast between the effeminate servant and the assassin, George, a strong, virile man. The male characters of the film are clearly divided into the weak and the strong, a thematic opposition at work throughout the film. Second, this is the only instance in the film where Mabuse praises (in a title) the work of his acolytes. Mabuse never ceases, from this moment on, to criticize his accomplices; and the fact that we have seen him capable of praise foregrounds the image of 'chastizing' father, essential to the character. Finally this title seems to mark the end of a utopian past for Mabuse and his gang, when all went well; and it marks the beginning of another era, when things will go from bad to worse. (The end of this era corresponds, as well, to the end of Mabuse and Carozza's love affair.)

7. George gets hurt when he jumps out of the train, and is clutching his wrist when he gets up. There is room for human error in the machinery, human error which 'demechanizes' and naturalizes. Later in the film, Mabuse smashes a glass out of anger at von Wenck – who thereby draws first blood, as it were – and refuses any help from La Carozza (the incident marks the end of their intimacy). Mabuse takes no notice of his injury, like George jumping out of the train. For the powerful (i.e., real men), humanizing traits are synonymous with the traits of masculinity.

8. The movement and gestures of narrative are much more important than its content. This is amply demonstrated by the manipulation of the stock market, from the 'x-ray' of the briefcase to show the 'commercial contract' to the triumphant expression on Mabuse's face superimposed on the empty stock exchange. The title summarizing the content of the contract is barely comprehensible, Mabuse's orders to his men are enigmatic and in one instance indecipherable (cf. 9), and the explanations given about the fall and subsequent rise of the stock market are at best schematic. But none of this makes the slightest difference. What counts is the mythology of power.

9. Mabuse uses real bank-notes for writing paper, and counterfeit notes for money. Writing on the bank-notes sets the Doctor outside the social order at least as much as any counterfeiting. The message he writes is undoubtedly in code, and in any case it is illegible, but again, as always, the substance of narrative barely matters: what does matter are the archetypal, symbolic gestures enacted by the movement of narrative.

10. The traffic 'accident' marks a first supreme moment in the system of camouflage that is characteristic of the film. Mabuse's car runs into a cab, and Mabuse invites the rider to continue his trip with him. Lo and behold, the rider is Spoerri – although Mabuse has just left him at the house. Spoerri gives Mabuse the stolen briefcase, probably delivered by the driver of the first car. The scene borders on the ludicrous, on the useless – but who would think so at the time? For example: the 'accident' is seen from afar (the only close-up shot is quite brief), and Spoerri is unrecognizable until we see him in close-up, next to Mabuse inside the car. Our attention is so quickly focused on

the briefcase that the surprising appearance of Spoerri is accepted as a momentary titillation; with no second thoughts of how unrealistic his presence might be. Indeed, the only indiscreet gaze to be mystified in this scene is that of the spectator, dutifully awed by this new demonstration of Mabuse/ Lang's powers. For from one end to the other, this scene is a prime example of 'useless' complications.

11. After the initial exchange with Spoerri, Mabuse threateningly reprimanded his aide, Pesch. Now we witness an even more insistent demonstration of Mabuse's reign of terror over his men. In an attic room, Pesch expresses his discontent to George, who reminds him of the 'Commission for Liquidations'. Indeed, the script has already begun to plan Pesch's execution (it will take place during the second part of the film), and the theme of the weak versus the strong is further developed. Like Mabuse and von Wenck, George is one of the strong, and he will even be associated with sophisticated 'anarchist' culture at the moment of his suicide: he writes the name of the sixteenth-century rebel knight Götz von Berlichingen on his cell wall. (This is the only indication, except for the final shoot-out, that the adventures of the Bonnot gang actually did inspire Dr Mabuse, as has been claimed.)

12. Essential to the characterization of Mabuse is that he is classless. Mabuse is always in his element, whether as a drunken labourer, a peddler or a union organizer, or as scientist, theatregoer or aristocratic snob. He runs his counterfeit money operation in a tenement basement, acts the role of the millionaire at the stock exchange and lives in a petit-bourgeois apartment. Mabuse is the Absolute Evil that transcends class – that is, that transcends History.

13. And who are these blind workers in Mabuse's counterfeiting shop? There are obviously too many of them for the task at hand. And why should they be blind? In a film where the ultimate power resides in Mabuse's look (Mabuse as director), to be deprived of sight is to be totally powerless. In Mabuse's world, slavery again becomes an alternative to 'fair' exploitation. Here again, what is meant to pass for 'expedient' goes over in fact by the power of its symbolism.

14. The use of an iris (for instance: to frame Pesch as he finishes his

lament, and after George has reminded him of the price to be paid for desertion; or to isolate Mabuse in the midst of the crowd at the stock exchange) is one of the many technical survivals in *Mabuse* of the primitive and post-primitive eras (such as one finds in many films up to 1925-6). One thinks, also, of certain long shots in the film that are decentred in the primitive manner (at the 17 + 4 Club as well as the Hotel Excelsior). But at the stock exchange, there is a clever mixture of the primitive and the Institutional 'language' of cinema. First a rapid, 'impressionistic' montage creates the atmosphere – or rather, the *presence* – of the stock market (the 'casino'). Then, beginning with a high angle long shot, the iris closes and singles out Mabuse's disguised face in the crowd. Rather than intercalate the close-up within the total tableau (as frequently occurs elsewhere in the film), the close-up is extracted from the scene. The contrast between those proximate, nameless bodies and that terrifyingly distant Him, like an emissary from the primitive Id unleashed, is remarkable. We encounter what is certainly a particular code of this film; but a code that also marks the historical position of *Mabuse*: the primitive system has by and large been surpassed, but many of its figures remained in the memory of the contemporary spectator and in the hands of the technicians, figures that can still serve now and then *without yet appearing dépassé*.

15. Superimposed over an image of the empty stock exchange is a dissolve comparing Mabuse's stock-broker face with his 'real' face. The shot of the stock exchange is unusually long (12 seconds until the first appearance of Mabuse's face, 22½ more for the slow dissolve from one to the other). The shot stands as an abridged echo of the very first, showing Mabuse in his various disguises. Bracketed by these 'face-parades', everything seen thus far has been a prologue: only one character has been introduced and he has demonstrated his apparently absolute powers; conflict has yet to manifest itself on the screen, let alone plot. Lang and Harbou delay the 'beginning' of the plot for more than 20 minutes (although it is true that the film lasts for over four hours and that they have time ahead of them). This long delay at the beginning of the film reveals, I think, something essential about what a beginning

means in the archetypal version of the classical narrative, and could shed light on the appetite-whetting role of a more recent phenomenon, the 'credit-sequence'.

16. The plot proper is engaged at the music hall where La Carozza performs. Hull just happens to come to the performance for an evening's entertainment, and the same terrain is chosen by Mabuse as his 'hunting grounds' for the evening. In classical narrative, such coincidences are natural occurrences. The whole affair is self-evident: Mabuse comes to the theatre and finds a victim in the audience and what's more Hull is becoming enamoured of Carozza – Mabuse's official mistress – at precisely the moment Mabuse spots him. Distinctions between the 'planned' and the 'fortuitous' dissolve. This is, to be sure, melodrama – the dramatic form so directly engaged with 'the popular unconscious'. But with its powerful capacity to 'naturalize the mechanical', cinema disengages melodramatic forms from their limited, stereotyped associations, to establish a pervasive narrative mode.

17. If everything preceding the music hall scene is prologue, then it is remarkably appropriate that the plot should begin as a stage curtain opens. But this is yet one last false beginning, since the curtain opens to reveal nothing but an empty stage – that is, empty of movement: the frozen figures on stage are the last scene in a tableau-performance. In the cinema, to be motionless is to be non-existent (to 'fall back into' photography): movement is life in the cinema, and in this film, life is Cara Carozza. After a bleak encounter between that 'empty' dead stage and a row of stone-faced male spectators, she is the one who at last brings life – that is to say, plot, conflict – to the film.

18. Displacement is handled with remarkable skill: Hull's attraction to Carozza is displaced onto, magnified in, the erotic frenzy of the little old man who can't find enough flowers to throw at the feet of his beloved idol. It is well-known that such displacement is fundamental in classical narrative (the internal externalized through a specific figure: this is the armature, expressionist in origin, of all psychological cinema, at least until the 1960s).

19. What visual irony there is in the image of Carozza responding to

the enthusiastic audience while holding a large doll in her arms – the 'child she will never have', not by Mabuse, not by Hull!

20. That the first encounter with face-to-face hypnotism (Hull becomes Mabuse's victim in the empty corridors of the theatre) occurs entirely in profile seems to me crucial. Mabuse does not direct his dangerous look at the camera, but leans rather towards the edge of the frame, towards an invisible Hull. Could it be that 'we' (the public in 1922) are not yet ready to accept that look? For, central to *Mabuse* is a ritual of initiation to the look. The following scene at the 17 + 4 Club, where Mabuse does indeed 'capture us' with his look, might seem excessively long; a clumsy moment, perhaps. But to be effective, initiation rites have to be performed slowly.

21. Apropos of the 'hypnotism' scenes, we need to recall the history of glances aimed at the camera/spectator. First, there was the 'innocent' look of Fred Ott, sneezing at Dickson's Kinetograph; or that of Lumière's conventionites in Lyons; or the crowds of bystanders who would watch films being shot, from within the frame. And then, the less innocent look of Williamson's camera-swallower (*The Big Swallow*, Britain, 1900); or the comedians and villains accustomed to leering directly into the camera, until producers succeeded in putting a stop to this practice. A particularly eloquent moment in this history occurred in 1908, with the comparison evoked by the perspicacious journalist to encourage, precisely, the prohibition of gazes into the camera. When an actor looks at the camera, he said, it is like a hypnotist snapping his fingers to bring a subject out of a trance.

Such prohibitions soon became veritable taboos. In 1919, a director as familiar with modern techniques as Maurice Tourneur, had a character who was supposedly addressing the audience directly aim his look 30° off-camera (*The Bluebird*). By 1922, shot-reverse-shot had existed for at least three or four years as a common though not yet universal practice (undoubtedly less common in Germany). Still, however, the component eyelines seldom came anywhere near the camera. Thus the spectator-subject's identification with the camera was not yet complete – or at least this is how it seems to us today. We can only speculate as to whether or not *Mabuse* was the first film to use this face-to-face encounter systematically (and perhaps Lang was ahead of his time merely by virtue of the requirements of his script – somewhat like Griffith in *The Drunkard's Reformation*, in which, as early as 1909, shot-reverse-shot is used to show an alcoholic learning his lesson from a temperance play).

Mabuse's gaze may be framed and situated in the same way, but it has nothing to do with the comedian Dranem's look into the camera in the Gaumont *Phonoscènes* (talking pictures!) of 1905. The significance of Mabuse's look and the way it interpellates the spectator are entirely different. In 1922, the taboo was still strong, and gazes grazing the camera were at best rare. But the camera-as-subject had already been assimilated into the Institution of cinema in a variety of ways, and Lang could rest assured of the dissolution of the *spectator-in-the-movie-theatre* into the *subject-in-the-film*. In other words, spectators were prepared to identify with Mabuse's victims in the same way that they surrendered to the powers of the director, i.e. surrendering but 'not for real'. This is a remarkable instance of self-reflexivity. If this scene is inordinately long, that may reflect the need firmly to codify the camera-directed gaze with which the spectator must engage as unseen voyeur, and not as real spectator, seated comfortably in a movie theatre. He must come to recognize that when Mabuse looks at 'him' it isn't him he looks at, but an *other*, within or through him. It is the keystone of the Institutional structure that is being patiently fitted into place in this scene.

22. The stupendous boredom reflected in the lengthy game at the club and the endless post-mortem that follows it is the boredom of upper-class men. Gambling is represented (in the film's first three sequences of this kind) as a movement up and down the scale of social class; from Schramm's vulgar bourgeois elegance we move to a sleazy gambling den, and then we proceed upwards from the disguised gambling-room (the woman who emerges from the ceiling in case of a police raid is just like the leather-bound book on the boss's desk which is in reality a cigar box) to the aristocratic drawing-room where Mabuse disdains to gamble but abducts the woman. If Mabuse transcends class differences, it is to terrify everyone, regardless of class: 'We

must unite against the bogy-man' (or inflation, or the Reds . . .). But gradually it appears that Mabuse does have a class identity, his mobility is not his nature but a strategy. Mabuse is the petit-bourgeois of his appartment who dreams of 'marrying Princess Grace'. And in the madness of the Weimar years, there must have been more than one shopkeeper who deplored the fall of the Habsburgs, only a few years prior to the making of this film.

23. Mabuse is so sure of his plans that he sends Carozza to the Excelsior Hotel to flirt with Hull even before he has encountered Hull in the wings of the theatre. But why does Mabuse send Carozza to the Hotel? Unless Mabuse knows that von Wenck is going to turn to Hull (and there is no way he could know), there is no reason to plan Carozza's seduction of Hull. Mabuse 'riposts' to von Wenck's investigation, but *before the fact*, before it has even begun (that is, before it has been represented on screen). The narrative of *Mabuse* is not as linear as it appears, but nonetheless *it retains the appearance of linearity*. Each series of gestures has phantasmic, archetypal value. The elements of the obvious, surface intrigue of the film simply do not hang together. Rather, what 'counts', what 'matters', is the kind of 'magnetization' that is fundamental in classical cinema between Carozza and Hull; or the power of the magician Mabuse over all of these paper silhouettes. In short, what 'matters' overall is the constant and continual reaffirmation of a set of mythological givens. The flow of narrative is like a body of water that is like quicksilver on the surface, but is frozen solid underneath.

24. We enter the real Hugo Balling's room and discover, before Hull does, that Balling had nothing to do with the man who, in his name, won so much money from him the night before. Thus, the text establishes a solid distance between us and Hull. We must not for a moment be allowed to mistake Hull for a central character, or to empathize with him, because Hull is going to die. Hull is a weakling, incapable of resisting either Mabuse's powers or Carozza's charms. Hull cannot be compared to von Wenck, for instance, who later in the film will successfully resist Mabuse's psychic powers. During the scene in Balling's room, Hull is slow to realize the obvious: that his opponent from the

night before gave him a false name and address. Nor is he quick to figure out what in fact happened to him at the club. Hull is a puppet and will soon cease to have any autonomous role to play at all. La Carozza having got him under her thumb, and the state attorney having placed him under police protection, Hull becomes a mere pawn between two masters. This is what makes him a killable character, easily disposed of. Moreover, from the moment he sees Carozza in the hotel and picks up the handkerchief that she intentionally drops, he is physically and morally transformed into a cartoon character (a puppet indeed). He becomes a stick figure, scurrying about, rushing down the hotel stairs and knocking over a portly gentleman, or greeting La Carozza at his home with child-like enthusiasm (two scenes in long shot, an allusion to primitive cinema that accentuates a farcical quality).

25. The first scene with von Wenck, the state attorney-hero, takes place in front of a magnificent futurist/expressionist stained-glass window in the living-room of the very wealthy Hull. Modern art is shown for the first time; in Mabuse's house, everything is very dull, very petit-bourgeois. There is one exception: the Oval Room, reserved for Woman (first Carozza, who resides there willingly, then the Countess, who is taken there by force). The room is decorated in Empire style and there the Countess will play the role of Mme. Récamier. The image and the room evoke an era when the relations between ruler and ruled were still those of rapist and victim. Modern art is thus a characteristic of the weak and the rich (in the film, to be rich is to be weak): Hull and the Count. Modern art underlines the decadence present in the corridors of wealth (corridors populated in the Germany of 1922 by the Herr Hulls and the Graf Tolds of the real world), leaving the State – in the person of von Wenck – to confront . . . Napoleon? Hitler? In this fiction there is of course no question but that the State will win, even though Doctor Mabuse, in the role of 'returnee from Elba', has his charms. And his petit-bourgeois interior made identification with him easy for large sections of the audience.

26. In the 'bestiary' of this film, where men are divided into the weak and the strong, women seem, rather, to be both weak and strong. Love strengthens La Carozza, and love kills her: if she is

strong, it is in the terms of the female stereotype: strength equals sacrifice (she willingly swallows the poison sent to her). Like her husband, the Countess – who is given to languishing on sofas – has the weakness of a 'dying race'. But she also possesses the strength of female solidarity (with Carozza in prison, she realizes the nature of a woman's love). And in addition, the Countess has a certain virginal purity, that is, the strength to resist the advances of men. (The complexity of these female characters is attributable to Thea von Harbou; in this respect, her absence is glaring in Lang's American films.)

27. A cinematic rhyme based on 'question and answer' occurs in the film during von Wenck's first conversation with Hull. The two men are discussing 'Hugo Balling': 'Maybe he's one of them' says the state attorney (he still believes that a gang of card sharks is responsible for what Mabuse, with his disguises, does alone). After this title, we see a white-smocked Mabuse in his laboratory: thus invoked, the Demon appears. This kind of rhyme, intensifying the rhetorical links between sequences, was a characteristic of Lang's work for ten years. German cinema in general (Murnau, Lupu Pick and Dupont were also attentive to these implications of montage), and Lang's work in particular, made decisive steps forward in the 'alternating syntagm' bequeathed by Griffith. Griffith moved from one parallel action to another in such a way that the exact timing of the match was neither decisive nor even significant. Throughout this film, however, Lang attempts to construct very precise transmissions of meaning, of which this scene is a particularly obvious example. This question and answer has the effect of authorial comment. The articulation of title and image 'says': 'And here is this monster, in the flesh'. Aided by George, Mabuse draws venom from a live snake. A more appropriate emblem is hard to imagine. But as the scene continues, the first reading is gradually effaced. We become involved in the scene and accept it, quite simply, as Mabuse making the preparations for another evil deed. But ultimately, this scene leads nowhere; it has no ties to either the present or the future of the film (never again will mention be made of the snake or of the venom, and the laboratory will never be seen again as such). Its extension – its 'apparent development' – served merely to naturalize the shot, to render its emblematic function less 'bold'.

28. Lang places Hull on his knees, lower in the frame than Carozza, as she scolds him for playing into the state attorney's hands. This was typical of the new dramaturgy, in which meaning was totally controlled by reduplication (here, through composition; elsewhere through framing; still elsewhere through lighting, staging, or music). It is not surprising that such an echo-effect should have developed so early and to such an extent in Germany, since this is certainly the most important contribution of expressionist style to the classical system of cinema.

29. The presentation of Schramm's combination grill and gambling den is a unique moment in the film. First, this is the only instance in which the narrative principles of chronological ordering and unified space are abandoned. To begin with, we see a series of shots representing details of the restaurant 'as concept': an aquarium for live trout, fowls on a spit and a display of cigars, all shown against a neutral background or through a mask; and then, a woman dancer in men's clothes (suggestive of 'bourgeois decadence') and a jazz band. Finally, there is a shot of the entire restaurant. We then move on to a peculiar little biography of the proprietor, Schramm, who went from peddler to convict, and from fence to owner of a prosperous enterprise. When we return to a long shot of the restaurant, the brief sequence – unlike any other portion of the film – appears to have been a sardonic parenthesis: 'Today, anyone can get rich, by fair means or foul'.

There is only one 'partisan' voice in the film and that is Mabuse's. He does not hesitate to give free rein to his right-wing anarchist philosophy. But in this parenthesis, a voice intervenes which the film-makers designate as their own. This voice will never intervene again on the image-track, only in a very occasional title. By virtue of the elliptical, ironic tone of the parenthesis, their voice is firmly situated in the realm of 'editorial lucidity'. Thus, the petit-bourgeois German viewer, whether social-democrat or liberal, is reassured: the 'people behind the camera' see things more clearly than the characters they have created. Such an editorial pose serves here to camouflage the profound identity between Mabuse's fascist ideology, tinted with Bonapartism, and the real-life shopkeeper mentality which indeed looks with a jaundiced eye on 'all those Jews getting rich on the backs of ordinary working people'. Such methods for establishing a tacit editorial complicity with the audience are part and parcel of the Institution.

30. Representations of private life (usually relations between the sexes) are an important way of naturalizing filmic characters. (Films where both cops and robbers are perceived only from an administrative view-point are quite rare, especially on American television, where, more often than in the past, the criminal remains an 'other' without a home, so to speak; while the human centre, the 'hearth' of the diegesis, is the private life of the policeman or policewoman.) Hence, when the state attorney flirts with a beautiful woman in a clandestine gambling den, he emerges with the indelible mark of Humanity. From now on, von Wenck can no longer be defined only in his official capacity, for he is a man sensitive to a woman's charms – and yet this fact will be evoked only once again, with admirable restraint, at the end of Part II.

(The private lives of women are always present on the screen, and often represent the sum total of their existence. Even when a woman is 'on duty' she is personalized.)

It is indeed remarkable that von Wenck has no family and no home, only a modest office that will soon be destroyed. Mabuse, on the other hand, is often seen at home. Thus, an interesting question is raised: who is expected to identify with the film's only character to be seen so much at home, and who reigns not only over his servants, but before too long over his kidnapped bride as well?

31. Mabuse's values permeate every level of the film. All of the characters killed at his command are weaklings. Hull is undermined by his playboy lifestyle, the Count by the decadence of his race, while Pesch is a pathetic lumpen. As for Carozza, her weakness is to believe in love ('There is no love, there is only the will to power,' says Mabuse to the Countess, whose strength is that she does not believe in love.) Mabuse does not die; he goes mad – a fate much less definitive, as the *Testament* was to show. Hence, the film is informed by the fundamental principle of the survival of the fittest (a principal common to the majority of mainstream films in Western culture).

32. Here is an example of a 'premonitory' rhyme: 'I prefer watching other people's passion for gambling, without getting too close to them myself,' the Countess tells von Wenck, to explain why she is a passive observer in the gambling dens. Her words are followed by a close-up of Mabuse at the gambling table, keeping track of the bank.

33. There is a remarkable symmetry between the sequence where von Wenck converses with the Countess in an alcove situated apart from the gaming table and the final scene of Part I, in which the Countess faints and Mabuse carries her away in his arms. In this latter scene as well a card-game is in progress, and in the background the Countess converses with a man. But this time the man is Mabuse, and one of the poker players is her husband, whom Mabuse hypnotizes from a distance to make him cheat at cards (in the previous scene, it is Mabuse who cheats, by hypnotizing the Russian woman). Both scenes conclude with a flight. Whereas in the first of these two scenes the Countess flees her husband under the protection of the gallant state attorney, in the second it is Mabuse who flees with the woman in his arms, removing her from von Wenck's protection. Together, these scenes provide a compact résumé of the intricate relations between these four main characters.

34. During the alternation between von Wenck's 'idyll' with the Countess and the card-game, an ambiguous structure emerges. The state attorney leans toward the Countess and speaks to her. Mabuse, who sits facing the camera, turns to his left with an evil look in his eye. Is he looking at the Countess and von Wenck (up until now he hasn't paid them any attention), or at the Russian woman, whose gigolo is taking out his wallet? It would subsequently appear as though Mabuse had been looking at the Russian woman, since he proceeds to swindle her. Considering the narrative structure of the film in its totality, however, it seems that the first impression, a kind of topological reading, is also 'correct', that Mabuse is indeed leering at the Countess as well. Just as he covets the Russian woman's pearls he also covets the Countess's body (not to mention her 'race').

35. At the end of this sequence, the threads connecting characters are tied together in such a way that the unity of the film is confirmed before we move into another alternating montage.

Carozza's remark, that 'At the gambling table no one looks like a saint', suddenly reminds us of her love for Mabuse. Count Told appears for the first time (though in such a way as to be absolutely unidentifiable, thus underlining the overall transparency of his character). The attorney offers a proof of devotion to the Countess by turning off the lights so that she can leave unnoticed by her husband. La Carozza rushes to watch her leave, and asks: 'What does that mean?' Her jealousy of the woman who will replace her in Mabuse's affections is reflected *before the fact*.

Finally, the directional machinery of the scene is stamped with Mabuse's inimitable trademark when an employee hands Hull a card. One side of the card reminds Hull of his gambling debts to 'Balling' and the other warns him against any co-operation with the police.

36. The 'Tsi Nan Fuh' sequence is crucial. Here we are reassured as to von Wenck's psychical and moral superiority over Mabuse. Actually, the Doctor's powers are hypnotic in appearance only. Closer inspection indicates, rather, that we are dealing with an occult power. Indeed, while the word 'hypnotism' is used quite incidentally to describe the show put on by Mabuse in his role as Sandor Wiseman, it is never used in reference to Mabuse himself. During the Wiseman performance, however, the mystical nature of Mabuse's power is definitely confirmed. We see him covertly manipulating the envelopes in which he has enclosed instructions for his subjects, but it is only to give a harmless text, totally different from the one that is to send von Wenck to his death, to the woman who has been serving as his foil. And since von Wenck executes the secret command without any verbal instructions, what we witness is, indeed, mystical thought-control.

In this connection, Mabuse's masquerade as a man of science is ambivalent. On the one hand, the attempt is made to discredit science (and psychoanalysis in particular, which proves to be Mabuse's 'cover' and which was widely thought of then as a fundamentally threatening domain). This is a familiar procedure for ideologues sensitive to ruling-class pressures when the system breaks down: blame (explicitly or implicitly) social evils on science (or progress), and thus encourage obscurantism and 'turning the clock back'. Similar phenomena are very much in evidence in our time. On the other hand, giving Mabuse's occult powers a scientific rationale tends to legitimate the 'charisma' of Great Men. A writer such as Kracauer would not be mistaken if he saw in this aspect of the film a 'ludic' manifestation of the pseudo-scientific theories that were part and parcel of Fascist and Nazi ideology.

It follows from this sequence that the Law will prevail indubitably, since von Wenck succeeds in resisting Mabuse's 'fluid'. In the universe of the film, von Wenck is the only one capable of putting up such resistance. Which allows us to conclude that the science of the Law is as illusory as Mabuse's criminal science, since in the final analysis it is only by sheer psychic force that von Wenck triumphs over Mabuse.

37. Question and answer: von Wenck asks the manager of the Excelsior Hotel, 'who is staying in room 231?' We see Mabuse in a long shot, wearing a different disguise and walking cautiously down the stairway. The implications of this scene are complex. We assume that it is because of his mastery of disguise that Mabuse can freely leave the hotel. But in point of fact, this mastery is not put to the test. At this particular moment, no one is even in pursuit of him. Mabuse gets an unexpected break only because of the state attorney's absolute respect for legal procedure. So that while the scene appears to be just another variation on the theme of Mabuse's power (he tricks his enemies one more time), there is an additional motif. von Wenck is a prisoner of social conventions, while Mabuse flies free as a bird.

On close inspection, this detour through the hotel bureaucracy is a bit crude. But, of course, it is characteristic of the classical text that one never *does* inspect it closely. Such crude proceedings are naturalized by the 'laws' of the links between images, and by the *coherence of the ideological sub-text*. The sub-text is held together by a commonly shared assumption: the police are hampered; their hands are tied by petty regulations. Hence, it is normal that a state attorney does improbable things in order to prolong the fantasy; things that are accepted *because they illustrate what 'everybody knows'*.

38. We abandon von Wenck, gassed by one of Mabuse's henchmen,

in the back seat of a sealed cab, only to rediscover him immediately, adrift in a rowboat. This abrupt ellipsis poses an enigma of narrative logic (as do so many other moments in the film, but this is the most spectacular). If we suppose this to be the film's original editing scheme (and the use of a double iris, closing and opening in the same part of the screen, authorizes this), certain questions emerge. If Mabuse really wanted von Wenck dead, wouldn't there have been a more effective plan? The boat is drifting close to shore, and the rescue that ensues is practically inevitable. In any case, the rescue happens so quickly that there is no time for any sense of real danger to develop. Von Wenck in his rowboat is much more suggestive of the baby Moses than of impending tragedy. Meanwhile, the men responsible for the operation return to Mabuse. They are embarrassed, and are ridiculed by their colleagues. Mabuse curses and strikes them. They were supposed to kill von Wenck, it appears. But even before their return, Mabuse knows that von Wenck is not dead (if not, why the outburst about that 'damned bloodhound' when he finds the list of gambling dens in the attorney's wallet?) Yet von Wenck has not yet been rescued, so how does Mabuse know that he has escaped?

Spectators who are unattentive to such contradictions – as are most spectators then as now – might well accept everything in the order presented: von Wenck was in danger, and was then rescued; Mabuse assumed him dead and is furious to discover that he is alive. In this reading method, each new bit of information cancels out that which has preceded it. On the other hand, spectators more atuned to the 'mystical' struggle which is going on here might catch a mental glimpse of another scene. For these petty crooks, the idea of killing this particular man – symbol both of the power of the State and of paternal benevolence (Mabuse is the wicked father; von Wenck, the good) – is so intimidating that they are not about to risk a straightforward murder. They choose, rather, an ancient gesture: exposure of an unwanted child to the elements, leaving the onus of the actual death to the gods. But not only is this scene not shown, it is barely even suggested (and this is unusual for the film). Partisans of the 'internal deconstruction' of the classical text will see in this a moment when the narrative mechanism proclaims its own arbitrairiness. They are not mistaken, as long as they take note also of this confused multiplicity which legitimates many possible readings, including the very real possibility that this is also ('simply') a point at which the machinery – intoxicated with its own efficiency – momentarily runs away with itself.

39. The second scene in Hull's appartment (shorter than the first) shows Carozza with a new, unfamiliar characteristic: her head in the clouds, she keeps dropping her belongings on the floor. Perhaps this is a pose designed to strengthen Hull's attraction to her (isn't clumsiness supposed to be endearing in a woman?), or perhaps this is simply a way for Carozza to 'accidently' leave a piece of evidence for Hull to discover, dropping it like she drops her gloves or her boa. The discovery of the note – in which Mabuse tells Carozza to take Hull to the opening of a new nightclub – endangers the Doctor's plans. Hull's discovery, however, does not in any way protect Hull himself from the ambush being planned for him. But the police have been alerted, and Carozza is sent to prison, where she will eventually die. This is the true result of Carozza's strange behaviour, dictated by the film-makers 'disguised' as Mabuse, so to speak.

40. The prepared descent from the ceiling of the Petit Casino of a woman dancing to conceal the game area with her 'performance' in case of a police raid could also be an emblem of the film itself: a game with serious stakes – sexual, mystical and political – is disguised, by an ingenious mechanism, as an 'innocent' diversion.

41. The seance (introduced with the title 'The Other World', a type of commentary that is rare in the film) occurs as a kind of break in the narrative, a moment whose privileged quality is enhanced by the enormous coincidence of Mabuse's and the Countess's presence. During this scene, a 'spiritual betrothal' is consolidated between Mabuse and the Countess, and that 'mystical struggle' so implicit throughout the film is finally concretized. The seance is disrupted by an 'alien spirit'. The Countess takes the blame and leaves the room. Mabuse accompanies her into an adjoining room. At the beginning of the conversation there is an image – unfortunately cut from the version for commercial distribution – of the Countess tracing

the spiral design on her dress with her finger. When her finger reaches the centre of the spiral, Mabuse's hand enters the frame to rest on her shoulder: she is caught in the web.

42. There is a remarkable alternating montage of increasing acceleration, between the action leading to Hull's murder and the arrival of the police at the Petit Casino. Such moments are particularly effective in drawing the spectator into the movement of the film. And then, a prodigious condensation: Carozza is arrested and taken to prison; Mabuse in his apartment, surrounded by his gang, writes her off once and for all.

The murder of Hull, however, does little to further Mabuse's plans. (Hull was merely an instrument in the hands of the police, and their investigation continues unhindered; moreover, he could easily have remained tied to Carozza's apron-strings – were it not for the note that announced his murder.) The only reason for Hull's death is that it provokes Carozza's arrest and thus leaves an empty place for the Countess (Mabuse immediately has the Oval Room prepared). Does it not begin to be clear that the 'serious' centre of the film is not the detective story, and that only indirectly (by ideological association) is it political allegory? The 'serious' centre of the film is, rather, of an erotic-metaphysical order with shades of Spenglerian neo-caesarism, that was all the rage amongst German intellectuals of the day.

Notes

1. A film that was shot and shown in two parts, entitled *Ein Bild der Zeit* (*Portrait of an Epoch*) and *Menschen der Zeit* (*People of an Epoch*). The action, however, is continuous from one to the next (although the beginning of the second resumes the end of the first, much as in the old cliff-hangers). In the USA, these parts are titled respectively *Mabuse the Gambler* and *The King of Crime*.
2. Or, before the First World War, Danish films like Gad's *Abyss* (1910), German films like *The Student of Prague* (1913) by the Danish director Rye, or Italian films, like Gustavo Serena's admirable *Assunta Spina* (1915).
3. See Chapter 1.
4. Needless to say, I precisely do not regard films like *The Man with a Movie Camera, Gertrud* or those of Straub, for example, as extreme instances but as singular texts indeed, whose textual system opposes in some crucial way that of the Institution.

1987

This group of notes was my first attempt to come squarely to grips with issues of meaning in film. They were written during the stay in the United States which finally enabled me to take stock of the ravages caused by the formalism which I had helped to promote there. The fact that I was unable actually to write an article but only to accumulate these discrete notes attests to the difficulties of this first venture into an area so familiar to others.

The article on which these notes were an attempt was commissioned by Judith Mayne, and they first appeared, in her English translation, in *Cine-Tracts*, No. 14.

11 Harold Lloyd vs. Doctor Mabuse

As represented by a scant handful of prestigious signatures and classified masterpieces, the Soviet silent cinema seems today to be a known quantity, assimilated once and for all. Yet in the last few years, several series of screenings, in London, Paris and elsewhere, have reminded us of the existence in that cinema of a kind of experimentation wholly different from that of Vertov, Eisenstein and Dovzhenko; different in that it does not privilege the 'work of the signifier', and constitutes instead an effort to appropriate and overturn the narrative codes of popular cinema, in particular that of the United States. I refer to the films that derive directly or indirectly from the teachings of the first great theoretician of classical film language, of 'readable' cinema in the Barthesian sense, Lev Kuleshov, to whom homage must be paid here, even though the exercises of this type signed by him (*The Death Ray, Mr. West in the Land of the Bolsheviks*) seem less achieved than a number of films by film-makers trained by him: Ozep, Barnet, Komarov, Zhelyabuzhsky, etc. This type of experimentation atained its apogee as early as 1926 with the three-part film *Miss Mend*, produced by the Mezhrabpom-Russ Studio, where all four of the above-named directors then worked.

Historians seem to feel that the actual direction of *Miss Mend* should be attributed to the elder of the two co-signatories (Ozep was thirty, Barnet twenty-two), while to the younger man should go credit for a decisive role in the writing of the script. I shall leave to the devotees of auteur theory the task of sorting out the stylistic and thematic affiliations which might justify this or that paternity attribution, and to the prophets of reductive intentionality that of disputing in its name the following reflections. Let me simply express my amazement that this film, one of the most *enjoyable* of the silent era, has been neglected for so long, as well as my fear that its rediscovery today may come too late (or too early).

Indeed *Miss Mend* would no doubt have spoken to our

Miss Mend (Barnet and Ozep, 1926)

community of critics and film-makers far more urgently some fifteen years ago, when the search for a materialist pedagogy of images and sounds was still at the centre of our collective preoccupations, when we impatiently awaited the next Godard, or the latest film from Cuba or Brazilian Cinema Novo. For *Miss Mend* was one of the very first films to integrate a pedagogical distancing (Brechtian before the letter) into a form of popular cinema.

It is no doubt as much on account of the Rocambolesque nature of the film's story-line as of the auteur politics which now saturate cinema historiography that *Miss Mend* has fallen into such utter neglect. Indeed, its outward appearance is that of an adventure melodrama very much in the tradition of Ponson De Terail himself. (It even contains the theme of concealed, prestigious paternity.) A superficial appreciation might conclude that the film is an artificial grafting onto the age-old melodramatic formula of a timely story. And indeed, the aim was to make the Soviet public of 1926 aware of the very real threat still posed by capitalist encirclement (this was the time of the NEP, with all the illusions of *détente* which were associated with it in the minds of many).

However, if Barnet's and Ozep's script is indeed faithful to the newspaper serial by Marietta Chaginyan from which it was drawn, then this latter already contained a dialectical conception which went far beyond a simple 'graft' in the way in which it overturned one of the stock themes shared by so-called ladies' literature (*presse féminine*) and by old-fashioned melodrama: the Great Love Affair between the boss's son and a working girl employed by the family firm. Bemused – precisely as in a Girls' Own romance – by a series of extravagant misunderstandings, Miss Mend remains, until the very last, oblivious of the bitter truth: that the handsome 'Technician Johnson', who carries the torch for her throughout the film, is none other than Arthur Storn, her enemy on two counts – her enemy as a woman (he is the accomplice of her adoptive son's murderer) and as a worker (he is manager of the factory that fired her for strike action). Viewers, of course, know the truth from the very beginning. Here, again, we are dealing with an appropriation/overturning of a basic trait of 'popular' melodrama – those asides in which the villainous seducer thrills the audience with the disclosure of his lewd intentions, but never avows his own class status, which in *Miss Mend* is explicitly conveyed with each of Arthur Storn's interventions.

Now, the film-makers' great *trouvaille* is to have transposed and extended this narrative subversion to *the cinematic codes of 'typage'* (by genre, by style, by national traits); it is to have made the confrontation between the Champions of the Land of Socialism and the Evil Spirits of Capitalism a struggle between clearly identifiable film types. And this option acquires its full critical significance whenever a collision between different types destabilizes the dramatic illusion without suspending the 'flow of pleasure' which anchors the spectator 'inside' the film.

It seems to me that through this attempt to dialecticize a popular genre for agitprop purposes, *Miss Mend* raises problems and proposes solutions that, no matter what some may think still concern us today.

Four young, progressive Americans – two reporters, an office-worker and a secretary, Miss Vivian Mend – accidentally stumble on a diabolical plot hatched by a mysterious organization of businessmen who are implacable enemies of the Soviet Union. The idea is to sell the Soviets a shipment of high-tension insulators containing deadly germs, to be released by wireless remote control. The three heroes and the heroine track the plotters by sea to Leningrad, where the plotters are ultimately exposed before they can execute their fiendish plot.

The conflict at the heart of the film, then, in accordance with a pattern that, however familiar, corresponds with a permanent reality, pits a group of North American progressives against their capitalist oppressors. And this conflict between two sets of class interests, between two ideologies, is paralleled by a 'battle' which opposes two cinematic *types*. On the one hand, we have the democratic types: the acrobatic reporters Barnet and Vogel[1], the comic office-worker Tom Hopkins and the dynamic Miss Mend are all drawn directly from the popular American film, be it the adventure serial – Miss Mend and Barnet – be it slapstick comedy – Tom Hopkins – or be it both at once – the photographer Vogel, a blend of Harold Lloyd and Douglas Fairbanks. And on the other hand, we find arrayed against these fugitives from Hollywood two characters who are straight out of the Teutonic universe of Fritz Lang and Thea von Harbou: Arthur Storn and his evil genius Tchitche, in whom audiences of the period could not have failed to recognise Freder Fredersen and Doctor Mabuse. Moreover, the images which depict their sinister doings are laden with all the signs of that German cinema which is somewhat loosely but quite commonly called 'expressionist'.

So, on the one hand we have a set of references to specifically American popular genres which anchors the popular character of the heroes and heroine in cinema itself ('these are the people because they are from the people's movies'): the chase after tickets in the steamship offices, as the windows are banged down one after another by order of the plotters, is reminiscent of Chaplin; the night spent in the hay-loft is a cliché of the romantic Hollywood comedy. On the other hand, we have references of a completely different order, since they are to an explicit *style* and even to explicit films: *Mabuse der Spieler* is evoked in the character of Tchitche but also in that of Elizabeth Storn, who loves him with that same masochistic passion that the unfortunate Carozza had felt for the fascinating doctor; Arthur Storn and Tchitche's laboratory remind us of *Metropolis*; and Gordon Storn's coffin, slowly opening in the empty cabin of a ship at sea, recalls a certain scene in *Nosferatu*.

Other notations refer more generally to the 'style' of filmic Expressionism: the monumental staircase climbed by Arthur Storn's funeral procession; the giant arm-chair that dwarfs the mediocre figure of Arthur Storn; Tchitche's 'medieval' interior, with its armours and baroque candelabra. True, this is only pastiche; in their new context, these borrowed traits continue to function in the expressionist manner. But in conscripting characters out of Harbou-Lang to people these sets, the film-makers – and possibly Chaginyan before them – *reveal them for what they are*. Arthur Storn, like Freder Fredersen, is the heir to a super-trust; he too falls in love with a woman 'from below'. But Storn is like the shadow of Fredersen, his hidden underface. He is, so to speak, the subconscious of his class – beneath the 'pure passion' lies the naked concupiscence of the rapist, beneath the deference to the father, lies the selfish calculation of the parricide. And just as Arthur Storn objectively acknowledges the incomplete, truncated nature of John Fredersen, so, too, Tchitche brings to light the truth that lies hidden in Mabuse, a character so overdetermined as to achieve a kind of innocence. Indeed, Mabuse's 'human foibles' placed him outside and above the capitalist machine (it is in this way that he prefigures the Hitlerian mythology): the demigod who manipulates the stockmarket *as if in sport*, who is capable of a mad passion and who is susceptible to insanity is, at bottom, one of us – he cannot belong to the perfectly rational system of our real oppressors, cannot be confused with them. Tchitche, on the other hand, is a machine totally devoted to the perpetration of evil. His faultless rationality is that of those sinister offices from where, forty years later, poisoned cigars would be sent to Fidel Castro. He is insensitive to love and, it would seem, to any form of pleasure; he is beyond the reach of madness, for he is combatting the 'destroyers of culture', and he knows full well in the name of what. He possesses the cold, cruel determination of Big Business itself. Tchitche is the reality principle lurking behind the Mabusian play of masks; he needs neither disguises nor hypnosis, for this is the Power of Money. This is shown with a Brechtian simplicity in one of the incidents which are like so many cracks in the overt system of the narrative: a policeman raises the lid of Gordon Storn's coffin, which our reporter friends have told him is empty; in it he finds Tchitche, alive and well, who slips a bundle of dollars into his hand and orders him to be silent; immediately the policeman turns on the reporters for wasting his time. Now this kind of contamination of the drama by the incongruous – a Brechtian strategy if ever there was one – is the chief function of that key character in the film, Tom Hopkins[2].

From the very beginning of the film, it is through Tom Hopkins that a certain tone of mockery is brought into play. In the midst of a violent confrontation between striking workers and Pinkerton cops there appears a shot that shows Hopkins standing on a window sill over which Barnet and Vogel have just leapt to rush to Miss Mend's defence. This gag-shot, in which Hopkins plays the attentive on-looker, craning his neck to see what's going on, introduces a discordant note of levity into a context which otherwise bears all the distinctive marks of *gravity* in accordance with the codes that prevailed at that time in the USSR (dramatic frame-composition, dynamic editing, tense acting style, etc.). It is true that this is the only time when a comic distancing will manifest itself *in opposition to gravity* (rare in this film, in any case). However, it does recur with each of Hopkins's 'grand solos'[3], and later in the scenes involving his bizarre Soviet 'double', the street waif Nicolas.

Although the primary degree of gravity – which grounds the

diegesis in the real world – is never again the target of the clown's innocent logic, the sham seriousness of the villains is not spared: Hopkins asks Elizabeth Storn to repeat for Vogel's camera her distressed-widow act over Gordon Storn's coffin (when the audience knows that she is Tchitche's accomplice and that Tchitche is holding her poor husband prisoner). This is a privileged moment in that, like the other major distancing gestures that Hopkins is to deploy, it concerns the idea of *illusion*.

It was only cumulatively that incidents such as this, or *coups de théâtre* such as the handing of the dollars to the policeman, could succeed in putting spectators on guard, as it were, against the narrative system at work, could provoke them into taking it less seriously than they had been inclined to do by reflexes built up by some fifteen years of post-primitive cinema, in particular the American.

These distancing gestures are often endowed with a certain theatricality which makes them even more incongruous. The one that most explicitly enlists the *theatrical sign*[4] shows Hopkins spying on the plotters at work, using a rolled-up newspaper as a telescope, and apparently incapable of *acting* in response to what he sees. This is the third time in the film that he finds himself in this role of passive, innocent spectator, who can ask nothing of *those who act* except to begin over again (he is in the position of the film's spectator, who, incapable of intervening, can only wait for the next scene).

The high point of Hopkins's role, dramatically but also pedagogically (a 'point' which actually covers several sequences), occurs when he finally finds himself face to face with the redoubtable Tchitche, in a train compartment. Having realized that Hopkins has just read a lurid tabloid article about hypnotism, Tchitche decides to resort to the power of suggestion, but so susceptible a 'subject' is Hopkins that he anticipates, as it were, his hypnotizer, immediately declaring himself in a trance when everything indicates that he is not (if he feels no pain when he pricks himself, it is because he is running the pin through his sock, not the skin of his leg, etc.). However, the ambiguity of this hypnosis is such that one could imagine that he has indeed been hypnotized but without his knowing it, and that he at the same time believes it. Indeed, one of the strengths of this theme is its introduction of comical uncertainty into an issue which, above and beyond the melodramatic context, is eminently serious, since it refers us to our status as spectators both of the film and of the world: once more, Hopkins is a passive witness of events – 'Don't bother with me', he says to Tchitche's henchmen, who are about to manhandle him, 'I'm hypnotized anyway!' In the end, however, this sleeping spectator awakes to consciousness – 'By gosh, it seems I've been taken in with this hypnosis business!' – and joins actively in the fight against the criminals – an exemplary trajectory in which the audience were no doubt being invited to recognize themselves.

Each of Hopkins's appearances skews the codes of the serial towards those of slapstick (a bit like the clowning of the actor Levesque in Feuillade's *Les Vampires*, for example). However, one singular episode, situated about halfway through the film, skews them, on the contrary, towards tragic pathos. When the cute little boy who is Vivian Mend's adoptive son is kidnapped by Tchitche because he is actually the heir to the Storn millions, we thrill to a familiar melodramatic twist. When, following Vivian's appeal to Arthur, Tchitche decides to free the child, we are relieved but scarcely surprised. When he gives the child a poisoned apple before sending him on his way, we dutifully relish this additional proof of Tchitche's evilness – and the fertility of the authors' inventiveness. But when the child, after a number of false alarms, actually eats the apple and falls dead at his mother's feet, we suddenly find ourselves in another film; we instinctively protest – 'they' haven't respected the rules of the genre. At this point a kind of breach is opened in the text, leading perhaps to a moment's reflection (on the real victims of the real Tchitches?). True, one may conclude instead, more simply, that the authors were merely following an age-old recipe: a woman needed reasons of a personal nature to chase off to the ends of the earth in pursuit of criminals and she also had to be relieved of her domestic burden in order to be free to undertake this journey. But the fact remains that in the economy of the popular cinema of the West during that period, such a solution was *unacceptable*. One is reminded of the child whom Hitchcock did away with in a similar manner in *Sabotage*, and of the 1936 article in which he ascribed the failure of the film to this violation of spectatorial expectations and swore never to do it again.[5]

However, it is important to note that at the symbolic level, the taboo is nonetheless observed in *Miss Mend*. For while Sylvia Sidney's child is killed for good by the bomb he has been carrying quite unsuspectingly, Miss Mend's little boy is destined to 'live again', within the narrative logic of the film. Borrowed, perhaps, from Chaplin's film *The Kid* and more generally from the street-wise children who so abound in the cinema of America (and of France), little Nicolas clearly represents here the Soviet people. In fact he is the only Soviet *character* in the entire film (the pale silhouettes that appear here and there, from the quarantine doctor to the business-like militia-men, each arrives *in extremis* as *Deus ex machina* figure and cannot qualify as such. Dressed in rags, living off his wits, sleeping on a building site, Nicolas embodies that stage of development then reached by a nation that was scarcely older than he was. At the same time, to give this symbolic role to a street urchin was to confer a slightly ironic cast upon the patriotism which underlies the film, not unlike Hopkins's mockery of the conventions of the adventure serial.

Even if Vivian scarcely comes into contact with him, this child replaces, in the film's 'extended family', the one she has lost. And the moral of the story is that when the building where Nicolas 'squats' is finally built, when his people no longer have to dine on sausage ends, then the USSR will be able to restore hope to the working people of America, crushed under the heel of the Pinkertons and their masters, the Tchitches and the Storns, that American people to whom Vivian's child was in a sense a martyr. For two decades, this was more than just a fantasy for the workers of both the USSR and the USA.

I know nothing of the intentions of the makers of this film. It is not at all certain that their manipulation/deconstruction of the codes of popular cinema was dictated by theoretical considerations of the same order as those of directors such as Eisenstein or Vertov, or of the Cuban film-makers of the ICAIC, for whom the 'subversion' of the popular codes was, for a time, a major concern (*Death of a Bureaucrat*, *Giron*). At the same time, this film is at once too beautiful and too strange to have happened quite by accident, in that country, and at that moment in history.

Notes

1. Played by Barnet himself and by the actor V. Vogel – a little joke which invites us not to take these 'Americans' too literally.
2. Played by the remarkable Illinski, star of Kormarov's *Kiss of Mary Pickford* (Kormarov himself plays the role of Tchitche).
3. Including the scene in which he blackens his skin so as to be able to go home half-naked. This scene is like an 'innocent' anticipation of the death of an anonymous Black, felled by a stray bullet in the following scene ('A Negro! Pooh, nothing serious', says a policeman).
4. Which Jiri Hönzl once defined in terms of its functional mobility: an actor representing a tree, a tree signifying a forest, etc.
5. And he kept his word, at least until *Psycho*, when the codes of expectation had considerably evolved, especially in the USA, Hollywood finding it more and more difficult to cast a veil of modesty over the realities of the modern world's most violent society.

1987

First published in F. Albera and R. Cosandey, *Boris Barnet: Écrits, Documents, Études, Filmographie*, Editions du Festival du Film de Locarno, 1985. This English translation is my own.

Index of Film Titles

Index of Names

Naruse Mikio, 193, 194, 198
Nash, Mark, 92
Nizhny, Vladimir, 64–5, 131, 136

Ophuls, Max, 195
Orrom, Michael, 125, 136
Osanai Kaoru, 191
Oshima Nagisa, 68, 200, 201
Ozep, Fyodor, 122, 228–37
Ozu Yasujiro, 68, 97, 191, 194–5, 198, 199, 202

Pabst, Georg Wilhelm, 195
Parain, Phillipe, 91
Perret, Léonce, 5, 120
Pick, Lupu, 50, 218
Poirier, Léon, 45
Porter, Edwin S., 6, 12, 108, 117, 118, 138–56, 160, 167, 168–70, 171
Pradot, Marcelle, 34
Preminger, Otto, 31
Protozanov, Jacob, 30
Pudovkin, Vsevolod, 46, 49, 85, 122, 124, 125–7, 133

Raizman, Yuli, 69
Raynal, Jackie, 182
Renoir, Jean, 31, 85, 195
Resnais, Alain, 85
Richard, Jacques, 139, 154
Robbe-Grillet, Alain, 60
Rossellini, Roberto, 32
Rossen, Robert, 31
Rye, Stellan, 226

Sadoul, Georges, 139, 142, 152, 154, 173, 180, 185
Sebestik, Miroslav, 106
Serena, Gustavo, 30, 226
Shimazu Yasujiro, 194, 195
Shimizu Hiroshi, 97, 194, 196, 198
Sidney, Sylvia, 236
Sinclair, Upton, 64
Sirk, Douglas, 31
Sitney, P. Adams, 179, 185, 187
Sjöstrom, Victor, 30

Skolimowski, Jerzy, 65
Smith, G.A., 117, 171
Snow, Michael, 174, 180, 185
Sternberg, Joseph von, 45, 85
Stevens, George, 125
Straub, Jean-Marie, 85, 226
Stroheim, Erich von, 205

Tasaka Tomotaka, 198, 202
Tati, Jacques, 85
Teshigahara Hiroshi, 200
Tourneur, Maurice, 214
Toyoda Shiro, 193
Trauberg, Leonid, 46
Tuttle, Frank, 31

Uchida Tomu, 194
Ulmer, Edgar, 31

Vassiliev, Sergei, 46
Vertov, Djiga, 48, 71, 94, 98, 100, 101, 110, 122, 133–7, 157, 159, 184, 228
Victor, Henry, 40
Vigo, Jean 85
Viota, Paulino, 183–4
Vogel, V., 236
Volkoff, Alexander, 39, 45

Walsh, Raoul, 44
Warhol, Andy, 145, 180, 181, 185
Welles, Orson, 65, 199
Wiene, Robert, 177, 201
Williams, Raymond, 125, 136
Williamson, James, 117, 214
Wollen, Peter, 183, 186
Wyler, William, 199

Yamamoto Satsuo, 200
Yamamura So, 200
Yamanaka Sadao, 194
Yoshida, 68, 201
Yutkevitch, Sergei, 46

Zecca, Ferdinand, 144, 174, 187
Zhelyabuzhsky, Yuri, 228